TOSSERS AND ARSEBLOWERS

Raised on a ranch in Colorado, J. R. Daeschner won a Fulbright Scholarship to Latin America after university and gained firsthand experience of carnival, cholera and military coups. Between blackouts and water shortages, he also freelanced for the *New York Times*. He later worked on Fleet Street and Wall Street, with stints in Mexico, Brazil and Peru before putting down roots in Britain and writing his first book about his adopted home, *True Brits: A Tour of 21st Century Britain in all its Bog-Snorkelling, Gurning and Cheese-Rolling Glory*.

When not Shin Kick or Arseblowing, J.R. endeavours to live as quiet a life as possible.

THE 'KING' OF THE ARSEBLOWERS . . . AND J.R.

Also available by J.R. Daeschner

True Brits

TOSSERS
AND
ARSEBLOWERS

J.R. DAESCHNER

arrow books

Published in the United Kingdom by Arrow Books in 2008

1 3 5 7 9 10 8 6 4 2

First published as *Eurotripping* in the United Kingdom in 2006 by Century

Arrow Books
The Random House Group Limited
20 Vauxhall Bridge Road, London, SW1V 2SA

Addresses for companies within The Random House Group Limited can be
found at: www.randomhouse.co.uk/offices.htm

The Random House Group Limited Reg. No. 954009

www.rbooks.co.uk

A CIP catalogue record for this book
is available from the British Library

ISBN 9780099484523

The Random House Group Limited supports The Forest Stewardship Council
(FSC), the leading international forest certification organisation. All our
titles that are printed on Greenpeace approved FSC certified paper carry the
FSC logo. Our paper procurement policy can be found at
www.rbooks.co.uk/environment

Typeset by SX Composing DTP, Rayleigh, Essex

Printed and bound in Great Britain by
CPI Bookmarque, Croydon CR0 4TD

For Dominique and Nina

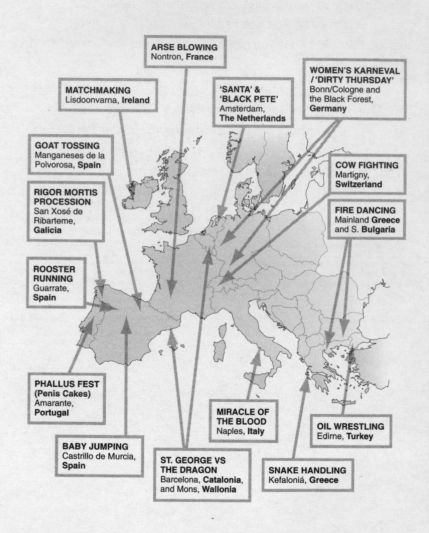

ARSE BLOWING
Nontron, **France**

WOMEN'S KARNEVAL / 'DIRTY THURSDAY'
Bonn/Cologne and the Black Forest, **Germany**

MATCHMAKING
Lisdoonvarna, **Ireland**

'SANTA' & 'BLACK PETE'
Amsterdam, **The Netherlands**

COW FIGHTING
Martigny, **Switzerland**

GOAT TOSSING
Manganeses de la Polvorosa, **Spain**

FIRE DANCING
Mainland **Greece** and S. **Bulgaria**

RIGOR MORTIS PROCESSION
San Xosé de Ribarteme, **Galicia**

ROOSTER RUNNING
Guarrate, **Spain**

PHALLUS FEST
(Penis Cakes)
Amarante, **Portugal**

MIRACLE OF THE BLOOD
Naples, **Italy**

OIL WRESTLING
Edirne, **Turkey**

BABY JUMPING
Castrillo de Murcia, **Spain**

ST. GEORGE VS THE DRAGON
Barcelona, **Catalonia**, and Mons, **Wallonia**

SNAKE HANDLING
Kefaloniá, **Greece**

'As Europe is becoming more and more the same, people are starting to realise that it's important to keep your own identity – and that you can have two identities: you can be European, but you can also be proud of your own nationality.'

> – a museum curator in the Dutch Bible Belt, on the renewed popularity of the original 'Santa' and his controversial Muslim sidekick, Black Pete

'They say "Spain is different" – not any more.'

> – a Spanish town councillor, on the (British-led) campaign to ban Goat Tossing

CONTENTS

A Year of Tossers and Arseblowers

Goat Tossing/Fiesta de San Vicente Mártir
Manganeses de la Polvorosa, Spain – 22nd January

Rooster Run/Correr el Gallo
Guarrate, Spain – Last Sunday in January

Wenches' Feast Day (Weiberfastnacht)/Karneval
The Rhineland/Black Forest, Germany – usually February/March

Arse Blowing/Mascarade des Soufflaculs
Nontron, France – Usually the first Sunday in April

St George's Day/Diada de Sant Jordi
Barcelona, Spain – 23rd April

Fire Dancing/Anastenariá
Ayia Eleni and Langadás, Greece – 21st May

Phallus Festival/Festa de São Gonçalo
Amarante, Portugal – First weekend in June

St George vs the Dragon/Combat dit Lumeçon
Mons, Belgium – Usually in May/June

Baby Jumping/Fiesta del Colacho
Castrillo de Murcia, Spain – Usually in May/June

Kirkpinar Oil Wrestling Championships
Edirne, Turkey – Usually the last weekend in June

Rigor Mortis Procession/Coffin Festival
San Xosé de Ribarteme, Spain – 29th July

Handling the Virgin's Snakes
Markópoulo, Kefaloniá, Greece – On and around 15th August

Matchmaking Festival
Lisdoonvarna, Ireland – September/October

Miracle of the Blood
Naples, Italy – 19th September

Cowfighting/Combat de Reines
Martigny, Switzerland – Usually early October

Sinterklaas and 'Black Pete'
Amsterdam/rest of the Netherlands – Mid-November to 5th December

*For exact dates, visit www.daeschner.com

CHAPTER ONE

KIDS' PLAY

GOAT TOSSING AND BABY JUMPING IN SPAIN

PART ONE:

A TOUGH ACT TO FOLLOW

For a man about to jump over babies, Rafael Benito is remarkably relaxed. Whereas other devils talk about their legs quivering like jelly, he claims he's never been nervous about his make-or-break role in the annual Baby Jumping Festival. Every summer, the village of Castrillo de Murcia in northern Spain puts its very future at risk in one of the world's most bizarre blessing ceremonies. Dozens of infants born during the previous year are laid out on mattresses in the streets while the priest and his entourage shuffle through the pueblo. Then, amid clouds of prayer and incense, a couple of 'devils' in Reeboks take running leaps through the baby obstacle course, knowing full well that just a few centimetres' shortfall could be catastrophic. As a father of two, though, Rafael is a veteran baby jumper: he's the Evel Knievel of kiddies. 'The way I look at it is nothing's ever happened before, so why should it happen to me?'

Of course, there's always a first time.

When I initially heard about Baby Jumping, my reaction was the same as that of any apparently sane person with a self-destructive sense of curiosity: *I have* got *to go see that*. At the time, I was working on a book on some of Britain's more colourful traditions. However, long before I'd stumbled into the alternate realm of Shin Kickers, Mob Footballers and other *True Brits*, I was in thrall to the strange customs of Europe; in particular, the Spanish practice of Goat Tossing (more about that later).

The idea behind this journey is to go where few foreigners have gone before, exploring the Continent's most obscure customs to find out what they reveal about the people and places that inspired them. The events also provide an excuse to delve into the big issues facing Europe today – controversies over race, sex, religion – you name it. The row in the Netherlands over the original Dutch 'Santa' and his black Muslim sidekick, for instance, reflects the culture clash between immigrants and 'native' Europeans, while the furore over the gay fanbase for Turkish Oil Wrestling highlights the problems of East–West integration. Similarly, Arse Blowing in France offers a chance to vent dissent over a certain (ahem) superpower's foreign policy. Of course, that's not to say that all Spaniards are Baby Jumpers, all Swiss are Cow Fighters, all Portuguese are Penis Worshippers or all French are Arse Blowers (though if you said Arse *Talkers* . . .). My goal is simply to discover an unfamiliar side of otherwise familiar countries. *At the very least,* I thought while outlining my itinerary, *it'll be fun.*

So I've come to Castrillo de Murcia, a winsome village two hours north of Madrid in sprawling Castilla y León, a region that's arguably more representative of Spain – at least the ironfisted Catholic core that unified the country – than the guitar-strumming, flamenco-dancing, *Viva España* south. As every road sign reminds you, this is also *Camino de Santiago* country. The famous pilgrimage route culminates four hundred miles away at Santiago de Compostela, the last resting place of St James, the disciple whose body was miraculously 'discovered' here in Spain. The Castilians built their churches to last till kingdom come, and Castrillo's is a fine example: fat stone walls with just a few windows punched in the sides as airholes. Like so many churches along the way, it's dedicated to James in his peculiarly Spanish incarnation. Rather than a pacific saint padding around and turning the other cheek, James is tooled up and charging into battle, cutting down Moors left and right and trampling them underfoot. This is *Santiago Matamoros* – James the Moor Slayer – the icon of Spain's long history of hostility against Islam: a symbol with uncomfortable resonances since Muslim terrorists murdered 191 men, women and children in the Madrid train bombings of 2004.

The official line on Baby Jumping is that it's a religious event coinciding with Corpus Christi, the uniquely Catholic festival that celebrates the miracle of Mass, when the bread and wine are supposedly transformed into the very body of Christ. However, it isn't entirely clear what that has to do with devils leaping over infants, so many observers have jumped to the conclusion that the *Fiesta del Colacho*, or Devil, has pagan roots stemming from the prehistoric Celtic Iberians.

'It's a fertility rite,' a villager explains matter-of-factly.

I don't get it. The local population is barely two hundred and fifty – and falling. How does endangering newborns improve the town's fertility? One wrong step, and you're down on your headcount.

The man patiently waits for my lips to stop flapping.

'It's a fertility rite.'

That's his story, and he's sticking to it.

The only group ever to oppose the event has been the Church, which, incidentally, is often blamed by animal rights activists for perpetuating beastly abuse at many of Spain's religious festivals. Bizarrely, the Church hasn't baulked so much about the fact that Baby Jumping involves well, *jumping* over *babies*, but that it features the Devil as part of the religious proceedings.

'The Church has tried to stop it many times because certain priests thought it wasn't very devout,' says organiser Angel Manso. 'Also, the Devil used to mimic and make fun of the priest behind his back in church.'

Definitely not the done thing during Mass, much less at Corpus Christi.

Angel's the drummer in the select Brotherhood of the Most Holy Sacrament, a group of sombre men in black who walk in formation behind the brightly coloured *Colacho* as he runs through the village terrorising children. The Devil chases the kids with a horsehair whip and clacks a giant castanet, while Angel bangs the bass drum strapped to his waist in a holy war of percussion instruments. The Brotherhood was formed in 1621, partly out of piety no doubt, though you can't help thinking that it also allowed the Brothers to indulge in the peculiarly male tendency to wear silly outfits while still thinking themselves cool. The theory is that the Brothers represent Good driving Evil out of the village, but in their dark capes and anachronistic black trilbies, they look more like Hit Men for Christ: *He died for your sins. Now it's payback time.*

The *Colacho*'s jerkin and trousers are eyesore yellow with red trim, matched with a yellow mask with black mouth- and eyeholes and cute little red circles for cheeks. Every couple of hours, one of the besneakered *Colachos* emerges from the town hall for a *corrida*, similar to running with the bulls; only here, the kids run with the Devil. While the Brothers drive the *Colacho* through the narrow streets, the boys and girls get as close as possible to taunt him. Whenever he can, he dashes after them and slashes at them with his whip, avoiding their heads, though everything else is fair game. Back in the day, the kids used to shout obscenities at the Devil, but the language has been cleaned up in recent years.

'The aim is to annoy without causing offence,' a former *Colacho* explains. 'Say, if I've bought a new tractor, they'll make fun of it by yelling: "Your tractor's worthless."'

Now them's fightin' words.

The run-up to Baby Jumping goes roughly like this: *corrida*, church, *corrida*, then more church, another *corrida*, some more church and so on, with breaks for eating, drinking and sleeping. Angel and the Devil attend the final Mass, standing in the alcove next to the altar, though Rafael doesn't wear his mask during the service (or the actual Baby Jumping, for that matter). Occasionally Angel, the Brother in top hat and tails, will interrupt the ceremony by pounding on his drum, but that's as raucous as it gets for now.

'This fiesta is above all about the victory of Good over Evil,' the priest exhorts us.

5

Provided that there are no missteps.

The altar boys lead us out, accompanied by the thunder of Angel's drum and the clacking of the Devil's oversized castanet. Outside, the village has been transformed into a baby obstacle course. Instead of bunting, the villagers have lined the street with sheets of elegant handmade lace hung from their windows. The babies are already in position, ready to be jumped, whether they like it or not, lying on a chain of mattresses set out barely ten feet from each other in the road. Despite what Rafael told me, I had expected the mattresses to be shorter than average – baby-sized, even – with just a single row of infants scrunched towards the front, where they'd be less likely to get squashed. However, these are full-sized mattresses – they really *are* six feet long – big enough to hold three babies in not one but *two* rows, so that the kids at the back are only inches from touchdown when the *Colacho* lands on the other side (hopefully). God forbid he should fall backwards. Not only that, but the mattresses stand at least ten inches high. If the babies roll off, it's a straight drop to the tarmac; for an adult, it would be the equivalent of a three-foot tumble out of bed. 'Every once in a while a baby will roll off and bump its head, but it doesn't hurt them,' an elderly señora assures me.

And if it does, well, every village needs an idiot.

Three mattresses have been laid out on the small plaza, full of babies who have been laced, bowed and taffetaed within an inch of their potentially shortened lives. The infants are squirming in the sunshine, frantically kicking and waving as if to flip themselves over and make an escape if only their parents would let them. One of the first babies in the line-up is a little blond boy just two days away from his first birthday. His parents, Oscar and Nagore, are from the Basque Country. Oscar's family has a cottage in Castrillo, and he's sure there's nothing to worry about.

'Why should I be scared? They say it frees the child from evil spirits. I don't know about that, but at least it doesn't hurt them.'

Notably, his wife remains tight-lipped and silent.

The two *Colachos* descend the steps from the church and survey the plaza. Now, if this were Britain or America – and that's a ginormous if – a clichéd hush would descend on the crowd right about now and there'd be a nerve-tingling build-up for the spectacle, probably a drum roll or at the very least a solemn warning not to try this at home. But the scene here is controlled pandemonium. The church bells are clanging like Quasimodo's gone mad as the two *Colachos* plan their approach. Their masks off, they take running leaps over the mattresses, clearing them with less fanfare than if they'd jumped a puddle of water. There are no trumpet blasts to hail their safe landing, no cheers of relief from the crowd, and certainly no quick jogs around the plaza to soak up the adulation. These men have just jumped over three mattresses laden with eighteen babies, and they act like it's no big deal!

That's because there's so much else going on. As soon as the *Colachos* touch down, two columns of Castilian dancers in jinglebells and espadrilles hop into action, somehow keeping in sync despite the lunatic rhythm of the church bells. The priest follows the *Colachos*, flanked by six men who carry a golden canopy over him to protect the big sunburst relic in his hands. He makes the sign of the cross over the babies right after they've been jumped – surely he should've done that beforehand – and someone scatters rose petals over them, while another attendant busies himself wafting incense. The priest is braying a prayer over a portable tannoy that squawks every time he starts to sing, and the faithful in the crowd are chiming in with the response while the babies kick and cry for all they're worth. Throw in some little girls in lace dresses, a few banners, and of course the Hit Men for Christ and their beating drum, and you've got a full-fledged assault on the senses. In this ten-ring circus, Baby Jumping is just one of many distractions. You half expect to see a chimp swing past on a trapeze or a dwarf fired from a cannon. The whole jumping, dancing, jingling, praying and braying cavalcade makes its way from mattress to mattress through the narrow streets, with men clearing the crowds as much as possible to give the *Colachos* some semblance of a landing strip.

A woman screams: 'Your baby! She's going to fall off!'

The mother in question runs into the mayhem to catch her newborn.

There are babies everywhere. I'm crouched down taking photos, so stunned by the drama in front of me that I don't realise there's another mattressful of infants immediately behind me. Scuttling backwards to get out of the way of the *Colachos*, I nearly trip and wipe out half a football team of posture-sprung offspring. By the time we finish the circuit and make it back to the plaza, the *Colachos* have bestowed their airborne blessing on at least a hundred children.

Oscar comes up to me, grinning. 'See? I told you – nothing happened. My son was tired, so he was crying. But apart from that, nothing happened.'

Thank God for that.

Now it's back to the church for more blessings. After the last amen – and God knows there've been a lot of them – I strike up a conversation with a couple of mothers: Isabel, a slender redhead, and Ana, a plump brunette who's bottle-feeding her baby. Coming from Burgos, they've heard about Baby Jumping for years before finally seeing it for themselves. And once here, Ana couldn't get enough. She smiles as she tells me that two-month-old Nicolás was jumped not once by the two *Colachos*, but twice. She missed seeing the first time, in the plaza, so her friend saved her a spot – that's right, *saved her a spot* – down in the village so that she could watch Little Nick be jumped all over again by Old Nick. Ana has four other kids, but Nicolás is the first to have been blessed by the *Colacho*.

'I wasn't going to put him there, but when we came here, I thought, *Why not?*' she says, shrugging her latest newborn in her arms.

And anyway – one more, one less . . .

'But it wasn't out of any religious fervour,' Isabel interjects, wagging her finger.

'We do it for the tradition and because it's of touristic interest.'

And who wouldn't sacrifice their baby for touristic interest?

'Actually, I am Catholic, and I like him to be blessed.'

'It can't hurt, can it?'

'Well, it could hurt them. It could definitely hurt them if the *Colachos* stuck their foot in it,' Ana admits, using a particularly apt expression. 'But so far they haven't.'

The first time, Nicolás was in the front row of babies – the safest spot; for the second, though, he was at the back.

'There was a moment there when the *Colacho*'s foot barely cleared my baby's head, and I thought he was going to be *aplastado*.'

'What?' I know what the word means, but her nonchalance doesn't match the definition.

'Y'know – *aplastado.*' Ana's hands are full, so Isabel mimes it for her – by smashing her fist into her palm.

'But then it happened so quickly, by the time I saw it, it was over.'

Isabel tells me that she has two kids, aged seven and twelve.

'So they're too old to bring here.'

'Well, I could have, but I was too scared.'

'Ah!' Ana gasps. 'You never told me that!'

She places Nicolás in a pram the size of a VW Beetle and thumps down the stairs outside. Thanks to the shock absorbers, though, he remains blissfully oblivious, swaddled in a baby-blue suit spun from the finest linen.

I compliment her on his clothes.

'Oh, that's just his ordinary, everyday clothes.'

'Yeah – some of those babies were dressed up like they were going to a wedding,' Isabel laughs.

Even so, Little Nick looks pretty well turned out to me. 'Spain produces some of the prettiest baby clothes in Europe,' I venture.

'*Sí,*' Ana agrees, her face irony-free. 'In Spain, we take very good care of babies.'

'So what other traditions have you seen here?'

I mention that my journey around Europe began back in January, with another event in Castilla y León: *El Salto de la Cabra* – the Jump of the Goat.

'I've heard of that. But they don't jump *over* the goat, do they? It's more of a *hurling*, isn't it?'

Ana's appalled. 'They hurl the goat? From where?'

'From the bell tower.'

'Ah! Poor thing.'

I try to explain that the goat was never killed, but that

doesn't make much of a difference to Ana: having her baby jumped repeatedly is one thing, but throwing a goat from a tower – *Ah! Poor thing*.

'That seems very wrong to me.' She shakes her head. 'Do they still do it?'

PART TWO:
ATTACK OF EL NANNY STATE

It's hard to say. What I do know is when I came to Spain back in January, I definitely had my doubts about having chosen Goat Tossing as my starting point. Why had I picked one of the most controversial – and potentially dangerous – events first?

As far as I can work out, it's probably in my blood. I must have inherited my fascination with odd customs from my Swedish-American grandfather, who revelled in ambushing people on their birthdays by smearing butter on their noses 'to help them slide through the next year'. Whether this was a grand old Swedish tradition or his own peculiar practical joke, I don't know. For the German side of my family, it provided further proof, if any were needed, of the inherent stupidity of Swedes. Given my background, then, it's no wonder that I was drawn to the Jump of the Goat from the moment I read about it after moving to the UK over a decade ago. I wasn't motivated by any self-righteous horror or moral outrage; it just seemed an intensely stupid thing to do . . .

When I arrived in the home of Goat Tossing, though, the

mayor's warning was as strange as it was serious. 'You'd better put that notebook away,' he muttered. 'Otherwise, people will think you're *un ecologista*.'

An ecologist? Frankly, I've been called worse. But in this red-dirt town in northern Spain, the term is synonymous with any number of epithets involving one's privates or mother or both. Being mistaken for *un ecologista* – an animal rights activist – can get you run out of town by pitchfork-toting pig farmers and assorted rustics. For it was the 'ecologists', particularly a long-haired animal lover from Liverpool, who cost this town its tradition. And poor Manganeses de la Polvorosa has yet to bounce back from the loss of its beloved Goat Toss. For years, its sons and daughters would celebrate their coming of age with a surreal ritual: throwing a live goat from the church belfry onto a canvas sheet below. The locals swear the bleating projectile always survived the sixty-foot drop, but that didn't stop the hate mail and protests by fauna defenders from around the world, agitators who spread rumours that the barbaric Spaniards would dance in the blood of the dead beast and copulate themselves silly at witches' sabbaths.

The villagers, in turn, blamed an Englishwoman for twisting their screwy tradition out of proportion. Notorious in Spain, she travelled the country in wigs and dodgy disguises to secretly film so-called 'blood fiestas', 'rescuing' unfortunate animals that became tabloid causes célèbres back home (*Save Blackie the Donkey!*). However, the interloper from Merseyside didn't fool the people of Manganeses. The last time she visited, the mayor and his brothers had to protect her from irate villagers chasing her through the streets. 'It was all we could do to keep them from tearing her clothes off!' he chortles. That may have had something to do with her apparel – at least if you believe the locals. 'She was protesting to save a goat while wearing a leather jacket!' snorts an old man in disgust. 'Hell! We may be farmers, but we're not stupid!' Unfortunately, *la inglesa*'s career as an undercover *ecologista* was cut short. She died after being gored repeatedly by the very bull she was trying to save at another *fiesta de sangre*.

Although the government banned the Goat Toss in 2001 (on pain of exorbitant fines), every year a few journalists and animal-lovers venture all the way to this otherwise media-forsaken town 200 miles north-west of Madrid just in case there's the odd clandestine toss. That explains why, when a strange *yanqui* turns up one night during the January festivities that used to culminate in caprine high jinks, the initial reception is a little chilly – almost as cold as the Castilian wind sweeping the streets outside.

For the record, *El Salto de la Cabra* was more of a 'push' or a 'shove' rather than a 'jump'; humans are the only animals that voluntarily hurl themselves off high points (contrary to myth, not even lemmings are that stupid). I may have never had a chance to see the Goat Toss in person, but, now that it's been cancelled, I have an opportunity to find out what happens when a town loses the custom that made it unique (for better or worse). As the mayor put it: 'It's as if the whole town has been decapitated.'

But not defenestrated. In contacting some of the locals in advance, I've stressed that I live in Britain, but I'm actually American. Even so, that hasn't stopped them from confusing me with an animal-mad *inglés* (we all look alike). And although I am fluent in Spanish, it's the Latin American variety. The Castilian of my student days in Madrid is rusty, and I'm worried it will seize up entirely the moment I need it most, when I'm asking the really delicate questions such as *How would you like it if a gang of billy goats headbutted you off a cliff?* Last year, some frustrated tossers beat up four journalists at the festival – and *they* were Spanish. So as a foreigner who stands a head taller than the locals and is blond enough to be called *El Rubio* – I'm even a Capricorn, come to think of it – what hope do I have among the goat tossers?

On my way to the airport in London this morning, the music on the radio was interrupted by ads for not one but two Spanish property shows held at a couple of Britain's biggest exhibition halls: 'See how easy it is to buy your dream home in the sun!' the announcer cooed. But she was referring to the Costa del Sol or, for the more adventurous, possibly the bits around Barcelona and the lush northern regions of Galicia and the Basque Country. Few foreigners would consider moving to this part of Castilla y León, the hardscrabble land of El Cid and the countless warriors who led the long fightback against the peninsula's Muslim occupiers. Castile is also home to Europe's oldest human fossils, discovered in caves decorated with animal paintings, and to this day practically every town has its own animal-related festivity, if not its very own bullring. The local wine is so red it's actually called *Sangre de Toro* – Bull's Blood – and the russet soil that provides a living for so many is still yielding up the bodies of those 'disappeared' during the Civil War.

My hopes of slipping quietly into town vanish as soon as I arrive. Like so many depopulated Spanish villages, Manganeses does a convincing impression of a ghost town at night, even though 22 January is the feast day of its patron, St Vincent, one of Spain's most beloved martyrs. As I drive through the dark streets, the only signs of life among its 800 souls are a banner announcing this weekend's festival, some lights in the 'Disco-Bar Charlot' and the scent of garlic and olive oil emanating from the tightly shuttered houses. After asking directions at the Chaplin bar, I wander over to the auditorium where apparently there's some form of entertainment taking place. Unknown to me, the door marked 'Entrance' opens right next to the stage where a troupe of old folks is performing a musical comedy. I practically walk onto the set through the squeakiest door in creation: enter the *yanqui*.

The community hall is a big, stark, concrete rectangle. The walls are a scarred green, and the floor still bears the white lines marking the courts for jai alai, or *frontón*. There are barely a hundred people in the audience, huddled against the cold, while a couple dozen more stand at the back, next to two electric heaters and the concession stand turned bar. The mayor, Pedro Prieto, is among this group, a dark, squat man who eyes me suspiciously at first, clearly uncomfortable about being seen with a stranger.

However, a sense of duty overcomes his reluctance. After the performance, he takes me on a night-time tour of the village and even invites me home for dinner. While I'd like to think this is due to my winning personality, it crosses my paranoid mind that it could be a set-up: come this weekend, they'll be throwing a *yanqui* from the church tower. More likely, though, it's all part of the town's new PR offensive. 'Our mistake was that we didn't get the media on our side,' one of the organisers told me.

Pedro's wife is cooking dinner in her dressing gown, and we sit in the small kitchen dominated by an outsized TV. Carlitos the canary chirps above the doorway and a couple of goldfish circle nervously in a bowl right next to the hob. Angela has knocked together a feast of sizzling *gambas al ajillo* – shrimps in garlic served in earthenware dishes – plus croquettes, green salad, sliced pork loin with paprika and all the homemade chorizo and cured ham we can eat. Virtually every home around here makes its own stash of porkstuffs in the winter during the traditional *Matanza del Cerdo*. 'We also make a fiesta out of that,' Pedro says with a grin. While it's not everyone's idea of family fun, the Slaughter of the Pig brings young and old together, with the labour divided between the sexes. The men kill and butcher the pig on the backyard patio, leaving the women to turn the meat, fat and intestines into food. Very little is wasted, and the members of the family pose happily for photos with the carcass throughout the preparation. Out in their shed, the Prietos have hung hams and pork loins to cure, along with dozens of stick-like *salchichones* and the fat, meaty necklaces that are chorizos. They even eat the pig's snout and ears: its face is draped over a rafter like a grisly party mask.

Compared to their porcine counterparts, then, the goats had it easy. Pedro tells me that it fell to him to enforce the ban on the Goat Toss, despite opposition from his own family: his son was due to take part in the event that year. 'I didn't have a choice,' the mayor shrugs, keeping half an eye on the sitcom blaring from the TV. Practically everyone in town could have been fined for breaking the law: the goat throwers, the Church and the entire town council, including himself. And anyway, he says, the move hasn't affected his popularity; he was recently re-elected. 'I still haven't had to pay for cancelling the event,' he grins, tearing off another hunk of chorizo.

'But who started the Goat Throw in the first place?'

He shakes his head. 'If you go around asking questions like that, people really *will* think you're an ecologist!'

*

When it comes to baroque acts of cruelty, the Spanish are renowned for their creative flair. Besides bullfighting, Spain has hundreds, if not thousands, of fiestas and traditions involving animals in often cruel but always unusual ways, typically as part of religious celebrations. In many places, particularly here in the Castilian heartland, bulls are forced to run with burning balls of tar stuck on their horns, facing a gauntlet of abuse before being killed. In the town where I'm staying, five miles from Manganeses, the big event of the year takes place during Corpus Christi in the summer. The Tied Bull, or *Toro Enmaromado,* of Benavente is a tamer version of the bull runs at Pamplona: a bull stampedes through the streets with a long rope tied to its horns, the local youths proving their machismo by getting as close as possible without being gored. Elsewhere in Castile, the town of Tordesillas honours St Vincent the Martyr by having blindfolded girls slash and bludgeon roosters to death with blunt swords. Then there are the outrageously absurd customs on a par with Goat Tossing: in the Galician village of Laza, the locals celebrate carnival by dowsing ants with vinegar – to get them good and angry – and then throw them at each other, along with handfuls of dirt and flour.

'Lovely people, the Spanish,' joked a friend of mine back in London. 'If it moves, abuse it.' But outsiders should be wary of throwing the first stone. From bull- and bear-baiting to cock 'threshing' and even cat throwing, countless European customs have revolved around the suffering of animals – and some still do. In fact, the only forms of abuse that haven't officially been sanctioned over the years are monkey spanking and chicken choking (for those, you'd go straight to hell).

During much of the past millennium, animals were tried in courts throughout Europe, squirming in the dock while they were prosecuted. Strangely, they never had much to say in their defence. Once convicted, they were sentenced to exile, torture and execution by hanging, burning or assorted gruesome methods. Beginning with a hive of murderous German bees in the ninth century, people brought cases against cows, pigs, dogs, roosters, rats, beetles, caterpillars, worms and even leeches. Cats were particularly loathed for being witches' sidekicks and just plain evil. In the Belgian town of Ypres, the Flemish used to hurl live felines from the top of their Cloth Tower – a seventy-metre drop – right up until 1817 (nowadays, their Cat Throwing Festival uses stuffed kitties). The practice of trying animals seems to have died out in Britain in the late eighteenth century, but the last-known case in Europe comes from Switzerland, where two brothers and a dog were convicted of murder as late as 1906. The men got life in prison; their canine accomplice, death.

Of course, most 'civilised' countries have now put a stop to animal abuse (apart from battery hen farms, foie gras and the odd spot of rebel foxhunting). However, it's no coincidence that the nations at the forefront of the animal rights movement, namely Britain and America, are also among the richest in the world: people can afford to worry whether their roast chicken died humanely because they don't have to worry where their next meal is coming from. In contrast, to get an idea of the economic situation around Manganeses, consider this: the locals have been petitioning the government to build a new hospital in the district; without it, they won't be able to attract new companies or young families to the area. One newspaper headline warns that the existing hospital doesn't have enough facilities to perform autopsies: never mind the living, it can't even take care of the dead.

Over the years, the villagers have trotted out several stories to justify Goat Tossing, none of which makes much sense. The most popular legend is that some time in the eighteenth or nineteenth centuries, the local priest kept a goat in the church to produce milk for the poor. One day the beast fell from the bell tower, and the locals caught it in a blanket. The less heart-warming variation on this theme has it that the villagers wanted to eat the goat during a famine, so the priest locked it in the tower; once the danger was past, though, the beast refused to budge, so he threw it out. At some point the locals supposedly began commemorating the Jump of the Goat with a party that was stopped during Franco's dictatorship (along with many festivals – the *Generalissimo* was paranoid of public gatherings) but restarted once he died in 1975.

However, the truth is that Goat Throwing is just a few decades old. Over drinks during the weekend, Pedro tells me that his parents were part of a *peña* at the time, one of the many groups that club together to buy food and drink and even dress alike during fiestas. One day, after a skinful, some of the men decided (as you do) to sneak into the church and throw a stuffed goatskin from the belfry. Maybe it was a drunken homage to the legends about the goat and the bell tower or maybe it was because the animal was very much on their minds at the time – the mainstay of the St Vincent festival has always been the Dance of the Goat, when couples are allowed to switch partners and flirt in ways that wouldn't normally be tolerated. Then again, it could be that a stuffed goatskin was the most convenient projectile on hand. Whatever the reason, the prank soon became a rite of passage for kids who had just turned eighteen, the age of national military service. Another group of conscripts, or *quintos*, started throwing a live goat from the tower around 1978. As a result, Pedro didn't feel that bad about putting a stop to it. 'People talked about it being a tradition, but what tradition? It had been around for only about thirty years.'

Then again, the same could be said of Spain's Constitution. All traditions, venerable or not, have to start somewhere, and within a decade, the Jump of the Goat had become 'as old as the river bank', attracting up to four thousand spectators to the town, along with the national and international media. And that's when the trouble began. In 1989, an English animal rights activist travelled to Manganeses to film a video exposé of the event. Vicki Moore was a former cabaret singer and bunny girl whose debut as an international animal defender had been a highly public success. Just a couple of years earlier, she had been working at an animal shelter in Southport, when, as one admiring interviewer put it, she 'got the call to save donkeys'. Surprisingly, this call took the form of a tabloid article. In the finest Fleet Street tradition, the newspaper and its rivals sensationalised the facts to the point that they verged on fiction, reporting that the despicable Spanish – aka the 'Sick Señors' or 'Fiesta Fiends' – were about to murder a beast of burden at their annual 'donkey-crushing' festival. Outraged by this apparent barbarity, Vicki and her husband Tony felt duty-bound, indeed *called*, to travel from dreary Merseyside to sunny Spain to stop the poor little ass from getting smashed.

In reality, of course, 'donkey-crushing' didn't quite live up to the cartoonish violence implied by the tabloids. For foreign do-gooders, though, the spectacle in dirt-poor Extremadura was bad enough – and to be sure, it's more than any donkey should have to endure. During the Pero Palo carnival celebrations, a drunken fool rides an ass through the village of Villanueva de la Vera while equally intoxicated yokels let off shotguns and firecrackers near the donkey and its rider. Not surprisingly, the animal sometimes stumbles and collapses in the mêlée – hence the reports of 'donkey crushing'.

The villagers defended their custom by arguing that the donkey didn't suffer any more than the rider (the crucial difference, of course, being that the man *chose* to take part in the scrum). For the British media, though, Operation Save Ass was already well underway. In their zeal, the tabloid hacks resorted to fistfights to rescue the donkey – not so much from the locals as from their competitors. The *Sun* and the *Daily Star* launched a bidding war, with both sides claiming victory and ponying up thousands of pesetas for donkeys that fit Blackie's description (namely, they were black). At least one of these alleged Blackies was shipped out of the country ('On His Way, You Cruel Señors!') to Britain, which, despite being one of the most crowded countries in Europe, miraculously still has land to spare for not one but at least a dozen donkey sanctuaries. Although the Moores didn't stop the fiesta – truth is, it's still going strong – the international donkey rescue encouraged them to keep trying. Back in the UK, they founded FAACE, a charity to Fight Against Animal Cruelty in Europe.

Faced with the media-savvy 'saviour' of Blackie the Donkey, the Goat Tossers of Manganeses didn't stand a chance. Within three years of Vicki Moore's first video exposé, the Jump of the Goat came to symbolise Spain at its worst – and its weirdest – particularly after she claimed a 'little goat' had fallen to its death (hotly denied by the locals to this day). Desperate to prove that Spain was no longer a backward country, the local authorities caved in. Not only did they ban the toss, they also sent riot police to block the belfry at Manganeses. Outraged at the sight of Robocops armed with shields and billy clubs, the tossers targeted the usual scapegoat – the media – attacking a photographer from the *Daily Star*, smashing up cameras and chasing some journalists out of town. Several people wound up in hospital, including a Spanish reporter suffering from 'acute shock'. Before the confrontation turned really ugly, the mayor and the Civil Guard cut a deal allowing the kids to lower the goat to the ground using a rope. Unfortunately, this meant the animal spent more time in the air. As it struggled, the rope slipped, and the kids ended up throwing the goat anyway just to keep it from being strangled.

The following year was even more farcical. The *quintos* rigged up a pulley contraption to lower the goat the first twenty feet or so and then drop it the remaining forty feet to the tarp below. At least that was the plan. In reality, the goat ended up banging against the church wall. Scrabbling against the stones, it managed to find its footing and then quite reasonably refused to budge. As a result, a couple of the boys had to lean out of the bell tower to push it off its perch.

'We almost lost two kids that way,' a local tells me.

Which is precisely *not* the purpose of a rite of passage.

Ironically, he says, that was the only year the goat was ever injured. At the time, José Manuel Martínez was a *quinto*; now he's one of the organisers trying to revitalise the fiesta. 'We realised that the goat landed on its feet if we threw it from the tower; if we didn't throw it, it didn't land on its feet,' he continues authoritatively, as if reporting the results of a particularly bizarre scientific study: *Research shows that nine out of ten goats land on their feet when thrown, not lowered, from a belfry.*

So Goat Throwing bounced back, supported by the then mayor, who weighed in with bizarre statements to the press.

'This is not a pig. It is a goat, an animal that jumps great distances in its natural environment,' he said, ignoring the fact that goats aren't naturally prone to hurling themselves from bell towers. As a sign of defiance, Manganeses had a heraldic shield drawn up in 1997 showing a palm branch of St Vincent next to a goat's head and a church tower.

Increasingly, though, the Goat Throwers faced opposition both at home and abroad, reflecting the town/country divisions that exist within Spain – and the rest of Europe. 'They should throw an inanimate object, or better still one of themselves,' said a spokeswoman for the National Association for the Protection and Wellbeing of Animals (or ANPBA in Spanish). When the locals refused, ANPBA President Alfonso Chillerón complained that the event was a premeditated violation of the law. The town council was fined 50,000 pesetas (about 300 euros) in 1999, an amount that could multiply exponentially if the pueblo continued tossing goats. Even more importantly, the national media came out against the event. *Diario 16* newspaper denounced the Jump as an 'annual barbarity' on its front page: 'It is clearly not necessary to throw a goat from a belfry in order for a town to enjoy its fiesta. In fact, this should never happen again.'

And, in fact, it didn't. At least not officially. The locals tried to save face – 'No one has the right to interfere in our fiesta,' the mayor declared – but the threat of fines hit the cash-strapped village where it was already hurting. The crowds gathered around the church as usual in 2000, chanting and cheering when the *quintos* arrived with Obdulia the goat. One of the young men mocked the animal's defenders, joking that maybe they should kill the goat beforehand to keep it from suffering stress.

'The ecologists want us to kill the goat first!' he hollered through a megaphone. 'Do you want us to kill the goat?'

'Nooooo!'

In fact, a goat had already been killed and taxidermied to take the plunge. However, the young men refused to use the stuffed substitute, deeming it 'unmanly'. 'That would be ridiculous,' they scoffed.

But throwing a live goat, that's completely normal: macho, even.

The youths vowed to throw Obdulia if someone in the audience would pay their fines. However, at up to 2.5 million pesetas – or £10,000 – a pop, no one took them up on their offer: 'We've got plenty of *cojones*; what we don't have is money.'

And so the Jump of the Goat was officially grounded.

That same year, the event's arch-enemy died at the age of forty-four. Vicki Moore had never fully recovered from the injuries she sustained while exposing yet another spectacle five years earlier. The San Juan fiesta in Coria, way out in Extremadura, is a bull run with a difference. Besides playing catch-me-if-you-can with stampeding bulls, the locals shoot the animals with hundreds of steel-tipped darts before eventually killing them. Moore was determined to expose this cruelty. As 'Spain's Most Hated Woman' (and a former actress), she often travelled in disguise, though it's unclear just how effective she was at fooling the locals. After all, you wouldn't expect to see many English nuns or tarts trying to film blood fiestas. In Coria, for reasons best known to herself, she arrived with dyed blonde hair and the equally conspicuous pseudonym of Lucille Eva Valentine Hayward. No doubt she blended right in.

While trying to get close-ups of the violence, Moore was gored repeatedly by a bull. Even so, she continued campaigning for animals until her death and undoubtedly helped bring about change in Spain. All seventeen of the country's regional governments now have laws banning animal abuse, although that doesn't necessarily mean they're enforced. ANPBA estimates the country still has some 15,000 blood fiestas, including everything from ant throwing to bullfighting. Villanueva de la Vera's annual 'donkey crushing' continues, despite the tabloid victory over 'Blackie' and the best efforts of animal rights agitators.

In Manganeses, people agree that *la inglesa* was special all right, though strictly in the pejorative sense. 'She wasn't right in the head,' they say, tapping their temples knowingly. And it's hard not to wonder when you read the profiles of her, even the sympathetic ones. When she was gored, she said someone had tried to lift her out of the way, but she felt an 'almighty thump' on her back. 'At first I thought it was a gang of men, so when I realised what it was, I thought: Oh, that's all right – it's only the bull.'

'Only' the bull?

I mention to a farmer that Moore's death seems tragically ironic.

'We don't call that ironic,' he counters. 'We call that fucking stupid.'

Another old-timer laughs. 'Most people, if they saw a bull, would run the other way.'

The root of this hatred was Moore's claim that she saw at least one goat hit the flagstones and die. In talking with the locals, I try to get someone to admit as much by suggesting that an accident must have been inevitable at some point. Without fail, though, they insist, dead-eyed and adamant, that no goats were ever killed in their fun-making. 'The cameras always showed the goats falling, but they never showed them landing safely in the tarp!' What's more, they claim, the *quintos* had to make sure the goat hit its target: if it missed the canvas sheet held by the catchers below, it could've killed someone in the crowd. The goats were momentarily shaken by the trauma, but they always walked away unharmed: so much so that they were the guests of honour at the communal Dance of the Goat in the evening. As further proof, they claim that the goat would often be sold back to their previous owners; the farmers wouldn't have accepted them if they were injured. I end up meeting a soft-spoken farmer who was one of the pioneers of Goat Tossing back in his youth. For years, he used to buy the goats from the *quintos* for milking and breeding. However, he had to stop after his flock reached a dozen. 'Now, with all the laws and paperwork, it's too much of a hassle.'

The *quintos* still name a goat as their mascot each year during the festivities, parading it around town with ribbons on its horns, just like they used to, but the church doors are kept locked. Manganeses is struggling to come up with something to pull in the punters. In another bar – there are only three, but we keep doing the circuit – I ask a town councillor how they plan to go about replacing a spectacle like Goat Tossing.

She turns glum. 'Well, it *is* difficult . . .'

Which is an early candidate for Understatement of the Millennium. Back in 2001 – the first year without an official Jump – the council tried to fill the gap by organising a horse-riding contest on the outskirts of town. However, the *quintos* took advantage of the distraction to sneak up to the top of an old water tower and complete a Rebel Toss, dubbing their goat Chillerona, a pun on the fact that the name of ANPBA's president sounds like 'Squealer' in Spanish. Sure enough, the animal rights group protested, ensuring that the Guardia Civil have been on hand to guard the church during the festivities, along with plainclothes policemen mingling among the spectators. Even so, the year before my arrival some Spanish journalists got beaten up,. with the *quintos* vowing ominously: 'The goat will be thrown, that's for sure, but without witnesses.'

Javier, a wisecracking organiser who's fond of calling me *yanqui*, says the committee is trying to unite the village during this year's festivities.

'What divided it in the first place?'

'Two words,' he grins: 'fucking politics.'

A grey-haired pig farmer with lines burnt deep into his face is standing next to us. Though he's named after the town's patron saint, Vicente swears like a sinner. 'In this fucking country of ours nowadays, if you kill a bird, they put you in prison. But if you kill a person, they give you a prize.'

Javier nods bitterly. 'They say "Spain is different". Not any more. Now it's just like everywhere else.'

I can see what he means. On the eve of the big day, two bands are headlining the all-night concert in the jai alai court-turned-community hall. The first plays Latin music and some American hits, including a Spanish version of 'Achy Breaky Heart', no doubt translated by Satan himself. But the main attraction is a Top-40 metal group from Zaragoza that performs word-perfect covers of hits in English – copying them right down to the very last howl of universal angst, making them a tribute band in the truest sense, a paean to the homogenisation of world culture. Not only is the achy-breaky mainstream of Anglo-Americana piped into the backwaters of Europe, even the norms of nonconformity are happily swallowed whole.

Throughout the night, the lead singer, a wannabe rebel and *rawk gawd*, tries to match his multiple costume changes to suit the mood of the music: he wears black shades and a leather jacket for 'Born To Be Wild' by Steppenwolf; a hooded jersey and nihilistic sneer for 'In the End' by Linkin Park, and, most worryingly, a pair of Lycra biker shorts for Nirvana's 'Smells Like Teen Spirit' (as somewhere, the spirit of Kurt Cobain reaches for a gun all over again). Likewise, the kids do their best to bang their heads – though they also gamely try to dance to the music rather than just thrash. When the band unfurls a marijuana-leaf flag onstage (their prop for an anthem to pot), a few joints circulate in the audience, while the rest of the fans thrust their index fingers in the air in time to the beat, forgoing the traditional Horned God hand signal beloved of pseudo-Satanists elsewhere. In Spain, the horns can also be the sign of a cuckold, and questioning a *rockero*'s way with the ladies would be a cultural import too far.

Twice during the night the *quintos* drag their mascot onto the stage. The goat, twitching and disoriented, looks in vain for a way to escape as they sing. But there's no escaping 'The Goat Song' this weekend. At any excuse, the *quintos* and the rest of Manganeses will start hopping up and down, shouting the lyrics over and over again:

> The goat, the goat
> The whore of the goat
> Its bitch of a mother, too
> I had a goat once
> Its name was Asunción.

Believe me, it doesn't make much sense in Spanish, either. Whatever oblique irony there is – a bunch of goat throwers singing about an animal called Assumption – is unintentional: this year's goat is named Fresita, or Little Strawberry. Despite the public taunting, she seems to be holding up well. The only cruelty she suffers is exposure to the Lycra-clad rockers.

However, another event in the programme sounds altogether more ominous: the 'Goat of Fire'. I immediately (and stupidly) imagine the worst: *they're not going to throw the goat; they're going to* burn *it! At three a.m., when all the outsiders have gone!*

In reality, the Goat of Fire is simply a variation on the *toro de fuego* you see at fiestas throughout the country: a guy carries a wooden contraption on his head in the shape of an animal and charges the crowd, while the effigy spits fireworks and sparks. This one has a goat's face. Even so, I don't get back to my hotel until nearly six a.m.

I return for the big event at midday. Will the *quintos* stage a Rebel Goat Throw? On my way to the plaza, a chubby ten-year-old runs past me, singing. *How cute.*

Then I realise what he's singing.

'. . . Its bitch of a mother, too . . .'

Tra la la. The *quintos* are already jumping up and down, the long ribbons around their waists fluttering in the air with each bounce. The group numbers just eight this year – six girls and two boys – down from the annual harvest of twenty or so that Manganeses used to produce only a decade ago, but they're making a terrific ruckus with the aid of a brass band and clubs of kids and adults in colour-coordinated outfits. The plaza itself is actually more of a clearing than a square. A big culvert cuts through it, bypassing the eighteenth-century church and the new town hall, which has a few columns out front but is otherwise plain and featureless, seemingly made of flimsy chipboard compared to the sturdy huddle of stone walls next door.

I get plenty of suspicious glances as the parade starts – *The only tosser here is you*, yanqui! – but that's as bad as it gets. Despite last year's violence, there are no police on hand, at least none in uniform. The *quintos* are busy chanting, shouting and making as much noise as possible, all the while leading their frightened mascot through the streets. Occasionally, Fresita tries to bolt, but the kids yank on the rope around her neck and drag her back. As the cavalcade passes, I mention to one of the town councillors that the thousand-strong crowd seems to be respecting the law.

'Yes. But it's not coming from their hearts; more likely their pockets.'

The climax takes place around five o'clock, when groups of villagers in homemade fancy dress gather in front of the town hall for the parade that's meant to take the place of Goat Tossing. The locals take great pride in making their own costumes, and the most ingenious ones are Orcs from *The Lord of the Rings* and some tots embodying American food: a sandwich, a hamburger and a hot dog, each with Coca-Cola cans wrapped around their ankles. There's also a whole flock of goats in brown cotton suits with bells around their necks.

Suddenly, as the *quintos* arrive, some of the goats make a break for the church. But the real animal is nowhere to be seen: it's been locked up for safekeeping.

Instead, the eight *quintos* emerge on the balcony of the town hall. After jumping up and down some more and shouting 'The Goat Song', they produce some grey doves and release them into the air with a perfunctory shrug. To my surprise, there are no cries of defiance – Viva the Jump of the Goat! – or even criticisms of the status quo. I try to talk to their leader, a dark-haired girl who has the scowl of someone prematurely disappointed with life.

'Don't talk to us!' she snarls.

Later, though, during the Dance of the Goat, I bump into one of the boys. Javi's wearing baggy trousers and a skull-tight beanie cap: vintage American ghetto by way of Enrique Iglesias. Like his compadres, he's in a permanent sulk about not being able to toss the goat. 'You wait eighteen years, and because of what's happened, you don't get to do it. It's a bitch.'

Meanwhile, the organisers reckon the *quintos* will revert to throwing a stuffed goat from the church once the furore and hard feelings die down.

Failing that, there are always other options. 'I've been told it's possible to find *inflatable* goats,' one tells me.

They're available in all good Spanish sex shops . . . apparently.

PART THREE:
RUN, ROOSTER, RUN

Fortunately for me, the same weekend in January offers a two-for-one on fiestas. A hundred miles from Manganeses, still within sprawling Castilla y León, an even tinier village is holding another coming-of-age ritual. In the Rooster Run of Guarrate, however, the roosters don't do much running. The freshly killed birds are hung upside down on a line so that kids in military uniform can gallop past on horses and whack them with their swords. As with similar traditions elsewhere, the roosters used to still be squawking when they were strung up.

Nowadays, though, their necks are wrung beforehand as a concession to the squeamish. You might expect the tossers of Manganeses to express some solidarity with the hackers of Guarrate. But this is Spain, where a hundred miles might as well be a hundred light years: centuries of warfare have sharpened the very human urge to protect what's yours and yours alone: the rest of the world can go to hell (or God willing, purgatory). When I told Pedro's wife that I was planning to leave Manganeses to go to the *Corre de Gallo*, she frowned in disgust. 'That to me seems barbarous. The Jump was silly, but at least we never killed the goat.'

Driving into Guarrate on Sunday morning, I begin to worry that I have the wrong date. It's only a half-hour before Mass, and the village is virtually deserted, except for a used paella pan propped up in a doorway. The red-roofed buildings are made up of the usual patchwork of putty-coloured masonry, but Guarrate is built on more of a hill than Manganeses, surrounded by fields that somehow look greener and more fertile, even in January. The church's tiered bell tower juts up over the sanctuary – and everything else – while on the fringe of the village, another edifice competes for the villagers' devotion. Despite its minuscule population (only 300 inhabitants), Guarrate has its very own bullfighting arena, a temple to the local cult of the bull. In fact, the town of Toro is only half an hour away.

While I'm killing time in the church – it's got more statues of saints than places to put them – a barrage of rockets explodes outside. The fiesta has begun. A procession quickly fills the small sanctuary to standing-room-only capacity. The guests of honour are this year's crop of eight *quintos* and their families, not all of whom actually live in the village. The four girls have traditional silk Manila shawls draped over their shoulders, the long fringes skirting their ankles, while the boys are dressed in elegant black Castilian capes that protect them from the cold. The solemnity of the service is counterbalanced by the musicians belting out religious *jotas* from the balcony overhead, syncopating the songs with the clicking of *castañuelos* and the rasping of an unusual instrument: the knobbly surface of a bottle of anise.

Parched from all that singing, most of the congregation leaves the church to cross over to the bar for an aperitif and a snack before the serious drinking kicks in. A local photographer introduces me to Juan Cabral, an old-timer with a sun-weathered face and blue-grey eyes that match the sheen of his jacket. Over a sweet glass of *mosto* and a plate of calamari, Juan explains to me that the main draw for the crowds during the Rooster Run is the oratory. The *quintos* recite comic poems poking fun at their friends and families, satirising individuals in the community and cracking wise about local and national events. The rooster is secondary, he says. That's why no one baulks about whether it's dead or alive. Then he narrows his eyes and delivers an ultimatum: 'If you're looking for something morbid, you might as well leave right now.'

Next thing I know, a gunslinger moseys into the bar and shoots the piano player.

Not really. But that's the kind of place this is: if the locals like you, they'll do anything for you; if they don't, they're liable to do anything *to* you. Juan's eyes can beam all the warmth of humanity at you one moment, then turn cold and reptilian the next. It's a look that I always think of, for lack of a better term, as pure Hard-Bastard Castilian. That sounds like a terrible slur, but the truth is no group of humans could scrape a living out of this environment for hundreds (and possibly even hundreds of thousands) of years without the help of some cast-iron, carry-them-around-in-a-wheelbarrow *cojones*. It's no coincidence that many of the conquistadors hailed from Castilla.

Fortunately, Juan seems to take a liking to me, even offering to introduce me to the poet of the Rooster Run. First, though, comes the event itself.

Led by their captain, a square-jawed boy of eighteen, the *quintos* ride on horseback around the village, followed on foot by the *quintas*, a brass band and the rest of the village. This time, the girls are wearing the capes; the boys are dressed up like soldiers: green military dress suits over their shirts and ties, white gloves, black riding boots and officer-style hats. They stop for drinks at the homes of the mayor and other VIPs, then proceed to what must be the main street, banked on one side by a grassy incline full of humpbacked knolls with doorways. Though they look like the honeycombed entrances to catacombs, or possibly the front doors of very large gophers, they're actually bodegas. Anywhere else, having your own wine cellar would be an extravagance, but in the countryside of Castilla, virtually every family has a bodega. These alcoholic bomb shelters are passed down the generations, though no one seems to know how long they've been here. The assumption is for ever.

One by one the dead roosters are winched up over the street and the boys take turns addressing the community. Even in death, the roosters are magnificent birds, prime examples of the beauty and diversity of *Gallus domesticus*, their plumage blending from reddish brown to dark blue, shiny green to ink-tipped snow, the feathers glistening defiantly against the dull sky. Invariably, the young men begin their speeches by crowing about the glories of Guarrate, but after that anything's fair game. Mounted on horseback, with a dead bird overhead and the *quintas* giggling behind them, they lampoon village characters and embarrass their friends and families with jokes that are so specific the punchlines easily pass you by if you're not local. At the end, they turn their eyes heavenward to address the chicken, even though it's long past hearing them. With a final flourish, they unsheathe their swords and bat the bird's head more out of duty than malice. The other *quintos* gallop past, bashing the cock-on-a-string.

So far, so phallic. But perhaps the most bizarre aspect is that these are young men – *teenagers* – proudly reciting *poetry* – that *rhymes* – in *public* – as a rite of passage. Not just a few humpty-dumpty couplets, either, or raps about bitches and hos; they've memorised mini-epics with multiple stanzas. What's more, they're waxing lyrical in front of hundreds of people of all ages who have waited in the cold to listen to picaresque verse, perching on balconies, standing on walls and crowding right up next to them on the street to hear what they view as home truths, always laced with humour to avoid ruffling any feathers. In the spirit of *El Gallo*, the poems sound off about the plight of the countryside. 'I sing in honour of the peasants,' one of the cadets declares, before ticking off the usual complaints about immigration, environmentalists, the free market and the strings attached to EU aid. 'We don't want charity,' he shouts. 'All we want is justice!'

> We're losing aspects of our village life
> Our strange and amazing traditions
> Every year we have more bachelors
> But a smaller population.

As the applause turns to laughter, the *quinto* goes in for the kill.

> What's the matter with our *machos*?
> Have they lost their desire?
> Or is it that their balls and pricks
> Simply cannot sire?

The language turns even cruder with the arrival of the final speaker. The Fool is played by a different villager each year, incarnated in a topical disguise. Today, the figure coming down the street looks vaguely familiar. He's wearing a blond wig and some sort of football shirt, waving and shouting from the back of a haywagon. *It can't be.* With that fussy hairstyle, though, and the Real Madrid strip, it can only be one person. He turns, and the photo-mask in front of his face confirms his identity: David Beckham! He would've arrived sooner, he says by way of apology, but somebody hid his hair band. Then he starts flirting with the *chicas* in the audience.

> Feel free to take advantage
> And touch my ponytail
> But if I take my mask off
> You'll be off like bats out of hell.

And with that, he tears off the face of Beckham to reveal his true identity: Berto, *El Feo*. To be sure, The Ugliest Man in the Village is everything that Beckham is not: big-nosed, cross-eyed, snaggle-toothed and full of personality. Swearing like a true Spaniard, he offers himself to the mayor to help lure women to the village.

Don't worry about fixing roads,
creating jobs or other stunts
It would be better if you'd bring in
a trailer full of—

The audience howls at the c-word (*chumino*, since you ask) and some señoras gasp, but not for long. The jokes keep coming to the end.

So *adios*, you beautiful women
I have to go and train
And give my snooty wife
A tumble here in Spain.

Or America, as it happens.

El Beckham departs, and Juan introduces me to the author of this afternoon's entertainment. Luis Miguel de Dios is a radio and newspaper reporter who's written for most of the nationals at some point during his career. With typical hospitality, even though I could be an ecologist, he invites me to have a drink with a couple of friends in his bodega. I can't say *Sí* quick enough. The closest I've come to drinking in a bodega are the touristy *cuevas* in downtown Madrid. But Luis Miguel's is the real thing, a rustic drinking den with a barrel-vaulted ceiling and a long table and benches running down the middle. Wine-making equipment is stacked at the back and wooden casks are piled up in the corner, ready to be filled – or drunk. Here and there the brick walls are hung with miscellaneous farm tools, like the old wooden yoke over the central arch.

We start out on homemade muscatel (poured from earthenware jugs) before moving on to red wine. Along the way, we have a good ol' chat about the origins of the Rooster Run and its counterpart in Manganeses.

'The Jump of the Goat has only been around for about six days,' sniffs one of the men, whereas their ritual goes back to pre-Christian times. The theory goes that roosters, like bulls, embodied virility for the Celtic Iberians who settled in north-west Spain; by ritually killing and eating the animals, men literally absorbed their life force. At one time, the birds' blood probably would have dripped onto the boys, symbolising their passage to manhood.

It's a neat story. But the priapic theory withers when you consider that other towns use geese instead of roosters, and sometimes the riders are even girls. The more likely explanation is that spectacles like the Rooster Run developed in recent centuries, as ways to show off swordsmanship and riding skills.

Whatever its roots, Luis Miguel scoffs at any suggestion that Guarrate's event is cruel: the roosters are hand-raised by the *quintos'* godmothers and live in free-range luxury until their deaths. 'They have a much better quality of life than battery hens, which are the main source of food for most people.' It's the same with complaints about the wolf culls in the area. Spain is one of the last countries on the Continent to actually have a native wolf population – the English exterminated theirs long ago – and the only reason it's survived is because of farmers keeping them from overbreeding.

Meanwhile, the reverse is true for humans. 'Depopulation is the main problem facing Castilla y León,' Luis says, pouring me another glass. The situation is so bad that local boosters have tried to turn rural decline into a tourist attraction. A guide to *Abandoned Villages* promises urban weekenders 'more than seventy ghost towns chosen for their beauty'.

One of his friends leans forward. 'Economic surveys consistently rank Castilla y León as one of the poorest regions in the European Union. But they measure that by counting something ridiculous like the number of microwaves per person.' He laughs, his belly straining against the table. 'I ask you: if we can have locally produced food, cooked every day in wood-burning ovens, why the *hell* would we want microwaves?'

I'll drink to that.

The mention of sustenance inspires us to visit another bodega, owned by the parents of the *quintos*' captain. It's an altogether ritzier affair, like a private underground restaurant: all discreet lighting and earth-tone ambience, with candles and a fireplace. The food is casual enough to be unassuming but abundant enough to belie wealth: a never-ending supply of wine and cheese, chorizo and salchichon, puff pastries and empanadas for the fifteen of us gathered around the table. I'm sitting next to the captain's mother, a glamorous academic from the University of Salamanca. Mili and her husband live in the city but keep a country home here. Their guests are a mix of out-of-towners and villagers, including *El Feo*, who drops by to soak up some wine and adulation. 'When you tore off the mask, I couldn't stop laughing!' Mili tells him. 'You were the Anti-Beckham!' Rather than take offence, Berto accepts it as a compliment, seemingly resigned to – and at ease with – his physiognomic fate.

Across the table, a silver-haired businessman tells me that although he lives in the Canary Islands, he comes back every year to Guarrate, where he and Mili grew up. 'And you want to know why? Because this is the navel – the centre – of the world!'

Surrounded by the jokes and laughter, with enough food and drink to survive a nuclear holocaust, it would be hard to disagree. On a good night, the party doesn't end until ten the next morning, when the revellers emerge blinking into the sunlight. My new best friend is Berto, who's insisting that after this I must go to his house to have dinner with him and his family. But it's ten p.m. already, and I've got a long drive ahead of me. I really shouldn't drink any more; I've got an early flight tomorrow.

Before I leave, Mili mentions her friend's daughter, who travelled to the States as an exchange student and practically died of loneliness. Her hosts were friendly and their house a mansion, but they were never at home; they were too busy working to enjoy life.

The man from the Canaries nods and spreads his arms expansively. 'You're sitting here with people who have travelled the world. We know many places – China, the US, Britain – and they're nice to visit, but when it comes to the way they live, we have only two words to say' – he switches to English for emphasis – '*Keep it.*'

CHAPTER TWO

WOMEN ON TOP
CUTTING TIES AND TAILING SPIES IN GERMANY

PART ONE:

SWINGING IN THE RHINELAND

I wouldn't normally think of a necktie as a babe magnet, especially not the navy-and-orange number I picked up in London before coming here, a garish Disney design best described as Mickey Mouse in an acid-rain haze. The girl in the charity shop could barely keep from sniggering at my bad taste. But during the 'Crazy Days' of carnival in Germany, even a necktie like mine is bound to win me a kiss from a random Fräulein . . . provided that I first let her, uh, cut it off. Freudian implications aside, her scissors are the least of my worries. For all I know, there's a German detective, *ein* private dick, tailing me right now, to ensure that I don't indulge in that other time-honoured tradition of Wenches' Feast Night: adultery, coyly known as a 'sideways leap' in German.

To find out more about *Weiberfastnacht*, aka 'Dirty Thursday', I put in a call to the place where it supposedly all started. Now Bonn, you'll recall, was until very recently the German capital, a city so respectable as to be boring, full of politicians puffed up with sauerkraut and its attendant hot air. So it comes as something of a surprise to ring up the tourist office out of the blue and be given unsolicited advice on swinging.

'Brink lots of ties and you vill get lots of kiss. Iff you don't brink ties, no kiss,' the woman informed me.

'I'll be sure to remember that.'

'Do you haff a partner?'

'Uhh . . . yes.'

'Denn brink your lady and you can haff lots of fun. You can each haff separate party.' What followed was a laugh so dirty I had to clean out my ears after hanging up. Nothing sounds smuttier than an innuendo delivered in a German accent.

The receptionist at my hotel also gives me the wink-nudge treatment as he's checking me in (or out, as the case may be).

'Only a sinkle room, eefen though many vimmin?'

What on earth is going on? This isn't Rio; it's the Rhineland. As in football, though, German Mardi Gras gives Latin *carnaval* a run for its money. What the Germans may lack in creativity and spontaneity, they make up for with a dead-eyed determination to have fun or die trying. During *Karneval*, they tackle carnal abandon with all the seriousness they once reserved for questions of the mind and soul.

Deutschland's carnival heartland is the traditionally Catholic south-west, which, not coincidentally, encompasses some of

Germany's most famous vineyards. From 11 November, hardcore *Karnevalers* celebrate the so-called 'Fifth Season' of the year, culminating in a week's worth of intensive partying before the self-denial of Lent. 'If you plan it right, and you've got the money, you can have a party every night for about three months, from November right up until Ash Wednesday,' a Rhinelander tells me. In fact, you could follow carnival's mythical 'Ship of Fools' all the way down the Rhine, from Düsseldorf to Cologne and Mainz and across the Swiss border to Basle. Wherever you go, from Bonn to Bavaria and the Black Forest, the celebrations focus on fancy dress, satire, parades and carousing. The Germans have about a dozen different names for carnival – *Fasching*, *Fasnet*, *Fasnacht* or simply *Karneval*, to name a few – with peculiar greetings from place to place (*Alaaf!* in Cologne, *Helau!* in Düsseldorf), plus a multitude of idiosyncrasies reflecting regional rivalries and local – as opposed to national – pride. 'Carnival is local *everywhere*,' a veteran says. 'Because of our history, it's difficult to be proud of being German. But you can be proud to be a Bonner or a Black Forester.'

Despite all the surface craziness, there is a deeply Germanic method to the madness, including an abiding fondness for silly hats, formalised joke-telling and an obsession with the number eleven. Not only does the Fifth Season begin on 11/11 in most areas, but all the key processions start at eleven minutes past eleven o'clock. The reason for fixating on the number eleven is unclear: it could signify the missing eleventh commandment – 'Thou shalt be a fool' – or it may be a mockery of the revolutionary French, whose motto of *Egalité*, *Liberté*, *Fraternité* (or '*elf*', which is also German for 'eleven') didn't stop them from occupying the Rhineland. The double ones standing side by side may also symbolise the equality of master and servant during *Karneval*. Then again, it may just be a very particular manifestation of the Teutonic sense of humour. 'Eleven is a funny number,' a German man tries to explain to me.

Something's definitely lost in translation.

True to form, having identified a joke, the Germans have isolated it, sent it to the lab for testing and devised a specific term for 'a number consisting of the same digits' – *Schnapszahl* – so that future generations might split their sides upon its mere mention.

To ensure that everyone knows precisely when to laugh, the carnival societies have orchestras on hand to punctuate the humour. During the stage shows at their private fancy-dress dinner parties, a comedian or fool stands in an upright washtub and tells jokes about politicians and whatever suits his fancy, symbolically airing society's dirty laundry in public. For every punchline, the orchestra rewards him with an explosion of musical applause. Not just a little snare drum and high hat (ba-duh-bump-*ching!*); that would be way too subtle. The Germans go for thunderous drums and blaring trumpets known as a *Tusch*: duh-*DAH!* – or, if a joke is especially well constructed, duh-duh-*DAHHH!* Comedians in Blackpool would kill for that fanfare. It's the kind of accolade that other countries reserve for a magician or acrobat who's performed a particularly amazing feat: a German told a joke and – duh-*DAHHHH!* – it was funny!

Laughing on cue behind the performers sits a panel of middle-aged men in matching formalwear. The only thing remotely foolish about the governing 'Council of Eleven' is their headgear. Ever since the first Europeans pranced around caves with antlers on their heads, men seem to have had a primal urge to wear silly hats. In the case of *Karneval*, the hats are reminiscent of stiff, gold-embroidered tea cosies. One grand poobah of carnival says they represent the body of a cockerel – a link to the Rooster Run I witnessed in Spain. The story goes that during the Middle Ages, people would hang a rooster upside down, and the man who chopped its head off was named the biggest fool and made king for the day. So the typical carnival hat is shaped like a rooster, he tells me. 'It's the hat of a cock.'

That's one word for it. To me, though, the shape looks more like the prow of a ship, bringing to mind the two main theories about the origin of the word 'carnival': it may come from the Latin term meaning 'farewell to the flesh' – a pun on both the forty days of fish-eating and self-sacrifice during Lent – or it may refer to the Ship of Fools that floated through the crowds in medieval processions. We'll never know. One thing's for certain, though: during the modern incarnation of carnival, you can see plenty of fools wearing cutdown ships on their heads, the cloth vessels sailing on seas of hair – or cresting on combovers. For proof of how organised the revelry is, you need look no further than the local *Narrenfahrplan*, or Fools' Timetable, of events issued around the country: in Germany, even the fools are on the clock.

To be fair, many young Germans also fail to see anything fun in the clockwork formality. The structured side of *Karneval* dates from 1823, when the fragrant bourgeoisie of Cologne – Germany's oldest big city – decided to make their medieval debauchery respectable, keeping up with their counterparts in the rest of Europe, including Britain, where the royals were practically fresh-off-the-boat Germans. The Cologners turned the centuries-old folk event into an old boys' club, forming the first carnival societies (originally closed to women) and electing a ruling triumvirate for the Crazy Days: a Prince and a Peasant, plus a 'Virgin' played by a male.

By organising the revelry, the reformers helped ensure its survival. *Karneval* had always been a way for the masses to poke fun at their rulers, with the fool saying things that couldn't be said during the rest of the year. When Napoleon's troops took Cologne in 1794, the Gallic occupiers found the Germans' jokes so galling they banned *Karneval* for four years. Their successors from Protestant Prussia were slightly more tolerant, realising that carnival was too deeply entrenched in the Rhineland to stamp out. However, they did dispatch extra troops to keep the celebrations in check. The revellers responded by creating their own carnival soldiers, who disobeyed orders and made a mockery of Prussian military drills (a tradition that continues to this day). Typical of this bolshy atmosphere was Karl Marx, who edited Cologne's liberal newspaper before the Prussians shut it down. A hundred years later, the humourless Nazis also cracked down on the political satire and cross-dressing of *Karneval*, insisting that the female Virgin be played by a red-blooded Aryan woman rather than a cross-dressing man.

Nevertheless, *Karneval*'s satiric streak has survived. One of the more memorable floats of recent years depicted a naked Bill Clinton cowering before a pregnant Statue of Liberty and claiming, 'It wasn't me.' Another showed George Bush as Pinocchio with the words 'IRAQ HAS WEAPONS OF MASS DESTRUCTION' written on his nose, a phrase that's even lengthier in German. And these days, *Karneval* is as good for the goose as it is for the gander. The final countdown to Lent begins on the Thursday before Shrove Tuesday. *Weiberfastnacht* translates roughly as 'Wenches' Feast Night' but it's also known as 'Dirty' or 'Fat' Thursday – not so much a comment on the women's size or sexual proclivities – but a reference to the fat used in the special cakes and doughnuts served ahead of Lent. Throughout the Rhineland, from the smallest burg to the biggest cities, costumed females stage a day-long putsch, castrating men's ties, storming the town halls and seducing any males they fancy. On *Weiberfastnacht*, the vimmin run vild. 'Watch those German women,' an English friend warned me. 'They're allowed to be frisky by decree. And when Germans are ordered to have fun they go for it with the zeal of a Panzer battalion massing on the Polish border.'

Insofar as anyone knows, this proto-feminist tradition began in Beuel, a village across the Rhine from Bonn and about ten miles downriver from Cologne. For years Beuel's inhabitants made a living out of washing other people's dirty laundry. Given that 'Beuel' is pronounced like 'boil' in English, the laundry business seems like a natural choice for a local industry. Unfortunately, this is just a linguistic coincidence: in German, Beuel is simply an obscure place name. The town's location on the east bank of the river allowed laundries to soak up every last ray of sunshine to dry their clothes. To this day, in fact, Beuel is still home to a couple of industrial laundries and promotes itself as 'the sunny side of the Rhine', even though it's long since been a suburb of Bonn.

Then, as now, some of the laundries' biggest customers were institutions like the University of Bonn and the big hotels in Cologne. After Beuel's washerwomen had done the hard work of wringing, scrubbing, beating and folding, their husbands would return the clean laundry via horse-drawn barge and collect payment on Thursdays. Come *Karneval* time in Cologne, this proved a dangerous division of labour. The men suddenly found themselves in the big city, with pocketfuls of cash, surrounded by free-flowing wine, women and song. Needless to say, not much of the money made it back to Beuel, particularly after Cologne revamped its *Karneval* in 1823. Outraged by their husbands' carousing – and excluded from the new *Karneval* societies – the women got their own back by taking the Thursday off the following year and forming a group powerful enough to strike terror into the heart of any male: a kaffeeklatsch – a caffeine-fuelled gossip circle.

Since then, the sisterhood has never looked back. During the industrialisation of the nineteenth century, while Marx, a former student at the University of Bonn, decried the use of women as 'instruments of production', factories came to rely increasingly on their female workforce, and the women took to celebrating carnival by cutting off their bosses' ties to remind them that they were no better than their own working-class husbands. 'In those days, most husbands never wore ties,' explains Erna Neubauer, the former chief of Beuel's washerwomen. 'So to show the bosses who had the power, the women cut off their ties.' The symbolism seems obvious enough. But Erna denies any Freudian castration fantasies. 'It has nothing to do with sex,' she laughs.

Even so, I'll be keeping a close eye on the snipping.

Not content with grabbing men by the cravats, the washerwomen began storming the town hall in the 1950s. Since then, though, the rise of feminism has complicated their annual assault on this traditionally male bastion. The current mayor of Bonn, the *Oberbürgermeisterin*, is female. Not only that, but she's a Superwoman – an *Überfrau* – if ever there was one. Bärbel Dieckmann is a former school principal, a mother of four (two sets of twins) and a member of the national executive committee of the Social Democratic Party. Oh, and she's married to the Rhineland's ex-finance minister. Of course, her looks are unimportant, but if they *were* important, the 'Lady Mayor' would definitely stand her own against any attractive, intelligent women of a certain age – much more so than say, Chancellor Angela Merkel. Confidently feminine, Bonn's mayor wears just enough make-up to enhance her features. She's also been known to tie her blonde bob into a girlish bow to stand alongside the men of the town council. '*Weiberfastnacht* is a tradition of feminism,' she tells me. 'It's a really special feeling, and there is a *real* identification of women with other women. It's different from other parts of *Karneval*.'

When she first came to power in 1994, there was some debate as to whether she should continue the mock battle of the sexes by dressing up like a man. 'But the women and I decided that we didn't want to do that. We wanted to keep the symbolism to show that after a hundred and seventy years, there was a woman mayor. The washerwomen in the nineteenth century hoped that in the future there would be a female Lord Mayor, and so now I have the key to the town hall. I am a secret ally.' She smiles cannily.

Weiberfastnacht has sister events scattered around Europe, reflecting the near-universal popularity of one of carnival's oldest jokes. While some academics try to ascribe quasi-religious importance to gender swapping, it's more likely that humans are simply hardwired to find role reversal funny. People get a kick out of seeing the little guy made up as the big man or the great and powerful humbled for a day. When it comes to the battle of the sexes, the instinct may run deeper: at the back of his caveman's mind, even the most macho of men knows that he owes his very existence to women. And males know that if they don't acknowledge this ultimate power every once in a while, even if it's just one day a year, the women in their lives might actually start wielding it – at will and without mercy.

So it is that in villages in Macedonia in early January, men pay tribute to their local Gynaecocracy – that's ancient Greek for 'girl power'. The women leave their husbands at home with the housework while they have the run of the villages, including that most sacred of sanctums for Greek males: the corner coffee shop. Likewise, during Spain's Fiesta of the Female Mayors near Segovia, the women elect an honorary *Matahombres*, or Man Killer. I heard about it after the Rooster Run, while drinking in the bodega with the professor from Salamanca and her friends.

'In that fiesta, the women take power,' one of the men said.

'We've always had it,' *la profesora* corrected. 'But on that day, apart from private power, we have public power as well.'

'That's right. The rest of the year the women give us plenty of rope, but on that day, they rein us back in to remind us who's in control.'

Lest you think that this nagging suspicion is limited to macho, maternalistic societies, consider this anecdote. In 1960, a reporter supposedly asked Winston Churchill, a notorious opponent of women's rights: 'What is your comment on the prediction that in the year 2000, women will rule the world?'

The great orator simply grunted. 'They still will, will they?'

It isn't every day you get picked up by a woman in a feathered hat, but then again, this is *Karneval*. The day before *Weiberfastnacht*, the senior washerwoman swings past my hotel in her red jacket and matching tricorn to take me around Bonn with the Washer Princess and her entourage. Before I know it, I'm bundled into a people carrier decorated in party colours. I'm sitting next to an old man dressed up as a parody of a Prussian guard and across from this year's princess and her two scrubber handmaidens. Together, they've put in hundreds of appearances in the run-up to carnival, and tonight is their last big push before *Weiberfastnacht*. They've been visiting schools and nursing homes all day, and the princess, Silvia Emmerich, is beginning to show the signs. She's got a stomach bug, which may explain why one of her attendants was so quick to give up her seat to make room for me. If the princess hurls – and she could blow any minute – I'm directly in the trajectory.

Nevertheless, she soldiers on, munching the only thing she can stomach at the moment: a pretzel. Blonde and petite, twenty-two-year-old Silvia is pretty enough, though her laundry princess's costume doesn't do her any favours. It's a blue velvet bodice with cascading white lace – enough to put curtains in all the windows of the Reichstag – topped off with a frilly washerwoman's cap. Her sidekicks are also in caps, plus white aprons over their simpler frocks. One of them has a spike in her eyebrow, and her German reserve could easily be mistaken for surliness. Facing this trio gives me ample time to ruminate on why the German scrubber – unlike the archetypal French maid – has never found a place in the Pantheon of Male Desire. At a guess, I'd blame the underwear: real, old-fashioned granny pants, knee-length bloomers with an even uglier name: *Spitzenhöschen*. In a sex olympics, though, I'm sure the German washerwomen would give any Gallic floozies a good drubbing, scoring with ruthless efficiency and a technically flawless – if uninspired – finish.

For all I know, though, German guys may like knee-length knickers. 'We will fight against the men, and they will resist, but we will win!' Silvia laughs, explaining that with one flash of her bloomers, the male opposition will go ga-ga. Her other weapons in this war of the sexes are a doll of herself cradled in her arm – worryingly, it makes her look even younger than she is – and a wooden sceptre with a man baring his buttocks on top: the *Bröckemännchen*, the Little Bridge-Man. 'This is what I show to Bonn!' Silvia says with a smile, fingering the crack in the figure's backside.

From what I can see, the Washer Princess doesn't seem like much of a feminist; bloomers aside, though, I'm told she's a cunning stunt. At least that's what the Senior Washerwoman says. Evi Zwiebler tells me that the women added the princess to their tradition about fifty years ago. 'We use her to lure the men,' she grins. 'We have a saying in German: "Men can see better than they think."' Evi herself was the Washer Princess in 1973; now she revels in the much less flattering but powerful role of *Obermöhn*, the 'Old Married Woman' running the show.

We pay a visit to the local newspaper, where Bonn's official *Karneval* Prince and Princess also make an appearance for a photo opportunity. They're the formal side of *Karneval* – the private clubs and dinner dances – representing everything that non-carnival-lovers hate about the so-called Crazy Days. 'A German joke is no laughing matter,' Mark Twain quipped, and these people take their sense of humour way too seriously. Their golden costumes are so elaborately embroidered and bejewelled that they must cost hundreds, if not thousands, of euros. They could certainly stand their own against any eighteenth-century courtier's. The visual joke – such as it is – is their *Karneval* headgear. But a serious amount of work has obviously gone into their Ship of Fools hats. It's this forced jollity, this regimented mirth-making – *vee haff vays of mehkink you laff* – that some Germans dislike about *Karneval*, so much so that many leave the country during this time of year to go on holiday.

More silly hats await us at Beuel's town hall on the other side of the river. The Rathaus consists of two rectangular blocks cantilevered together in typical postwar fashion, though it's currently being given a facelift. The vertical bit is sheathed in scaffolding and green tarp. Inside, the members of the Old Washerwomen's Committee line up alongside the mayor and other public officials. Brandishing her mooning-man wand, Silvia addresses the men in that peculiarly doll-like voice she uses when speaking in public: 'Beware, gentlemen, today I am a little weak, but tomorrow I will show no mercy. Tomorrow you will know who I am. My greatest dream is to conquer the town hall!'

While I'm sampling some *Bönnsch*, the cloudy lager typical of Bonn, a man who's a doppelgänger for a scruffy Günther Grass shows me the medals and ribbons festooning his chest, identifying him as one of Beuel's City Soldiers. 'Which has nothing to do with the military – *nothing*,' he stresses, explaining the old chestnut about the Prussian occupiers. After two centuries, the joke gets funnier every year. 'But you must understand – it has nothing to do with the military.'

I know, I know – *nussing!*

In a similar vein, I meet my first Not-Nazi. A smiling old man comes up to me and introduces himself by announcing, 'I was a prisoner in the US during the war.'

I'm not quite sure how to respond. *Hold on, Herr – we're not meant to mention the war.* But he doesn't seem to care, and neither do the dozens of people around us. He informs me that 350,000 Germans were shipped to the States during the Second World War. I knew Britain held hundreds of thousands of German POWs; in fact, the British took their time returning them; they needed the captive manpower to help rebuild the country. But I didn't know that German prisoners were shipped all the way to America, much less that they were paid for their labour. Another ex-POW tells me he picked cotton in Phoenix, beetroots in Montana and peaches in California from 1944 to 1946, earning $27 a month – a decent wage, considering that a pack of Chesterfields cost only ten cents. What's more, the prisoners were allowed to play sports and eat as much fruit as they liked. One Christmas in California, the Germans even made wine: eighty litres for just eight men. That was practically a holiday camp compared to his brief stay in Britain en route to the US.

'England was *terrible*,' he says, shaking his head. 'There was nothing to eat. It was worse than Germany.'

That's because you bombed Britain to hell and back.

Like many of his compatriots, though, he seems blissfully oblivious to the fact that conditions in the UK were 'terrible' precisely because of the (two) war(s) started by Germany. It's strange, too, how you can find plenty of German veterans but never any Nazis. 'I was too young,' they'll say, or 'I was drafted; I never joined the Nazi Party' or 'My friend was signed up as a Nazi because he had very Aryan features.' It's as if they belong to a parallel generation of Not-Nazis – *die Nichtnazis*. Just as the French have rewritten history to imply that they alone liberated Paris, with Charles de Gaulle single-handedly sweeping the enemy from the Champs-Elysées with his freakishly wide hips, some Germans seem to believe that the only bona fide, card-carrying Nazis during the Second World War were Hitler himself and *possibly* Goebbels, if only to satisfy the grammatical diktat that 'Nazis' is plural. As for the rest of the armed forces, they weren't paid-up supporters of the fascist regime; they were mere soldiers, innocent conscripts stormtrooping their way through Europe. Human nature being what it is, though, you can't help but wonder if they'd be bragging had the war gone the other way.

This isn't to belittle the profound psychological burden that many Germans carry. To get your average German talking about guilt – even someone born well after the war – is to depress yourself with a case of secondhand *Angst*. But you also get the impression that many have coped with the past by compartmentalising it and distancing themselves from Those Nazis, a race of aliens who landed outside Munich in 1933 and somehow brainwashed the entire country into thinking that a dark, stumpy, lone-testicled dictator exemplified the Aryan ideal.

What's also striking is how one-sided the obsession is between Britain and Germany. Most Britons over the age of thirty can give you a list as long as the Rhine about why they don't like the Germans, even if they've never known one, let alone visited the country. The one English Germanophile I know – yes, there really is such a word – can't quite bring himself to admit he's stopped worrying about the war and learnt to love the Krauts. 'I'd say I'm more fascinated, really,' he clarifies. British TV schedules are clogged with Second World War programmes, a kind of patriotic porn, perfect for late-night when-we-were-greating. It's only a matter of time before documentaries like *Hitler's Lesbians: Nazi Women in Love*, *Gobbling Goebbels: A Prostitute's Tale*, or *Führerball:*

The Secret Life of Adolf's Lone Testicle goosestep their way across living rooms. After all, who can forget the ill-fated British sitcom about Adolf and Eva living next to a Jewish couple in America? The title was *Heil, Honey, I'm Home!*

If you ask Germans about their image of Britain, though, you're liable to get blank looks. If they think of the UK at all, they might mention the Royal Family (what with them being German and all), David Beckham, the glories of London and the clichés about lousy food and even worse weather. On the whole, though – and this is perhaps the truly insulting bit – you get the impression that Germans don't care enough about Britain to even bother forming an opinion about it; they're much more focused on America. And despite the protests against cultural imperialism, war and globalisation, they speak American English, listen to American music, watch American movies and even deign to eat American food: in Bonn, the McDonald's just up the street from Kennedy Bridge and the Rhine is cranking out Big Macs round the clock.

But enough of this Germanic contemplation. *Karneval* is about drinking, not thinking. 'Tomorrow is like Christmas, Easter, your birthday, all put together,' a former Washer Princess gushes. 'It's the best day of the year.'

Someone who feels decidedly less enthused is Lothar Wenzel, a proud native of Cologne – Germany's carnival capital – who's also a private detective. 'I used to enjoy *Karneval*, but not now,' he says with a frown. For him, it just means extra work. Ironically, the spiritual daughters of Beuel's washerwomen have been so successful in getting their own back during *Karneval* that nowadays many indulge in the philandery that used to be the preserve of men in Cologne. For their jealous partners, however, the old double standard still applies. As a result, *Karneval* is peak season for Herr Wenzel. He and his private dicks disguise themselves as clowns, pirates and even Scots in kilts to catch cheating Fraus and Fräuleins during the Crazy Days.

Herr Wenzel himself doesn't look anything like the guy on his website, which is actually a relief. The blond model online is dressed in a trilby and a shiny blue suit like the star of some trashy remake of *The Maltese Falcon*. He's even holding a newspaper; all that's missing is a trenchcoat. Likewise, Herr Wenzel's office is conspicuously located on a sidestreet near the old city, announcing itself in bold letters in the window – Detektei Lothar Wenzel – surrounded by a circle reminiscent of the opening bullethole credits in a Bond film. Inside, the decor is effortlessly retro: dark, Persian rugs on the white tile floor, black leather chairs with chrome tubing and a mirrored-and-marbled reception desk topped off with a bronze statuette of the *Venus de Milo*, for a touch of class with a capital K. The overall feel harks back to the Eighties, a time of limitless nostalgia here in the Land the Mullet Never Forgot. If you listen hard enough, you can almost hear the Scorpions ringing through the space – time continuum like tinnitus, even if it's been decades since the Winds of Change have blown through here.

Unlike his showy surroundings – he's even got little bumper stickers that read 'I ♥ DETEKTIVE WENZEL KÖLN' – the spymaster of love could blend in just about anywhere in Germany, what with his patterned jumper, taut beer belly, stubbly jowls and salt-and-pepper mullet. Sitting in the fluorescent gloam of his office, a financial news channel scrolling across the TV at his side, he tells me and my interpreter about his work, rubbing his eyes and chain-smoking pencil-thin cigars. Sometimes he allows himself a chuckle, but for the most part he comes across as a professional businessman who neither loves nor hates his job. If anything, he's simply weary of human weakness.

However, my ponytailed interpreter, who's costing me a bomb, is lapping it up. He counts himself among those who hate *Karneval*, but he's loving this interview, raising an eyebrow at every salacious detail. 'It's great to learn something I didn't know about my own city. I never would have connected *Karneval* and detective work.'

But Herr Wenzel is so busy during the Crazy Days he often has to bring in agents from other areas to manage the additional assignments. Such as the one I like to think of as the Case of the Hamburgers That Were Actually Bangers. An adulterous couple from Hamburg decided to use *Karneval* as a cover for a dirty weekend in Cologne. Wenzel's detectives noted that the woman arrived at the hotel without any festive gear. Bizarrely, though, her lover had smuggled in a pipe and drums – each to his own; maybe they liked some extra pomp and circumstance with their rumpy pumpy. Wenzel dutifully informed the woman's husband that his wife was holed up in a hotel with another man.

'But that can't be,' the husband said. 'I just spoke to her on the phone. She was right in the middle of a *Karneval* procession and having lots of fun.'

She may have been having a lot of fun, but Wenzel knew she was still in the hotel. Hence the musical instruments. While she'd been phoning her husband, her lover had been parading up and down the room providing carnivalesque sound effects.

Wenzel says his clients over the course of the Crazy Days are pretty evenly divided between suspicious wives and husbands.

'Their reactions are quite interesting,' he muses, blowing smoke out of his nostrils. He reckons that three-quarters of husbands are simply looking for reasons to divorce. 'Sometimes you say, well, nothing happened, and the husband says, "Oh, that's great." And others will say, "*Scheisse* – I was hoping something would happen!"' Most of his female clients, in contrast, are trying to save their marriage. 'But experience shows that if a man is unfaithful, he won't really change, even if he has been caught. Maybe he can change for six months to a year, and try to be faithful, but he won't really change.'

Take the Case of the Legless Kerbcrawler, instigated by the heiress who hired Wenzel to keep tabs on her husband. Every year, the man and his friends dress up like princes and party at one of the many private carnival sessions before rounding out the night with a visit to a whorehouse. 'He has many friends because he always pays for their visits to the brothel,' Wenzel explains. 'But it's his wife's money.' Normally the man pays cash, but last year the readies ran out, so he paid by credit card. That was his first mistake. Wenzel's men obtained a copy of the receipt. His second mistake was to be photographed staggering in and out of the brothel, in full uniform, carrying his toy rifle.

'Didn't he notice your men taking photos?'

'It isn't a problem during *Karneval*, because they are so drunk by five o'clock in the morning, they don't even realise.' Wenzel's agents also witnessed the man going into a room with a prostitute, though they don't try to take pictures inside or catch him *in flagrante*. 'It's impossible. The risk is too high that we'll lose the assignment. And anyway, it's clear what he's doing. You don't need pictures.'

Despite last year's damning evidence, the party prince has

been up to his old tricks this season. 'This year the wife said she wanted to do something about it but still save the marriage.' So his men have tailed him again. 'We took some nice pictures. One night he was so drunk he crawled into a taxi in his uniform on his hands and knees. His friends had to help him into the taxi.'

The Case of Berry the Clown seems to have had a somewhat happier ending. Two of Wenzel's detectives dressed as clowns to track a suspected philanderer, but they lost him in the chaos of *Karneval* because the man and his lover kept hopping from bar to bar. Determined to get the evidence they needed, 'Berry' and his partner went to the man's hotel for breakfast, still wearing their costumes, and bribed a maid to get into his room. Once inside, the clowns filmed the romantic champagne for two that the lovers had enjoyed, as well as the twisted sheets and the clothes shed around the room. They even rummaged through the wastebasket for condoms (rubber gloves are an essential part of the love detective's toolkit). They then delivered the video – and the used rubbers – to the man's wife. 'The thing was, Ash Wednesday was their anniversary, so she wanted to give the video to her husband as an anniversary present,' Wenzel laughs. 'Just to let him know that she knew about it.' He hasn't heard from her since, so he assumes that the couple managed to resolve the issue one way or another. 'She was satisfied,' he says with a grin.

Another big growth area is employees who call in sick during *Karneval*. The government has just announced that unemployment has hit five million, or 12 per cent of the population – the highest level since Hitler was in power. Part of this has to do with a change in the way the jobless are counted, but it also reflects a shift from the German work ethic to the out-of-work ethic. Germans famously rank at the top of Europe's holiday league, taking an average of forty-three days' paid holiday per year – compared to British workers' meagre allotment of twenty-eight – and even when they are working, the Germans don't necessarily live up to the industrious stereotype of old. A couple of anecdotes: an English friend who's a press officer at a European pharmaceutical company was puzzled to receive an invoice from a German freelancer; the man wanted to bill the company for having shown up at its news conference. Then there's the waiter here in Cologne who was recently sacked for downing up to *one hundred* bottles of beer a day on the job without paying for them. Somehow or another, he *won* his unfair dismissal claim: not only that, he was awarded £2,000, plus three months' wages. Of course, not all Germans have turned into work-shy skivers. But there's no denying a shift in attitudes. Just as the Spanish have turned their backs on anything remotely linked to Franco, the Germans seem to have enthusiastically (and very efficiently) rejected the values that predate the Nazis. Why work hard and go to church if all it leads to is fascism? In doing so, though, you can't help but wonder if they haven't thrown *das Baby* out with *dem Badewasser*.

Maybe it's because they've got more important things on their minds. Leafing through the morning papers, Herr Wenzel shows me the headline on the *Express* tabloid: *Wieverfastelovend: We're all thinking about SEX*. And, just in case you weren't, it provides some food for thought: a bare-breasted blonde on page one, her nipples jutting out just above the fold on the front of every street-corner kiosk in the city.

Over in Beuel, the parade's getting underway when I meet up with Martin Sauerborn, a journalist I met while doing the rounds with the Washer Princess. I ask him about infidelity during *Karneval*, having heard a tragic story from a washer-woman. A few years ago, a young couple were in a club called Rheinlust on the riverbank, when apparently the boy caught his girlfriend kissing someone else. He ran up to the bridge over the Rhine and jumped off, killing himself. 'Lots of relationships have problems after *Karneval*,' Martin says, guiding me through gangs of monks, clowns, Red Indians and American policemen outside the town hall. 'But there are also lots of new relationships. And lots of children.' So many, in fact, that the Germans have a special word for them: *Karnevalskinder*. 'Sometimes people drink too much – they forget what they do.'

Inside the Rathaus, the TV and newspaper journalists are working through the free beer, wine, coffee and cold cuts on offer, as well as the jam-filled doughnuts known as Berliners (or JFKs, as I like to think of them) that are typically eaten on *Weiberfastnacht*. I've got my acid-rain Mickey with me, but I have yet to put it on. Truth is, I haven't seen any other men wearing ties, and I've begun to think that maybe it's the kind of behaviour that marks you out as a tourist, like Americans in Britain who try to blend in by wearing London Fog trenchcoats. As soon as I slip the knot around my neck, Martin alerts the PR girl, a brunette in a miniskirt and an Oakland police shirt and cap, a woman whose personal theme tune could be 'Bad Girls' by Donna Summer – *Beep! Beep! Aaaah – Beep! Beep!* She dutifully fetches a pair of scissors. Having docked my neckwear, she gives me a prim little kiss, the kind of *Bützje* that the tourist brochures warn foreigners not to get overly excited about.

In the small square below, in front of a store called Kaisers, revellers in party gear are drinking and swaying to the carnival music churned out by a band onstage, a stein-swinging, elbow-locking rhythm that's as corny as oompah music, but more modern, perfect for clapping in unison. Some women manage to break the monotony with a little two-step or a shake of the hips, but a lot of the older men have difficulty moving in time to such *Karneval* classics as 'Love Me for Three Crazy Days' and 'Fat Girls Have Beautiful Names'.

From time to time, someone with a microphone will shout 'Beuel!'

'*Alaaf!*' the revellers shout, raising their right arms in salute.

But not *that* kind of salute. It's more of a flaccid, rubber-elbowed gesture, as if they're tossing their cares over their shoulders. Besides, anything rigid would be illegal.

On the balcony, the town councillors are waving stiffly and self-consciously to the four-four rhythm. They're wearing hard hats and work coats, and the mayor of Beuel is holding a big golden key and taunting the emcee below, a brassy washerwoman who's wearing bloomers and a plastic wash-tub round her waist. Of course, there could be a quicker way to end the pantomime. The mayor's superior, Bonn's *Oberbürgermeisterin*, is standing next to him in a fetching sailor's top, her blonde bob tied in a headband. All she'd have to do is punch the mayor, grab the key and throw it to her sister below and we could all get on with the drinking.

Around noon, Silvia the Washer Princess arrives on a float shaped like an old-fashioned washing machine. She's accompanied by Evi the *Obermöhn* and a gaggle of women in bright yellow hard hats carrying blueprints, in keeping with this year's theme, 'Renovate!', a nod to the scaffolding around the town hall. Silvia takes the mike for a bit, but the Old Married Woman's in charge. There's a lot of highly choreographed back-and-forth, with the Lady Mayor of Bonn expressing solidarity with the washerwomen.

'Men, come down and show us how to do the renovation work!' Evi shouts.

'Only if you give us a kiss!'

The price agreed, the council members descend a ladder. While they're distracted, the Washer Princess and the *Obermöhn* sneak up to the balcony and grab the key, waving it triumphantly at the men: 'You are nothing today! We are number one!'

Afterwards, I get a chance to speak to the mayor, Georg Fenninger, a tall man with an amiable sense of humour. He's changed into a black hat with horns and a cape, plus several *Karneval* chains around his collar and an emasculated tie that the Washer Princess cut while they were out on the balcony.

'We lost the war,' he shrugs.

'*What?*'

But he's not about to say *that* again. 'I am very sad to lose power for a day, but the women made it sweeter with their kisses.'

The party in the town hall features all the sausage-chomping, beer-guzzling, schnitzel-munching, bear-hugging German hospitality you can handle. Everyone is in fancy dress except for me. Stupidly, I didn't think it would matter, but my everyday street clothes mean I'm painfully and all too obviously out of sync with the lock-step jollity. 'Why didn't you bring a costume from England?' a local had asked me, laughing. 'Oh, that's right – in England, all they have are Nazi costumes.'

Prince Harry will never live that one down.

After a few glasses of *Bönnsch*, as the women leave for their private kaffeeklatsch, I venture out into the cold and head back to Bonn. Kennedy Bridge overlooks a Beuel landmark, a big yellow mansion on the Rhine. Costumed partiers are standing at equidistant spots around the geometrical garden, peeing. Women with pig snouts strapped to their faces bicycle past me. On the other side of the river, some Turkish kids are hanging out in ordinary street wear, either too cool or too foreign to act crazy. Four Germans are staggering along the pavement: two clowns, a tree-woman and a God-knows-what. They're laughing and joking, kicking at bollards and striking silly poses. I smile and overtake them, pulling my coat tighter against the cold. At the pedestrian crossing, the little man's red, but the traffic's clear. I know it's not the done thing in law-and-order Germany – *das ist nicht richtig!* – but there's no way I'm going to wait while an automated signal keeps me freezing in the street. Anyway, it's *Karneval*. I hurry across, and immediately a cascade of whistles and jeers hits my back like ice water. I glance behind me in disbelief. Surely they must be joking. But there they are, the four kids in their carnival suits, standing obediently on the kerb in the cold, waiting for the light to change. Even during *Karneval*, it's hard to walk on the wild side.

PART TWO:
GOING *VILD* IN THE SCHWARZWALD

I got a similar reaction when I told people I was planning to forgo the rest of the Crazy Days in the Rhineland to witness carnival in Germany's deep south.

'Where are you going?' asked a former Washer Princess, disbelievingly.

'A town called Elzach. In the Black Forest.'

She shrugged and pouted. 'But they don't do *anything* in the Black Forest.'

That's not exactly true. It's Sunday night in the Black Forest, barely an hour from the French border, and the Germans are marching in uniforms and torchlit processions.

But the French needn't surrender just yet. The only weapons the Black Foresters are wielding are inflated pigs' bladders, and their uniforms consist of red felt suits, wooden masks and big triangular straw hats decorated with snail shells and fluffy pom-poms. Although that doesn't sound overly frightening, the characters known as *Schuttigs* do exude a sense of mischief and menace, their faces carved into angry scowls, demonic grins and eerie animal expressions. At the very least, they're less than welcoming, especially if you're like me and happen to drive into town at the end of one of their processions. It's nothing personal, though; it's just to let you know that their version of carnival, or *Fasnet*, is very much a local festival, for local people, who understand local ways. The natives know, for instance, that when a *Schuttig* growls *ARRR!* at you, the proper response is not to consider punching him but to reciprocate in kind: *OO-ARRR!* I can't help but wonder if I've stumbled into a Devon vs Cornwall grunting contest that's been miraculously transported to the Continent.

However, *Fasnet* is as German as it gets, celebrated in towns and villages throughout the Black Forest, in the extreme south-west of the country, where the local dialect is Alemannic, named after the tribe that straddled the modern Swiss, German and French borders, harassing the Romans and the Franks. In fact, the French and Spanish still pay lip service to the fearsome Alemanni in their words for 'Germany' and 'the Germans'. Whereas *Karneval* in the Rhineland has evolved into a citified, even bourgeois, affair, its Alemannic counterpart has a much more primitive feel, tapping into the stereotypes of the Germans being at heart a barbaric race of semi-tamed and somewhat twisted pagans. *Alemannische Karneval* has many variations, but most feature mysterious masks and processions that involve brass bands, hopping around and beating members of the public.

The small town of Elzach is a stalwart of the Alemannic tradition, along with bigger and better-known Rottweil to the east and Freiburg in the south-west. And for the three days before Lent, Elzach's *Schuttigs* have the run of the town. Apart from the licence to drink and carouse from behind the protection of a mask, the main attraction of being a *Schuttig*, one tells me, is that 'you can touch women in a way that you normally wouldn't be allowed to'. For the local men, this means thwacking them with the pigs' bladders. As in some British traditions, the superstition is that the women will fall pregnant if they get porked, so to speak, by a *Schuttig*'s piece of pig-on-a-stick.

Given the masking and fertility links, the common assumption is that the *Schuttig* represents a prehistoric relic of paganism, in common with carnival itself. Never mind that most celebrations date from the Middle Ages (Cologne's was first recorded some time around 1341) and that Christianity had stamped out or assimilated paganism into insignificance centuries earlier (the Alemanni officially converted in the seventh century AD). What's more, carnival as we know it has always been linked to Christian days of feasting and fasting, shifting according to the idiosyncrasies of the Christian calendar – Shrove Tuesday can fall any time from the beginning of February to the end of March, depending on the year. Despite all of this, many people take it as gospel that something pagan has survived in carnival.

The source of this misconception can be traced back to the German Romantics, the philosophical heavyweights who enthralled Europe in the eighteenth and nineteenth centuries. Goethe and other literary giants idealised Germany's native folklore as evidence of a supposedly timeless past, a culture that was purer and possibly superior to industrialised society. Long story short, when these romantic ideals were imported to England, they fuelled the neopaganism and nature worship of the early twentieth century; back in Germany, they provided inspiration for the Nazis, who always had a strong interest in the occult and the 'ancient gods' of their 'master race'. Typical of these pseudo-academic scribblings is a passage written by one of the first folklorists to popularise Elzach, in the otherwise notable year of 1939: '[The *Schuttig*] still has deep connections to the activities of male cults in spring. He is gruff and carefree with the demonic ugliness of the masks he wears . . . He is wild for women and his noise and hits are unrestrained.'

Although modern academics have begun to debunk these theories, simply for lack of evidence, it's surprising how durable such mind-rot is. Trawling the Internet, I came across a discussion on a white-supremacist website about a festival's supposedly pagan origins. One of the correspondents – an American idiot who used a photo of a Nazi as his online alter ego – regurgitated a bunch of rubbish about the lingering influence of the Old German gods. 'It gives me hope because we continue to have connections with our natural past,' he concluded.

Fortunately, the Germans themselves seem to be slightly ahead of the rest of the world in taking a rational approach to folklore, which isn't too surprising given the national disgrace brought about by the Nazis and their perverted Romanticism. The truth is that carnival, like many other European customs, may very well have links to a pagan past; then again, it may not. There's no proof either way. And until someone finds a direct connection, any theories claiming to 'prove' the link are akin to academics in the year AD 2700 looking back at our era and concluding that a *Shrek*-themed children's party was a pagan celebration simply because it featured ogres but no overt symbols of Christianity. God knows what they'd make of the masked 'witches' that run wild on *Weiberfastnacht* in Offenburg, near Elzach. The German name sounds authentically ancient: the *Offenburger Hexen*. In reality, it was brewed up by a local couple in the 1930s.

To try to find out what is known about *Fasnet*, I've contacted Dr Ulrich Ruh, who recently stepped down from the local 'Fools' Guild' committee after fifteen years. A journalist for a local Catholic newspaper, he talks with the intensity of a man who could not only tell you how many angels can dance on the head of a pin, but also their names, weights and wingspans.

Dr Ruh reckons that all of Germany's *Karneval* celebrations began in the Middle Ages in cities like Cologne and then spread to the Catholic countryside over time. The first vague references to masking celebrations in Elzach date from the 1700s, and the *Schuttigs* probably get their names from the old term for Ash Wednesday: *Schauertag*. By the time the first known photo of them was taken in 1905, the *Schuttigs* were mainly working-class men in ragtag costumes who had become synonymous with drunkenness and brawling. Like Cologne's *Karneval* nearly a century earlier, Elzach's festival was cleaned up and regulated in 1911 to make it more respectable.

As with most public organisations in the run-up to the Second World War, everyone on Elzach's 'Fools' Guild' had to be a member of the Nazi Party. However, Dr Ruh claims the strong Catholicism in the area limited the party's influence. What's more, Elzach's size and remote location – not to mention its reputation as the home of a 'prehistoric' German ritual – spared it the Nazi meddling suffered by Cologne and other carnival epicentres. During the French occupation after the war, Elzach's carnival committee was purged of party members and filled with Not-Nazis: many devout Catholics.

Nowadays, over a thousand *Schuttigs* hit, growl and hop their way through Elzach during the three 'Crazy Days' before Ash Wednesday. Despite the potential for mayhem, there's only 'a minimum of organisation', Dr Ruh says, proudly contrasting it with the clockwork revelry in Cologne. 'You can't find a book of rules.'

Maybe not, but that's only because the Germans have already devoured the book page by page. The great debate about the German psyche is whether their love of order has come from deep within or been imposed to keep their inner barbarian from running rampant through Europe. Either way, come carnival time, a key distinguishing factor between the celebrations is whether they're 'organised' or 'Organised'.

Here are a few unwritten rules governing *Fasnet*:

I. A *Schuttig* must never remove his mask, except in the back rooms of bars and restaurants specially designated for private drinking or to verify that no women have infiltrated all-male carnival meetings.

II. One must never address a *Schuttig* by his real name. The correct greeting is a gruff '*Schuttig!*'

III. *Schuttigs* are allowed to personalise their masks within reason, but they must conform to the seven approved characters, such as the Long Nose, the Bear, the Fox and the Devil.

'So what would happen if a *Schuttig* showed up wearing a carved mask of, say, George Bush?' I ask in my unofficial role as devil's advocate.

Dr Ruh looks at me blankly, blinking through his lenses. My question simply does not compute.

'It couldn't happen,' he says, mystified. And in the remote-as-Mars chance that it did, the rebel *Schuttig* would be quickly reprimanded. 'You would tell him that perhaps it's better to leave the mask at home.'

Likewise, the role of the sexes tends to be clearly defined. Although women (and minors) are barred from key meetings – including the one featuring two men dressed as the town night-watchman and his wife – there's nothing to stop them from disguising themselves and taking part in the processions, gleefully whacking passers-by with pigs' bladders. However, female *Schuttigs* are not encouraged, Dr Ruh says. 'The women have a passive role. They get beaten.'

Which must be loads of fun for them. But the women get their own back tonight. *Weiberfastnacht* isn't a traditional part of *Fasnet* in Elzach, but the women have invented their own equivalent: the *Maschkele*, or 'little masked ones'. On Raving Monday, gangs of women prowl the streets and bars, teasing men and goading them with assorted unpleasantness. Just your average night on the town, then, but with one crucial difference: the women are all in costume, usually wearing masks to hide their identities. So when a *Maschkele* cryptically tells her victim 'I heard what you did on holiday', it has the potential to mess with the man's mind for infinity, particularly if he has something to hide. 'You better watch yourself,' the hotel manager warned me jokingly. 'Black Forest women get a little *vild* tonight. They can be very aggressive.'

Max Benz has offered to take me out on the town with his wife and another guest, a doctor from Berlin. Neither of us has a costume, so Max loans the Berliner an American hockey shirt (set off with a silk scarf that the doctor wraps sensibly around his throat) and lets me borrow his old national service uniform: a bright orange jumpsuit with a Red Cross patch and latex gloves stuck rakishly in the breast pocket. *If the rubber gloves don't do it, I don't know what will . . .* Max is a newcomer to Elzach, a natural-born charmer who used to play the fool at carnival celebrations in his hometown. Tonight he's dressed as a GDR navy officer, with his wife as first mate in a stripy sailor's outfit.

The four of us careen from basement discos to upstairs pubs and ground-floor bars, all blasting out Europap and *Karneval* songs, including 'Viva Colonia' from the Rhineland. My first shock comes just a couple of *Schuttigbiers* into the evening, when everyone around me joins in the chorus of 'Football's Coming Home', triumphantly oblivious to the song's meaning, specifically the references to the 'Three Lions' and 'years of pain'. Music truly is the universal language, but only because half the world doesn't get the lyrics. I mention to Max that some of my English friends might be surprised to see a pub full of Germans singing what is effectively England's national football anthem, but my observation doesn't go down very well with my host. The arrival of a faux footballer provides a convenient distraction.

'Oh, look – it's David Beckham.'

I manage to keep my mouth shut about the next surprise. In another bar, a guy in his twenties is wearing an army helmet and a long green coat *circa* 1940. All he needs is a Luger pistol and a potato-masher grenade to look like the flesh-and-blood version of a comic-book Kraut. But that's the only dubious disguise I come across – well, apart from the tribe of ululating *Maschkele* with blackened faces and bones stuck in their afro wigs. Carnival gives the Germans an opportunity to indulge in their passion for clubbing, not just in the narrow sense of partying, but partying as a synchronised group. After all, if it's funny for one person to dress as a nun, then ten fake nuns should be ten times as funny, right? So you see loads of Pippi Longstockings, clusters of Grinches who stole Christmas and Bob the Builders with papier mâché heads, a covey of cardinals and a murder of priests, eighteenth-century dandies with painted faces and long coats hired from the Berlin Opera and a bunch of gorillas lugging a cage through the snow. One of the few mixed clubs is a brass band pumping out the atonal noise known as *Guggenmusik* over the border in Switzerland: they're wearing feathered caps, checked shirts and suspenders holding up their tweed trousers. Otherwise, there are lots of men dressed as women, some women dressed as men, and a few women who look like men wearing dresses.

The groups of *Maschkele* take the guise of bunnies hopping around handing out carrots, female chefs in false noses cooking gherkins in crêpes and various sisterhoods wheeling big vats of booze through the streets. A gaggle of girls runs past, smearing my face with chocolate spread. A middle-aged group in black webbing stamps me with inky spiders. In one bar, some blonde Fräuleins in pigtails and sailors' caps encourage men to down a sachet of citrus powder followed by a slug of vodka. I do it twice. A female grease monkey squirts a pump-action bottle into my mouth, the kind used for washing windows. I thought the clear liquid inside was vodka, but maybe it really is window cleaner: I can't feel my tongue.

Snowflakes are drifting down outside, so fat and feathery that it takes only a puff of breath to blow them skyward again. The pubs have burst their thresholds, and costumed partiers are dancing in the snow to *Guggenmusik* and samba.

Full-faced and earnest, Herr Doktor takes all of this in like a northern anthropologist studying the behaviour of uncouth southerners who don't speak proper German. He claims to enjoy it, but he's a living reminder that the majority of Germans *don't* go crazy during the Crazy Days. In Berlin, *Karneval* is still a novelty, having been imported by the government's move from Bonn. 'Vaht I like is that it verks in the vintertime,' Herr Doktor tells me. 'People in the Mediterranean vould not belief sat you could do such a thing ven it is zero degrees outside.'

The rest of the world might take some convincing, too. The idea of carnival – in Germany – at the coldest time of the year – doesn't sound like much of an attraction. But once you see it, you begin to wish the custom had survived in Protestant Europe. Whether it's a full week or just three Crazy Days, carnival gives you something to live for during the depressing grey days between New Year's Eve and Easter.

On our way to another pub, we're accosted by a couple of giant red chillies. The girls are standing in the middle of the street in full-body costumes as if they're part of a promotional gimmick, challenging men with chillies on toothpicks.

'You have to eat one,' a talking red-hot tells me.

'What do I get in return?'

'Small talk with me.'

That seems like small compensation compared to the kisses in Beuel.

Next morning, the news is serving up the perfect hangover cure: hefty slabs of *Schadenfreude*. In the aftermath of Raving Monday in Mainz in the Rhineland, bodies are slumped in gutters and doorways, too intoxicated to move despite the subzero temperatures. You'd think they'd been attacked by invaders who strapped hoses to their faces and pumped booze down their necks until their livers liquefied. Ambulance teams are carting them off on stretchers. And to think *I* felt paralytic.

For several days now – and right up until Ash Wednesday – there's been morning-to-midnight *Karneval* coverage: news anchors delivering the news in wigs and bowties; televised 'Fools' Sessions' with stage shows such as a tiny devil and his minions taunting a fat angel by singing 'I Will Survive'; and audiences gathered at long tables as narrow as bratwurst, sometimes sitting and swaying, sometimes standing behind each other and bending over in time to the music. They've even shown black-and-white archive footage of classic comedians playing the Fool, proving that not much has changed in the postwar era: the revellers are wearing the same costumes and laughing on cue at corny one-liners.

Amid all the wonky camerawork and choreographed kerraaazy-ness, there's also plenty of music that would drive you to drink if you didn't already. As with 'Achy Breaky Heart' in Spanish, you should never have to hear 'Hotel California' sung in German or see a German Joe Cocker copying the woozy, half-cocked style of the man himself, all the while singing in his native tongue.

But the strangest thing is the documentary on another channel that undermines a pet theory of mine. I've long thought that the best (and possibly only) reason for moving to Germany would be to make a great escape from Second World War mania. As I'm getting ready in my Black Forest hotel room, though, I hear an unmistakable voice coming from the TV – that shrill, delusional *Nein!* from Hess – a pathetic yawp if ever there was one. They're broadcasting the Nuremberg Trials!

Meanwhile, back in Karneval Land, a mulleted crooner is singing earnestly about how we should all learn to live together, '*Juden, Islamisten und Buddhisten*'. It may be an ironic touch, but I'd take him more seriously if he weren't wearing an army cadet uniform. The crowd listens dutifully, paying their penance in musical suffering (it beats staying home and watching reruns of *Hogan's Heroes – on prime-time TV –* one of the lesser-known punishments imposed by the Allies).

I need to get out.

Down in the restaurant, a table of *Schuttigs* are glowering over breakfast, sipping glasses of beer under their masks. Their presence is vaguely menacing – not only are they anonymous and possibly free to do whatever they like, but you can't see their faces to judge whether they're liable to do it or not. From the listing of their heads and the limberness of their gait, though, it's obvious that they're already as soused as the herring on the buffet table, and it's only ten thirty in the morning. Is that German they're speaking or are they just grunting drunkenly? It's impossible to tell.

This afternoon the *Schuttigs* will stomp through Elzach in their last big carnival procession of the year. At midnight – and not a minute later – the men will remove their masks out of respect for Ash Wednesday and the beginning of Lent.

In the meantime, I decide to tramp around town in the daylight. Elzach isn't a full-on Brothers Grimm fairytale, but it's close enough, scattered along a narrow valley flanked by evergreens dusted with snow. The pitched roofs and steeples carry a heavier layer of frosting, but it's melting in the intermittent sunshine, replenishing the narrow stream that runs through town. Red-and-green bunting is strung across the streets, with banners of *Schuttigs* frolicking above the pavements. There's also a small statue of a *Schuttig* in mid-hop in the old part of town. In contrast to the modern town halls in many German cities, the Rathaus here is a neo-Gothic construction with stepped gables and a pointed tower. Many of the other buildings feature the dark, carved-wood balconies that you expect in the Black Forest, as well as Gothic lettering stencilled across their sides. A few even have paintings of wildlife decorating their façades.

On my way back, I come across a *Schuttig* headed home. Its mask is a ferocious man's face and its pig's bladder is limp and grey from beating.

I ask if I can take its photo.

The *Schuttig* poses obligingly, and I notice that it's too tall to be a boy, but its voice is too high to be a man's.

I thank the *Schuttig* and she growls at me merrily. One way or another, like the washerwomen of Beuel, this she-*Schuttig* has made carnival her own.

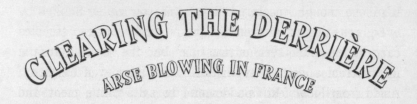

CHAPTER THREE

CLEARING THE DERRIÈRE
ARSE BLOWING IN FRANCE

PART ONE:

HOT AIR

First things first: I've never had anything against the French, but I've never thought they had that much going for them, either. Sure, France is famous for its wine, food, art and women, but so is Italy, Italy, Italy – and again – Italy. Without a doubt, the French do some things better than any nation in the world, namely champagne . . . pastries . . . industrial strikes and pretentious movies – but to my mind, the modern reality of the place is overrated. Rather than Francophobia, I think my problem is that I expect too much of *La Belle France*, having had its myths crammed down my throat over the years like corn down a goose's gullet. In fairness, many French have the same reaction when they visit my native land – I reckon a key factor in the Franco-American love–hate relationship is that both sides have more in common than they like to think. However, when the Arseblowers of the Dordogne hung a big stinking sardine around my neck, I knew they'd won me over.

Let me explain: for the most part, modern France seems to take itself far too seriously to celebrate the sort of national idiosyncrasies exalted by Britain, Spain and even Germany. Aside from local festivals devoted to salt, goat's meat and visceral etceteras, France is all but devoid of outlandish traditions. However, one of the rare exceptions to *la règle* survives in the south-west, a target of English invaders ever since the days of Richard the Lionhearted right up to the modern era of Nigel the Houseminded. Carnival in the town of Nontron has a name so risibly rude that it's guaranteed to raise a titter or Gallic gasp from Parisians and other northerners (or maybe it's just my friends). One English guidebook that really ought to know better translates *La Fête des Soufflaculs* as 'The Festival of the Whistle Arses', which would be something to see. And perhaps the confusion is understandable: thanks to the Spanish influence in the area, it was the south of France that produced the famous nineteenth-century Franco-Catalonian performer known as *Le Petomane*, or 'The Fartiste', whose bottom could burp in bass, tenor and baritone – and even play songs on the flute. Not for nothing does the south boast what must be the world's only Gourmet Prune Museum, plus a 100-kilometre Prune Route.

In truth, though, there's no polite way to put this: the *Soufflaculs* are nothing but 'Arseblowers'. On one Sunday in April, scores of men, women and children parade through the streets in broad daylight dressed for bed and armed with bellows in a tradition that takes its inspiration from the Middle Ages. Wearing old-fashioned nightcaps and long, white nightshirts, they liven up the proceedings by using their bellows to pump air up their neighbours' backsides or – even better – the skirts of unsuspecting women. While they're at it, they sing a ribald anthem about sex in a mix of French and Occitan, the original language of the troubadours. So far as anyone knows, the *Soufflaculs'* tradition may have something to do with local monks trying to exorcise Nontron and its notoriously loose women of evil spirits (not to mention foul body odours). Most likely, though, it's an example of etymology in action: the English and French words 'fool' and '*folie*' both come from the Latin word *follis*: an inflated leather bag, or bellows. At the very least, the *Soufflaculs* may help explain why the slapstick 'humour' of Jerry Lewis has found an abiding home in France.

What's most laughable to me – and even a little shocking – is just how arse-obsessed medieval Europe was. To wit: one theory holds that the *Soufflaculs* were originally connected to the commemoration of St Blaise, the physician-martyr whose saint's day is celebrated on 3 February. While writing *True Brits*, I came across St Blaise in his role as protector against sore throats (even though he himself suffered the ultimate sore throat: decapitation). At St Etheldreda's in London, England's oldest Catholic church, the priest still blesses people on St Blaise's Day by using two candles to make the Sign of the Cross on their necks. However, I didn't know that Blaise had been tortured with iron combs – which, somewhat perversely, makes him the natural patron of wool combers and weavers. I also had no idea that his Latin name, Blasius, sounds similar to the German infinitive *blasen*: 'to blow' (how I ever lived in such ignorance, I'll never know). St Blaise's Day comes during one of the stormiest months of the year in Western Europe, and it's said that some weavers would stop their work on St Blaise's Day to avoid weaving the ill winds into their cloth. Scandinavian sailors would supposedly refrain from mentioning the saint's name or eating flatulence-inducing foods for fear of provoking a tempest at sea – or in their intestines. After all, an old proverb warned: 'A fart on St Blaise's Day; wind and storms all year round.'

In France, the timing of the *Soufflaculs* celebrations may have drifted over the centuries to accommodate the purgative season of Lent and Easter, but an old snatch of doggerel makes it clear how they got their name:

> *Souffle lui au cul, la pauvre vieille,*
> *Souffle lui au cul, elle en a besoin.*

This translates – loosely, if you will – as:

> Blow up her arse, the poor old girl,
> Blow up her arse, she needs it.

I now know all this courtesy of a book with the innocuous title of *Le Carnaval en Périgord*. Although there doesn't seem to be any record of the *Soufflaculs* procession in Nontron before the nineteenth century, it could be that respectable historians didn't deem it worth documenting: as a vulgar custom, bottom-blowing was strictly below the belt. However, various carvings and engravings give the impression that bellows, or *soufflets*, were a kind of precursor to the whoopee cushion. Apparently, pumping air up the bum of a person – or animal – was one of the funniest pranks a joker could pull in the Middle Ages.

A sixteenth-century carving from a house in the German town of Goslar near Hanover shows a dairymaid churning butter with one hand and hiking up her dress and grabbing a big hunk of buttock with the other while a bearded demon with a jester's cap sneaks up behind her with a pair of bellows. Other carvings in France – including a detail from Troyes Cathedral – show jesters poking their bellows up the backsides of donkeys.

Even more bizarre are the fifteenth- and sixteenth-century illustrations that I initially mistook for the kind of sacred pornography you find in many religious depictions of hell: dirty girls getting gangbanged by the diabolical counterparts of de Sade and the like. In reality, the scenes portray a very peculiar carnival game: two men locked in a kind of standing sixty-nine position, one holding the other upside down, so that they both have their faces between each other's bare buttocks. This was *Le Jeu de Pétengueule*: literally, The Fart-in-Your-Gob Game. As with the old English pastime of shin-kicking, I reckon the French custom of face-farting would have been a lose/lose proposition for both players (assuming they found two fools stupid enough to play). And to avoid any confusion about the rules of engagement, an engraving from Dijon shows two Gob-Farters framed by cupid's heads blowing gusts of air at them.

Up until the Second World War, Bottom Blowers could be found throughout the south of France, particularly in Provence and the Dordogne, sometimes as part of the equally bizarre *Danse du Feu aux Fesses*, or the Pants-on-Fire Dance. Near Béziers, this apparently took the form of revellers wearing feathers on their backsides and trying to set each other's plumage alight. Today the only surviving epicentres of Arse-blowing are the *villes* of Saint-Claude, which is near the Swiss and Italian borders, and Nontron. Why two towns on opposite sides of the country should be bastions of Arseblowing is anyone's guess; predictably, they both claim to be the true home of the *Soufflaculs* (even though Nontron's *fête* is a revival: the original event languished after the war and finally died out in 1958). In addition to the general theories, the inhabitants of Nontron have developed some very particular hypotheses about the custom's origins. The most farfetched claims that French missionaries may have exported the rite to Latin America during the Napole-moronic attempt to occupy Mexico during the 1860s; when the French were inevitably kicked out, returning soldiers may have reintroduced the custom in Nontron and other parts of their homeland.

However, the most evocative theory holds that the *Soufflaculs* are satirising local monks who once tried to purify the town by sticking their bellows anywhere that sin might lurk, particularly up the skirts of *les femmes dangereuses* who gave the town a reputation for having 'more whores than chimneys'.

Having once been renowned for fallen women, Nontron has recently fallen on hard times, along with the French economy. The luxury brand Hermès produces its famous silk ties and leather goods at a local factory, but few of these seem to find their way onto Nontron's streets (though the *Soufflaculs* do sing about cravats). The town's neoclassical eighteenth-century château used to house a doll and puppet museum, but burglars stole the collection a few years back. Instead, the tourist office advises disappointed visitors – like one mother and daughter I saw – to see the town's state-of-the-art knife museum. 'It's not quite the same thing,' the Englishwoman muttered on her way out. However, knives are arguably Nontron's biggest claim to fame these days. The abundance of iron, wood and water in the area made it a natural for steel production since the time of the Gauls. According to legend, it was Nontron's workmen who forged the sword of Charles VII, the king who (thanks to Joan of Arc) finally ran the English out of most of France at the end of the Hundred Years' War. The Nontron Knife, with its distinctive honey-coloured handle carved from boxwood, is supposedly France's oldest knife, having been made locally since at least 1653.

Apart from cutlery, though, Nontron gets only a passing mention in most guidebooks. That's probably because the area as a whole is so fetching, there's just not enough space to fit everything in. Many maps ignore Nontron altogether, relegating it to the blank space between Limoges, Toulouse and Bordeaux where there aren't any sizeable cities. Although British homebuyers tend to know this *département* as the Dordogne, locals prefer to use its pre-Napoleonic name, Périgord, and Jules Verne gave a lasting gift to the tourist industry by dubbing this part *Vert*. The reason it's green, of course, is that it rains a lot. In April, the weather can be as mercurial as a certain national stereotype, sunny one minute and raining hail and gloom the next. In the late afternoon sun, though, the fields glow a golden green, studded with thousands of dandelions, and the forests of vine-cloaked trees strut across floors of rusted brown bracken. Located in the newly designated conservation area, the *Parc Naturel Régional*, Nontron overlooks the Bandiat valley, standing atop a promontory with terraced gardens descending gracefully down the side. The populated gorges of the town are banked by ageing houses with shutters that would look run-down anywhere else but seem inexplicably quaint in France. Some are coated in hardwearing pebbledash, others are hewn from grey stone or built from chocolate-coloured timbers filled in with a plaster-and-rock substance that looks like nougat and nuts.

As a result, this town of 3,000 forms an ideal backdrop for politicians when they're forced to leave Paris and rally the heartland, picking up a clod of earth (strictly metaphorically, of course) and declaring to the provincials: 'I am a Claude like you!' Jacques Chirac dropped by during his desperate re-election campaign against ultra-rightwinger Jean-Marie Le Pen in 2002, after nearly one in six French voters opted to elect a fascist as president (lest we ever forget). And it's no surprise that the percentage of voters who rejected the draft EU Constitution in 2005 was higher here than the national average. At the same time, though, Périgord has received so many British homeowners in the past decade it's become known as 'Dordogne-shire'. The likes of Le Pen may grumble about the English buying up what they lost in the Hundred Years War, but for the most part, the locals seem remarkably welcoming, mainly because a) *les Anglais* have money and b) they use it to buy almost completely into the French way of life. One Frenchwoman tells me that only five of the eighteen houses in her village are still owned by locals. 'But the English are very nice,' she adds quickly. 'They're old, but they're very nice.'

However, as a relatively young American arriving in the aftermath of the Iraq War, the lowest point in Franco-American relations since the movie *Green Card*, I'm a little worried that some of Nontron's famous knives may be out for me.

It doesn't help that I can only speak crash-course French, a level of (in)aptitude that's as likely to get me into trouble as out of it. My accent is passable enough for native speakers to gabble back at me, whereupon the whole charade collapses and

I wind up mooing 'like a Spanish cow', as the saying goes. Fortunately, a local Catalan remembers enough Spanish from his childhood to help me out of conversational cul-de-sacs, and many locals have a working knowledge of *anglais*: I reckon you'd be hard pressed to find more signs announcing 'English Spoken Here' in any other part of France. And anyway, my lack of fluency might actually be a plus: the key to being a Yank in Europe is knowing when to keep your mouth shut.

The President of the Arseblowers is plainly delighted to meet an American. 'I'm the Bush of Nontron!' he hoots, bending over and mooning me by way of introduction. Michel Meyleu, the Rearender-in-Chief, is clad in a nightcap, a scraggly grey wig, a white nightshirt and shorts beneath a pair of novelty plastic buttocks, the latex posterior decorated with bright-red lip prints on each cheek.

I've been invited to the *Salle des Fêtes* for a simple dinner to welcome all the caravanners who come here every year for carnival. Amid much mirth and merriment, I'm introduced to the group as an American who's come to find out about the *Soufflaculs*.

'Are you with the CIA?' someone shouts, and my red-faced disavowals are rewarded with an official Arse Blowing T-shirt and a seat at the head table next to Monsieur President and his daughter. Technically in his sixties, Michel acts young enough to keep Valérie continually embarrassed. Offering me a plate of long merguez sausages, he cracks, 'These are very good for your sex. They make you go –' he thrusts his left fist forward while slapping his bicep at the same time. As the river of alcohol flows from sangria to whisky-and-Coke and red wine, the Head Arse Blower becomes increasingly fond of this fisting gesture, telling jokes and singing songs, while slapping me on the back, thigh and head, even tugging my hair to cajole me into laughter.

Michel's been President for only a few years, but he was one of the original group that revived the tradition in 1979, after it had died out two decades earlier. Chewing a hunk of bread, he explains that the festival is usually held in April – this year it happens to fall on the Sunday after Easter. 'We would have held it last week, but the Pope, he no like,' guffaws Michel, ramming his fist up an imaginary backside yet again.

The other fools at the table include a contingent of policemen from Paris who've taken time off to play the *fou* at Nontron's carnival. 'It is good for me. It takes my mind off work,' says a bald cop named Franck, who's engaged to a local girl. Midway through the meal, a man with a fearsome limp and a wild beard joins the party. He's the *Buffadou*, the carnival scapegoat whose effigy is burnt at the stake at the end of the celebrations. His name comes from the old patois for a hollowed-out stick that allowed people to stoke the fire with their breath. 'That man is like a god in Nontron,' Franck the Fou tells me.

In that case, he's Bacchus incarnate, and his breath is best kept away from open flames. The *Buffadou* produces a liquor bottle that's been recycled for his homemade *gnole*, a strong *eau de vie* made from plums that tastes more like *eau de feu* and must be distilled right at the very magical moment when the alcoholic vapours turn to liquid. Fuelled by firewater, the evening ends with singing, drinking and joke-telling. The President of the *Soufflaculs* removes the bellows-shaped medal of the Brotherhood of Fools from around his neck and gives it to me to wear. Engraved on the back is the 'Song of the *Soufflets*' in Occitan, and he translates the opening verse for me by pumping his fist: 'While making love, I lost my cravat . . .'

The *Buffadou* and his bootleg liquor also put in an appearance the next morning as the organisers gather to prepare the stadium for the night's entertainment. Rather than coffee and croissants, this is a gutbusting *petit déjeuner à la campagne*, a country breakfast to set the men up for the rest of the day: rounds of Camembert and hunks of flat bread hacked off with a knife, served up with slabs of *rillettes du porc* – a chawed-up meat product as mysterious as any American hot dog – and steak so raw you wonder why they bothered cutting it off the cow. They could have plopped its twitching carcass on the table for us to tear strips off with our teeth.

Fortunately, there's plenty of drink to wash it down: several glasses of wine, a slug of *gnole* in my coffee, then in my *vin*, then a shot on its own, rounded off by a sample of the *Buffadou*'s batch of clear, unadulterated firewater, without the caramel colouring that makes it turn light brown.

Time and again, the refrain I keep hearing from people when I mention my nationality is: 'The Americans don't like the French.' Of course, *les Américains* are by no means alone. A recent study by a couple of Frenchmen asked Europeans to come up with five adjectives for *les Français*. With few exceptions, interviewees from Sweden to Italy and Portugal to Greece described the French as being 'pretentious', 'vain', 'shallow', 'nannied' or 'out-of-touch'. What's curious to me, though, is the way the people I'm meeting characterise Franco-American relations; if anything, I'd expect them to phrase the rejection the other way round. But the locals make the declaration with obvious embarrassment, almost apologetically – not for their point of view, but for the fact that political bickering has led to such an awkward bust-up. The unspoken hint coming through loud and clear is that if the Americans were to show any sign of friendship, the French would be more than happy to meet them halfway.

Not for the first time, it strikes me that the French and Americans are more alike than we care to admit. And here's where it gets a little too near the (pig's) knuckle for me. Like most nationalities, for instance, we're best taken in small doses; preferably one at a time. While it's easy for outsiders to hate 'the French' or 'the Americans' as amorphous groups, on a one-to-one basis, we tend to be fairly personable and even (if I dare say so myself) charming. Both countries also have a well-earned reputation for arrogance: the French think they invented civilisation as we know it; the Americans think they run civilisation as we know it, and neither group excels at accepting criticism from outsiders. From an early age, when their cerebella are still tender and unlined, French and American children are taught that France/America is the best in the world, so logically their actions are the best, simply because they're French/American. Like the US, France is a big, largely self-contained country with enough sun, snow, beaches and mountains to ensure its natives never need to travel abroad if they don't want to. As a result, they have a tendency to be inward-looking: navel-gazers par excellence. Here in the French south-west, as in the American Midwest, local news-papers sideline world news to the margins, so a headline like 'Nuclear Mishap: New Zealand Obliterated' would merit just a few inches of text. Both countries also adhere to the original consumerist slogan of 'eat, drink and be merry' (the notion being that if you consume enough, the merriness will eventually kick in as a natural consequence). The French pride themselves on doing this with more panache than my countrymen, though I'd argue that just because you can eat something doesn't mean you should (compare this with the American corollary: just because you can deep-fat fry something doesn't mean you should). So maybe it's these shared traits – the mirror-image arrogance and blindness to our own faults – that make the French and Americans quarrel with each other.

Or maybe it's just the *gnole* talking. As the alcohol blurs my brain, I'm trying to keep track of all the people I'm being introduced to. Shaking hands, they'll point to photos of themselves in the carnival guide. The thing is, all the people in the pictures are in costume and unrecognisably worse for wear. 'That's me in the parade car,' they'll say, 'slumped in the front seat.'

After all the drink and raw meat, I'm not feeling too perky myself. It's not even ten thirty a.m. I really do need to get some work done; then again, I could always go back to sleep. While closing the curtains in my hotel room, I vow never to complain about stingy continental breakfasts again.

PART TWO:
PLAYING *LE FOU*

The Hotel Pelisson in Nontron boasts a Napoleonic connection, with a certificate from 1867 and medals on the wall recognising it as an official purveyor of foie gras to the court in Paris during the reign of Napoleon III. 'The one with the beard,' the owner clarifies for me, stroking a cone of air beneath his chin.

It's been a long time since the hotel's ruptured goose livers passed imperial lips, but I slavishly ordered a portion anyway on my first night in Nontron. Sadly, the overstuffed birds died a horrible death in vain. I could barely taste the stuff. Ever since I've arrived, I've been besieged by hay fever so vicious I reckon I may die sneezing or wind up driving a spike through my head to put myself out of my mucoid misery. This morning I gave the locals a good laugh by staggering into the pharmacy and beseeching the clerk in my pidgin French for allergy medicine that was *'sans homéopathique – s'il vous plait! Sans homéopathique!'* I didn't want to have to swallow a homeopathic horse pill every two hours in the hope that the herbs might work a week from now; I needed a scientifically proven, laboratory-tested drug that would work *right now*. So she sent me away with a packet of tablets that I have to take every four hours.

Stupidly, though, I've forgotten them for the lengthy evening of dinner, dancing and bottom-blowing entertainment in the *Salle des Fêtes* on the eve of the *Soufflaculs'* parade. At the next table over, Valérie Meyleu is suffering even more than I am, her eyes puffed into red, weeping welts. But at least she doesn't have a little dog sitting across the table in its owner's lap. The woman insists on giving it kisses and yum-yums and combing it before, during and in between courses, raising an unusual question of *l'etiquette*: which fork does one use to remove furballs from one's mutt?

Apart from her and her spinster daughter, my other dinner companions are an English couple who've retired to the Green Périgord from the Black Country. 'Our son and his wife were looking to buy a house in the UK, but they couldn't find anything they could afford,' the wife says. 'So one day he said, "Why don't you just bugger off to France and leave us your house?"'

'We wish we would've moved earlier.'

'We reckon it's about a third cheaper across the board.'

'The French are soooo . . . welcoming,' agrees their friend, a dolled-up gal from Lancashire who speaks very good French. Her eyes suddenly glisten with emotion. 'At times it's almost humbling.' But she recovers to crack a joke. 'English people, on the other hand, can be a bit—' She flicks her nose up.

And that explains why the English who come to this part of France are so welcome. To a far greater degree than their countrymen in Spain or Greece, the English who buy properties here have also bought into the perception that French culture is superior to their own – so much so, that they arrive on bended knee.

'I wouldn't quite say that,' grumbles a friend who lived in France until recently, clearly rankled by my blunt assessment. 'I'd say the French are the only ones in Europe that we think we can learn from.'

Not an outright denial, then, but a clarification.

The Francophile from Rochdale articulates the snob appeal. 'I think of Spain as a place to go on holiday,' she says airily. 'But France is a place to *live*.'

No matter how long you live here, though, it's hard to match the French for sheer *joie de vivre*. The locals have converted the space between the long rectangular dinner tables into a dancefloor before the feasting has even started in earnest. For the English newcomers, the corridor between them and the French is suddenly as wide as La Manche. They're glued to their chairs, sipping their wine; they'd have to be legless to let loose like that. 'You wouldn't see that back home, would ya?' comments the Lancashirewoman, pointing out a French counterpart who's shaking her thing. 'Dancing by herself in a see-through white top with a black bra. They have no shame.'

The communal meal begins with *tourain*, a traditional cream of garlic soup made from eggs, goosefat and mushy vermicelli. This gives the immigrant couples the chance to introduce me to a local custom known as *chabrol*: after finishing your soup, you splash some wine into your bowl, swirl it around and then slurp it all down.

Now, when I was a true innocent abroad, this is just the sort of local practice that I would have lapped up and swallowed whole, choking it down and trying really hard to convince myself that I liked it simply because it was foreign and – even better – French. Unfortunately, I'm now old enough to see *chabrol* for what it is: an unappetising custom that was probably invented by hungry peasants who needed to soak up every last calorie they could. Maybe it helps if the soup is tasty to begin with. As it is, the only way to make *chabrol* worse would be if you had to lick your host's garlicky armpits afterwards. Having conned the newcomers into washing out their own soupbowls, the French probably cackle themselves senseless dreaming up new ways to bamboozle *les rosbifs*: 'Ah know – let's tell them to stick ze baguette up ze arse before zey eating it. Eez a vehry ancient Frahnch tradicion!'

The couples are recommending a restaurant in a nearby village.

'They drink *chabrol* one-handed there!' one of the women gushes.

'Brian has pictures of all his friends *chabrolling*.'

I wonder if they're all fully clothed.

The second course is *une salade de gésier*, which sounds infinitely posher than the plain English and is no doubt the best 'gizzard salad' I could have. After the inescapable *canard* for the main course, I duck out to dose myself with allergy meds at my hotel – and make it back just in time to learn that the judge of this year's Miss Soufflette Contest is . . . me. For many men, being named the sole judge of a French beauty pageant would be the stuff of fantasies, and I'm tempted to portray the nymphs of Nontron as a lineup of Bardots, Deneuves and Tatous. Alas, I'd be lying. They're no more or less attractive than you'd find in any small town. What's more, many of the mademoiselles are wearing nightcaps and less-than-flattering white nightshirts. Back in the nineteenth century, conjugal nightwear came with strategically positioned slots sewn in the front along with the words *DIEU LE VEUT:* GOD'S WILL BE DONE. But these nightshirts aren't even that risqué. I'm honoured to be asked to judge, but I reckon it's probably a privilege that the locals are happy to give up. The three girls I pick as finalists may think I'm swell, but the other twenty or so are going to hate me, not to mention their families and friends in the audience, who are liable to kneecap me in the dark afterwards (take *that* for not picking Sylvie!).

Each girl has to give the emcee a good reason why she wants to be Miss Arseblower, while he tries to rattle them with gags along the lines of 'I know your father – he's a drunk!' The candidates then have to sing the nonsensical *Soufflaculs'* anthem, preferably while jumping up and down:

> We're all children of the same family
> Our father was a bellows maker
> No, you will not see the colour of my gaiters
> No, you will not see the colour of my
> stockings

Yes, I will see the colour of your gaiters
Yes, I will see the colour of your stockings

If we're going to see anyone's stockings (the power is already going to my head), I'd go with an elegant blonde named Sonia, along with some buxom twins and a curly brunette who calls herself *La Rosa Española*. I pick the three – make that four – finalists, and they all sing the *Soufflaculs'* song one last time. Sonia and the Spanish Rose have the strongest support, but the French girl fluffs the lyrics; her rival, by contrast, not only knows the song backwards and forwards but can also sing it in Spanish, getting a laugh by updating 'gaiters' as 'panties'. One of Sonia's supporters is interpreting for me on the side of the stage; despite his affiliation, he's impressed with *l'Espagnole*.

'Maybe not so pretty . . . but she has the right spirit.'

And the fact that she's a foreigner – or at least the daughter of Catalonian immigrants – isn't held against her. Last year's Miss Soufflette was a Korean TV reporter. The *Buffadou* still mutters moistly about *La Coréenne . . . La Coréenne*.

By now, the scapegoat's gait is so loose his legs would amble off in opposite directions if they weren't attached to his torso. The *Buffadou*'s beard and hair are so wild and tangled it looks like he got his head stuck in a hedge and had to be cut out by paramedics using the Jaws of Life.

'*L'Espagnole, l'Espagnole,*' he slurs to me on the sidelines, leaning in so close his beard is bristling my face.

Personally, I'd plump for Sonia, but that's not what he wants.

'*L'Espagnole! L'Espagnole!*'

So the Spanish Rose it is. The new Miss Soufflette is dumped into a grocery cart with a lifesaver thrown around her neck and then wheeled helter-skelter around the auditorium. The entertainment concludes with a ballet of cross-dressers, including Michel Meyleu, and an ersatz nun jumping out of a cake.

So far, I seem to have avoided making any enemies, though only just. 'I wanted to kill you when you picked me,' one of the twins huffs afterwards. 'If I would've won, it would've meant I would've had to spend the day with the *Buffadou*.'

Having learnt the hard way in Germany about *Karneval* fun and conformity, I've come to France prepared with my very own long white nightshirt and cap. After a late lunch with Franck and the *Fous* of leftover gizzard salad and leg of duck (*how many legs do French ducks have?*), I join the other *Soufflaculs* who are having their faces painted in the *Salle des Fêtes*. One is a Frenchwoman from out of town who makes your average German sound like a barrel of footloose spontaneity. She may be made up to look like a clown in a frilly pink frock, but she takes her jesting in earnest. 'I am serious because I have something to do. For everybody life is difficult. But we forget all of that during an afternoon. And we try to let the people forget, too. So if the leader says to me, "You have to be mad," I obey.'

But having a good time would be a stretch.

Her partner is equally monomaniacal when it comes to the making of '*le fun*'. A theatrical type, he's invented a character for himself to play during the procession: St Buffo of Nontron, a fictional monk who came here to stoke the fires of love but was murdered by a jealous husband who stuck a pair of bellows up his bum and – well, you get the picture. It's a good joke, but the out-of-towner has gone to so much effort to fit in, he seems destined to remain on the fringe. Not only has he come equipped with a full-blown costume of mitre, long-flowing wig and robes, he's also carrying a 'saint's relic' in a chocolate box and, for reasons best known to himself, twirling a white parasol.

Outside the window stands a float with the effigy of the *Buffadou*, a crude papier-mâché mock-up of a *Soufflacul* smoking a pre-execution cigarette. 'The *Buffadou* represents everything that's wrong with the world,' I've been told. And it's not hard to guess who the main hate figure is on this side of the Atlantic. While a woman paints a clown's face on me, one of the organisers explains that this year the *Buffadou* has been rechristened the 'Bush-adieu'. 'The "Bush-adieu" is the illegitimate child of George Bush Sr and Lola Ferrari, the porn star. His parentage was discovered only recently.'

The grand procession is due to start at three o'clock, but everyone is having so much fun getting ready, it takes an unseasonably freezing shower and a smattering of hail finally to get the show on the road. Several dozen *Soufflaculs* in white caps and nightgowns caper through the streets in masks and make-up, tweeting whistles, blaring horns and banging drums, accompanied by a brass band and a couple of parade floats, including a vehicle disguised as a giant bellows-mobile. A man in a top hat and tails is directing them, and they're escorted by a handful of red-nosed clowns in the pillbox hats and buttoned uniforms of the gendarmerie. There's also a contingent of monks and a fat old man in a wig sporting a pair of bare latex breasts. The true leaders of the group, though, are the real policemen masquerading as fools who run up ahead with a bright red ladder allowing them to indulge in carnival-sanctioned breaking and entering. All five of the *fous* have on red half-masks with sharp cheekbones and pointed noses that contrast with the whiteness of their *Soufflaculs'* costumes and add a medieval touch to the revelry. One even has his nightcap stuffed so that it stands erect on the back of his head like a priapic headpiece. As a counterpoint, Franck has endowed himself with a flaccid, stuffed white shlong so long its red tip nearly scrapes the ground. All the fools are armed with bellows and hunting horns, and whenever Franck and his cohorts spot a pair of open shutters along the gulley of houses, they mount an assault on the building, the ladder trembling like a drunk's hand as they gallivant up the rungs to kiss the occupants hello and then climb inside the second-storey windows. The *Buffadou* often follows them up, even though he can barely manage walking in a straight line, let alone scaling a near-perpendicular ladder, and the fools often have to haul him to safety. Within moments, they re-emerge swigging bottles of wine and tooting their horns. Franck waves to me to follow them on to the next house – and café – and bar – and before I know it, we're drinking blue liquids, yellow liquids, pink liquids and clear liquids – pretty much any liquid on offer, so long as it's alcoholic.

Where the owners have been so inconsiderate as to lock the fools out or, even worse, try to ignore them, the *Soufflaculs* wind red-and-white emergency tape around their balconies and tie their doors shut. And for those unfortunate (or stupid) enough to have vacated their homes and left the windows open, the fools invade their apartments and scatter whatever they like to the crowd: magazines, flowers and the contents of their fridges, while the men pump their fists in the air and blast their trumpets amid the sickening splat of pâté on the tarmac.

Back on ground, in between raids, the fools are constantly on the lookout for a bit of skirt. On the rare occasions when they do find a woman wearing a dress, they rush up to her and do their best to puff it up with their bellows, while Franck waggles his fake willy lasciviously around her legs. However, given that few women wear dresses these days, much less during the Fête of the *Soufflaculs*, most of the suitable targets are on the far side of fifty, clad in bulletproof polyester skirts stretched tight by their haunches.

Finally, in an apartment-house above a café in the main square, the fools spot a youngish mademoiselle who's not only wearing a skirt . . . but also standing on a balcony . . . with all of her windows open and only her pet dog for company.

'Celle là!'

That's the one! A shy brunette armoured in the ankle-length skirt favoured by the matrons of the *ville*, plus a long cardigan, wrapping her arms so tightly around herself that you wonder if she's about to perform a disappearing act. The fools storm the ramparts, pumping up her skirt as best they can, and she laughs, alternately relishing the attention and embarrassment as Franck waves his dildo in her face. In no time, the fools are running rampant through the three storeys of her flat, stringing emergency tape between the balconies and shutters to crisscross the façade as they hang out the windows, guzzling wine and toasting the crowd.

'Vive les Soufflaculs!'

The sky begins to spit rain, and a few umbrellas mushroom in the crowd below. The revellers assemble on the steps of the town hall, in front of the EU and French flags and the arches engraved with LIBERTÉ, FRATERNITÉ and EGALITÉ. On the locked gates, the *Soufflaculs* have hung cutout bellows declaring their own motto, the levelling *esprit du Carnaval*: 'We're all part of the same family.'

For the thousandth time, everyone joins in the *Soufflaculs'* anthem, including the bawdy doggerel at the end. The gist is unmistakable, particularly given that a couple of men are enacting it in front of the town hall. The old guy with the fake breasts is being bounced by a monk from behind in rhythm to the Occitan chant:

> While making love
> I lost my cravat
> My cravat that was splendid
> And my waistcoat that was violet
> And my hat that was made of cotton.

Then come the speeches and adulations and the awarding of the *Soufflaculs'* highest honour to the dignitaries *du jour*: *La Sardine Valeureuse* – the Priceless Sardine. Throughout the procession, one of the merrymakers has been carrying a contraption strung with striped ribbons and big dried sardines, an apparatus that looks like the kind of mobile a family of ghouls might suspend above their baby's crib. To get an idea of just how horrible the dead fish smell, consider this: even the French think they stink.

It's all a liqueured blur to me. I'm off somewhere on the sidelines sampling yet another liquid of mysterious hue when I hear the master of ceremonies call my name, or rather 'Gérard' Daeschner.

'*Gérard!*'

'*Gérard!*'

The *Soufflaculs* clap me to centre stage and I suddenly find myself on the steps of the town hall, with a dead fish strung around my neck and a certificate identifying Monsieur Gérard Daeschner as 'an Epicurean, Reveller and Party Animal recognised by all'. *They must have the wrong guy.* Before I know it, there's a microphone thrust in my face, and the crowd hushes to hear me. With all the collective attention of Nontron focused on me, I stutter my thanks over the loud speaker: *'M-merci!'*

The disappointment is as palpable as the stench of the sardine: *We go out of our way to welcome this Yank, letting him judge the beauty contest and awarding him our most Priceless Sardine, and all he can say is 'Uh, thanks'?!?*

So I reach deep down into my grab-bag of French vocab for something more profound. And all I come up with is: *'Merci . . . merci beaucoup!'*

They're too kind to heckle or throw rotten fruit – besides, I've already got a dead fish around my neck – so they applaud and cheer instead.

Franck the Fou grabs me by the shoulders and gives me not one, not two, but *four* kisses on the cheeks. 'If all Americans are like you,' he gushes, 'they're very welcome in Nontron.'

The *Buffadou* also gives me the quadruple-kiss treatment, his smackers made all the more memorable by the fact that the bushy hole in his beard is smeared with lipstick and fish: he's actually eaten half of his sardine.

Miss Soufflette is much smarter, avoiding the *Buffadou*'s affections as best she can. After pausing at another bar, the noisy cavalcade stumbles to a car park at the top of town where the robed effigy of the *Buffadou* stands on a pyre of green tree branches. As the sun finally emerges from hiding, the clown-faced gendarmes lead the human scapegoat onto a stage, where a judge in a ridiculous wig condemns the *Buffadou* to the flames while the *Souffaculs* gather around m'lud and try to pump wind up his scarlet robes. The *Buffadou* is crying and carrying on and makes one last attempt to kiss Miss Soufflette, but she turns her face from him and the buffoonish policemen drag him to his fate. The *Soufflaculs* set fire to the effigy of carnival, singing and dancing around the bonfire as the flames purge the world's wrongs for another year.

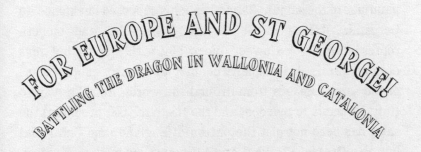

CHAPTER FOUR

FOR EUROPE AND ST GEORGE!

BATTLING THE DRAGON IN WALLONIA AND CATALONIA

PART ONE:

ON HOW *NOT* TO DO IT

'This could almost be the flag of the European Union,' the proud Catalonian tells me, caressing the miniature banner on his desk.

It's a nice thought, but I can't help thinking it would be a tough sell to the French, the Welsh, the Scots and the Irish, not to mention Europe's Muslim and Jewish communities. Why, even the self-effacing English might be embarrassed at the thought of replacing the EU's elite circle of stars with the stark, red-and-white, do-or-die angularity of their very own flag of St George.

To his credit, though, Narcís Sayrach does practise what he preaches. A former priest, he's turned his elegant, Gaudí-inspired apartment in Barcelona into a veritable shrine to Sanctus Georgius – or Sant Jordi, as he's known in this part of Spain. The high-ceilinged walls are festooned with graven images of the saint: everything from photos of the earliest wall paintings of the saint in Cappadocia, his supposed birthplace, to Germanic statues of St George Über Alles and modern representations of a sweet, blond boy with a spear but *sans* dragon. Narcís also has hefty country-by-country photo albums of the saint's images from around the world, from Norway to Italy, Romania to Sweden, and the US to the UK: proof that the saint has been not just the patron of England (and Catalonia) but also Greece, Portugal and Lithuania, as well as Moscow, Istanbul, Genoa and Venice, not to mention Germany and even parts of France.

Considering that he knows more about England's patron saint than most Englishmen do, Narcís is shocked to learn that St George is all but neglected in the UK. 'Maybe he's more closely related to the monarchy than the people,' he ventures.

It's as good a guess as any. For a foreigner, one of the more baffling aspects of life in England is the incessant handwringing over the question of patriotism and, in particular, St George. Every 23 April, the media churn out lengthy thumbsuckers about what it means to be English and why so few people celebrate St George's Day. The short answer is: most of them don't even know the date. According to surveys by Mori and ICM, anywhere from 54 to as much as 80 per cent of the English are clueless when it comes to pinpointing St George's Day. Granted, some of these are probably paid-up members of the Moronic Minority, the hard-crusted core of idiots who skew every poll going: they're the 17 per cent who confuse Churchill with the dog in the insurance ads (and the 9 per cent who don't believe the former prime minister ever existed); the 15 per cent who think the Battle of Hastings never took place; the eleven per cent who think that Adolf Hitler was a fictional character; and the 5 per cent who think Conan the Barbarian was a real person.

The reasons for the long-term decline in St George's popularity are well known: the Reformation and the secularisation of British society . . . two devastating world wars that led to the loss of the empire and a backlash against imperialism . . . and the hijacking of the saint, his flag and the Union Jack by racist 'nationalists'. But St George also runs up against another barrier in our perma-titillated, brazenly unchivalrous age: he just isn't sexy enough. Although he gets the girl, he doesn't do anything with her. That's partly what made the saint so appealing to the Victorians, but nowadays it may provide a clue to England's identity crisis. Put simply: the English don't have a romantic myth that can be sexed up to arouse patriotic pulses.

This (admittedly half-cocked) notion occurred to me on a trip to Ireland, while I was visiting the home of an American woman who loved anything Celticky but nothing Anglo or Saxon. 'Because the English always had to control things – to conquer people and steal their land,' she explained. 'When I think of what they did to the Welsh, for instance, and Welsh history . . .'

At the mention of 'Welsh history', she turned to gaze at the posters papering her walls, masturbatory fantasies of mythic babes, 'empowered' women in fetish-wear slicing the heads off serpents and dragons and so forth. It wasn't clear to me what relevance they had to the sad reality of Welsh history, but . . . *phwoar*. Now *that's* a national myth. When you look for something similar in England, well, *Beowulf* is bloody, but it doesn't have enough girls (viz. Hollywood's ill-starred attempt to sex it up with Angelina Jolie), and St George is positively G-rated, too goody-two-shoes compared to the rape-and-revenge stories in *Rob Roy* and *Braveheart* or the adultery and betrayal that destroyed the Celts' King Arthur. In terms of scope for gratuitous sex scenes, English myths and legends just can't compete. At no point in the canon did Shakespeare write: 'Then verily did Ophelia getteth her tits out.'

But – what ho? If you search hard enough, you can sense the stirrings that could restore St George to something like his former glory. After England's turn-of-the-century identity crisis, national pride has been rekindled by a string of specific events that have boosted sales of St George flags. At the same time, broader issues such as devolution, terrorism and the debate over the EU have inspired a growing realisation among conservatives and liberals alike that Englishness may in fact be unique and worth preserving; there's nothing inherently wrong about being proud of your country's accomplishments.

In recent years, some historians have begun to reappraise the British Empire and conclude that, while it wasn't an unadulterated force for good, it wasn't all bad, either. In fact, England's imperialists may have been the best of a bad lot: so much so that its former colonies might ask themselves a version of the famous question posed by Monty Python. 'Okay – apart from a global language, parliamentary democracy, a flexible judicial system, an upwardly mobile religion, the Industrial Revolution, advanced education, and the bloodymindedness to overcome fascism and communism, what did the English ever do for us?'

Having all but disappeared at one point, St George's Day celebrations are becoming more widespread in England, and each year polls and petitions show increasing support for turning 23 April into a national holiday (though asking people whether they'd like an extra day off work is akin to offering them free chocolate for life). It may be too early to call a rally, but after decades of institutionalised shame, England may be on the verge of a full-blown Georgian Revival, in spirit if not yet in practice. Pale and anaemic, St George may yet make a full-blooded comeback.

So, in anticipation, I've decided to find out how other places celebrate the saint.

But first, a lesson in how *not* to do it.

As a general rule of thumb, whenever you're casting around Europe for an example of how not to do something, Belgium is always a good bet. I won't bore you with the old 'Belgium-is-boring' routine, except to warn against an insidious rumour making the rounds, often perpetuated by some of the most cultured people you know. Returning from a city-break on the Continent, they'll confess, shame-faced and *sotto voce*, 'Actually, I think Belgium is underrated.'

Take it from me: they're crazy . . . or lying . . . or secretly in the pay of some nefarious, EU-funded 'Up with Belgium' quango (motto: 'At Least It's Not Luxembourg').

The thing is, I should love the place. Belgium offers a bonanza of strange festivals – practically every event on my itinerary has a buffoonish Flemish or Walloon counterpart. I've already cited Cat Throwing in Ypres as the spiritual kin of Spain's Goat Toss, while the people of Binche celebrate carnival by parading around as Incas and pelting each other with oranges. Indeed, Belgium has so many daft events, you could write a book on them. (Don't worry; this isn't that book.)

What converts mean when they say the traditional marching zone between France and Germany is underrated is that Belgium has some truly weekend-worthy towns and cities: Antwerp, Bruges and Brussels. Unfortunately, my destination isn't one of them. The former coal-mining centre of Mons in south-west Wallonia is so close to the border it's almost France, in the same way that Flanders is almost the Netherlands and the whole of Belgium is almost a country . . . but somehow not quite. Mons is built on a hill – hence its name – and its winding, knobbly streets are marginally kinder on the eye than the feet. In typically Belgian fashion, its landmark church lacks a belfry and its *Beffroi* lacks a church. Victor Hugo compared the tacky, stand-alone bell tower to 'a giant coffee pot, with four smaller teapots under it. It would be very ugly if it weren't that big.'

As in most Belgian cities, Mons' great redeeming feature is its central plaza, a *Grand Place* in every sense of the term. It's more modest than the one in Brussels, but still manages to be more impressive than you remembered. The irregular, cobblestoned expanse is ringed by elegant buildings – the Gothic town hall, gabled townhouses and restaurants and cafés with fields of tables and chairs set out on the square – forming the perfect ambience for soaking up the sunshine and sampling some of the country's eight-hundred-plus beers. Even then, though, the names of the establishments indicate that they would rather be anywhere but Belgium: the Copenhagen Tavern, the Café de Paris . . . and Chi-Chi's Tex-Mex chain.

Every summer, the *Grand Place* is also the scene of the world's biggest – and most bizarre – celebration in St George's honour: on Trinity Sunday, usually in late May or early June, the local Walloons re-enact the saint's famous derring-do against the dragon. The 'Battle of the Lumeçon' is about 600 years old, dating from roughly the same era as Britain's oldest chivalric honour, the Knights of the Garter. Quite why Belgian francophones should make such a fuss over England's patron saint, forcing their beloved founder-saint, Waudru, to share her big day out with a foreign interloper, is something of a mystery, not least to the local Walloons. Chalk it up to the timeless appeal of St George and the Age of Chivalry. One of Mons' churches claims to have a bit of the saint in a box, though exactly which part is unclear. 'It may be his head. I don't know,' shrugged the caretaker. As for the Lumeçon, the official literature waxes poetic about St George and the Dragon representing much more than just a humdrum conflict between Good and Evil. *Au contraire*. It turns out they symbolise the fight between Continuity and Evolution, Identity and Otherness, Order and Disorder and the Conscious and the Subconscious, Light and Darkness, Life and Death . . . in other words, pretty much whatever you want to see in it. There's even some tired, sub-Freudian analysis about the sabre's phallicism, noting that the saint wears a glove on his right hand during the swordplay: 'the hand remains "pure", unsoiled'.

To be sure, it's always sensible for a man to wear a glove if he's going to go around poking dragons. It's just good hygiene.

But never mind the Belgian waffle: St George actually has a much more recent connection to Mons, by way of the Great War, a ghost story . . . and a vegetarian restaurant in London. If you've heard of Mons at all, chances are it's because of a battle. Waterloo is only half an hour away, and Mons itself was the site of the first major engagement between the British and Germans during the First World War – best known for a case of divine intervention known as the 'Angels of Mons'. In August 1914, the British Expeditionary Force was outnumbered more than two to one by the Germans pouring into southern Belgium en route to France. The Kaiser ordered his men to annihilate the 'contemptible little army', but the Brits managed to inflict twice as many casualties, fending off the enemy long enough to save their French allies and make a miraculous escape: a 200-mile fighting retreat that justified their new nickname, the 'Old Contemptibles'. Within weeks, the media back home began reporting that soldiers had seen a host of angels come to their rescue, led by St George/St Michael. The heavenly helpers supposedly appeared as the archers of Agincourt. In actual fact, the fighting coincided with the anniversary of the Battle of Crécy, when English longbowmen saved the day. Of course, in both of those medieval battles, England had been fighting against France. At Mons, however, instead of raining death on the French, the divine archers targeted England's other Old Enemy.

Sadly, the vague accounts of the Angels at Mons probably stem from a story published shortly after the event by an occult writer in London. In 'The Bowmen', Arthur Machen imagined St George and the medieval archers ushering British troops to safety. Given that it's a patriotic tale about red-blooded, beef-eating Englishmen, the inspiration for the *deus ex machina* is more than a little ironic. While mowing down Germans, a nameless machine-gunner suddenly remembers eating at 'a queer vegetarian restaurant in London' that served 'eccentric dishes of cutlets made of lentils and nuts that pretended to be steak'. All the plates in the place were inscribed with an image of St George and an invocation in Latin: 'May St George be a present help to the English'. Blasting away on the battlefield, the gunner starts muttering 'the pious vegetarian motto' in Latin, and lo and behold, *Sanctus Georgius* and his archers appear in the sky, slaying the Huns without leaving any marks on their corpses. Afterwards, the Germans attribute the deaths to some new-fangled poison gas. 'But the man who knew what nuts tasted like when they called themselves steak knew also that St George had brought his Agincourt Bowmen to help the English.'

Despite that closing line – surely one of the most improbable sentences in the entire English language – the story spread by media and word of mouth until it turned into a full-blown myth, an inspirational story that the British wanted to believe, particularly during the early setbacks of the war. By the time St George's Day rolled around the following year, the tale of the Angels of Mons had virtually become gospel. In Mons' town hall, a painting of the myth lists the soldiers from England, Scotland, Ireland and Wales who fought and died in the town's defence. The *hôtel de ville* also boasts a chapel to St George and, on the afternoon before the Lumeçon, its tiny Gothic courtyard hosts a rehearsal battle for the big event.

Initially, the officials guarding the main entrance wave through anyone and everyone – old folks, parents with prams and a woman in a wheelchair – so I decide to try my luck, too. I want to get some close-up photos of St George and the Dragon today because from what I gather, the actual battle is chaos. This pre-rehearsal scrum is bad enough as it is. People are jostling each other against the grey stone walls and bickering about their children not being able to see. Of course, all this aggro could have been prevented if the jobsworths hadn't let in twice as many spectators as the courtyard can hold. But that would have spoilt their fun: they wouldn't have been able to kick half of them out again.

A little policeman in a peaked cap and fussy moustache is having a high time swaggering around, dismissing people with a smile. Some try to argue with him, but he takes great joy in informing them that – *aha!* – they've crossed the line.

Line? What line? The official points to a faded yellow mark painted barely a foot from the wall of the courtyard's cramped interior. Unbeknownst to everyone but him, you have to be standing behind the line to stay. Given the size of my feet, and the fact that I'm already backed up all-too-intimately against another guy, I'm an obvious candidate for ejection. I manage to communicate, with a combination of pidgin French and simian sign language, that I'm an American writing a book on the Lumeçon.

'*Avez-vous une accreditation?*' he asks.

I reckon I now have two options.

Tactic #1: I can pretend not to understand anything and hope for some residual transatlantic goodwill; after all, the headquarters of NATO's military command is just north of here, and, well, *if it weren't for us . . . speaking German . . . yadda yadda yadda*. Very Ugly American of me, I know, but Belgium brings it out in me. Years of exposure to the EU-bashing in Britain hasn't helped, either. In terms of venerability, the Belgian state is a mere babe. Brussels, 'the village on the marsh', didn't emerge from the muck until centuries after Europe's great capitals: Rome, Paris and London. In fact, even Americans can scoff at Belgium: it didn't gain its independence until 1830 – after a revolt sparked by an *opera* (and even that was imported: *The Mute Girl of Portici* was composed by a Frenchman about a Neapolitan uprising against the Spanish). Belgium didn't exist, so Europe's powerbrokers let it be invented. As a result, Belgium is the perfect home for pan-European unification: the natives have never had much national pride in the first place.

In fairness, though, the ignoble reason why America and Britain have never taken Belgium seriously – apart from beer, chocolate and 'French' fries – is because it was never a credible imperial power (and has yet to win a World Cup). In retrospect, this relative lack of ambition on the world stage might seem commendable if it weren't for the atrocities the Belgians committed in the Congo, the one time they did have a crack at empire-building. Worse still, the Belgians were conquered on at least one occasion by the *French*. So I'm loath to take orders from a funny little man in a funny little uniform with a funny little moustache and a funny little hat.

With that kind of attitude, it's no wonder I don't get any joy from him. His hard little eyes glint like sapphires poked into a blob of dough.

'May I help?' a voice intercedes in American English with a Belgian twist. A knight in a black T-shirt has come to my rescue. The man is involved in another key part of tomorrow's event – pushing a Golden Carriage into the church.

The dough-faced policeman tells him to tell me that he wants to see my press pass, which I'm guessing would take the form of a long scroll of illuminated leather, embossed with official stamps, ribbons, seals and signatures.

This brings me to Tactic #2: pull rank.

'But I spoke to Madame So-and-So,' I aver. Technically, this is a fib, but only because Madame So-and-So hasn't bothered to reply to my numerous attempts to contact her. However, the mere mention of a senior bureaucrat, one of the main organisers, has the desired effect of creating a frisson of officiousness.

'He says he spoke to Madame So-and-So,' the carriage-pusher informs the cop.

'*Et qu'est-ce qu'elle a dit?*' the cop asks the carriage-pusher. 'And what did she say?' the carriage-pusher asks me.

We go round and round like this until eventually a face-saving solution is found: I have to leave because there's no room behind the yellow line, but the carriage-pusher assures me that I'm not missing much anyway: St George won't be in uniform today. However, if I meet him tomorrow morning outside the church, he'll get me into a building overlooking the *Grand Place* for the battle. All too easily mollified, I retreat to an outdoor café across the square to begin working my way through its directory of beers.

More fool me.

The Sunday morning warm-up for the main event is the stately Procession of the Golden Coach, a gilded title that belies its grim roots in the Black Death – or 'Great Pest', as one pamphlet puts it. As the plague cut through Europe in 1349, the people of Mons beseeched their obscure patron saint for protection, parading St Waudru's 700-year-old remains around town, a practice that was infinitely more appealing than the bloody rituals of the German flagellants who crisscrossed the Low Countries, whipping themselves, attacking Jews and preaching that the end of the world had come.

Fortunately, carting around St Waudru seemed to fend off Judgement Day, and the grateful townsfolk of Mons instituted an annual day out in her honour, coinciding with the 'game of St George and the Dragon'. However, both events ran into trouble in the late 1700s. First the Austrian emperor tried to crack down on processions and rein in the Catholic Church, and then the French Revolution tried to do away with the Church altogether. St Waudru was spirited away for temporary safekeeping in two batches: her head went to one monastery, her bones to another. Meanwhile, the French rulers hijacked her Golden Coach – the same model used today – to get the subjugated lowlanders to pay homage to new goddesses: ironically, Liberty and Reason.

The modern procession recalls Mons' glory days during the Renaissance, when it was, um . . . apparently more important than it is today, especially now that most of the area's coal mines have closed. Women in period nun-wear carry a litter bearing St Waudru's skull, encased in a life-sized gilded copper bust of what she might have looked like, while the rest of her remains travel atop the Golden Coach in a reliquary shaped like a church. At the same time, supplicants from other parishes have also dressed up in fancy costumes to parade their saintly bits and bobs. The whole shebang culminates with the triumphant pushing of the Golden Coach up the ramp and into St Waudru's cathedral-sized church. Legend has it that something terrible will happen to Mons if the carriage stalls along the twenty-degree incline, so the locals pile in to get behind it and push, even though it's already being pulled by some very sturdy draught horses. I'm told that a girl fell under one of the wheels and broke her leg a few years ago, but the coach didn't stop, so nothing bad befell the general populace.

And that's where Fabian, the friendly carriage-pusher, comes in. I meet him outside St Waudru Church, and he immediately apologises: unfortunately, the vantage point on the *Grand Place* is going to be too crowded, so I won't be able to go there, but if I stand next to the church, on that flatbed truck over there, he says, pointing, I'll still have a good view of the action. So, gullible as I am, that's what I do . . . for the next hour . . . like an eejit, waiting for St George as the endless procession of priests, relics, choirboys, marching bands, knights on horseback, soldiers in plumed helmets, and women in gabled hoods and veils file out of the church. *Still*, I tell myself, *there are worse things to do than stand in the sunshine and watch a parade*. Gradually, though, I realise that if I wait for the carriage to return to the church around noon, I'll miss the beginning of the battle on the *Grand Place* a couple of streets over.

'It's either one or the other,' a man standing next to me explains. 'One year you can see the *Car d'Or*, the other the *Combat*.' He favours the former. 'It's so crowded on the square, most people don't even see the *Combat*.'

But I have to. I decide to skip the cart-pushing, despite the heavily qualified praise in the brochure, which claims it's 'the greatest historical-religious procession in the French-speaking part of Belgium' (not to mention the only one involving Mons, a carriage and a saint called Waudru). I jump off the truck and rush to the *Grand Place*.

The Golden Coach is just now making its way through the square, and the priests have paused for an open-air service, with singing from the choirboys and murmured responses from some of the spectators. For the most part, though, the crowds are more interested in drinking and chattering. It's eleven a.m., and the beer is already generating a buzz at the stands outside the cafés. Red-and-white streamers are fluttering across the square from the hall's pepper-pot tower, and its balcony has been decked out in red velvet for local VIPs. No fewer than four flags adorn the façade: one for the EU (natch); St George (though it's a red-and-white tricolour instead of a cross); Wallonia (yellow, with a red cock nicked from the old French Republic); and, of course, Belgium (which I always confuse with Germany's). A couple of cafés on the square are also flying American and Italian flags, as true pantheists of patriotism.

In preparation for the battle, the Belgian Red Cross has set up shop in the Salle de St Georges of the town hall – *surely they're not expecting injuries?* – but with barely an hour to go, there's no sign of a battlefield. Then I notice a ring of metal bollards with holes in their tops in the middle of the square, forming a ring roughly forty by sixty feet. That must be it. Thinking myself clever, I position myself next to one of the low metal poles, alongside a pallid guy with a sunken chest who tries to tell me something about the tremendous pressure on the frontline. I smile blithely. *He's probably exaggerating.* Within minutes, a couple of trucks rumble onto the square, dumping mounds of butterscotch sand onto the cobblestones, and men with shovels start spreading the stuff to form a purpose-built island in the middle of the plaza. While they're working, the men who have been boozing it up at the beer stands begin to crowd around, greeting their friends with kisses – *mwah, mwah* – before tearing each other's shirts off and grappling in the sand. Many of the hard men sport the mullets and facial hair common on the Continent but oddly eschewed by the modern English yob (as far as I can work out, Europe's Great Mullet Divide overlaps the English Channel). In their impromptu wrestling bouts, they inflict half nelsons and full body slams that would break their necks if it weren't for the four-inch cushion of sand on the stone. As it is, the throws look painful. Before long, practically every man under thirty is shirtless, the Walloons' pale flesh turning red in the sunshine and their shredded T-shirts tied as padding around the rope that's pulled taut through the bollards.

And then the crushing begins. All the stragglers from the cafés are trying to barge their way ringside; failing that, they're pushing as hard as they can to make life miserable for those of us at the front. The guy who tried to warn me about the pressure has already been bullied to the back. I'm (stupidly) standing my ground – intent on photographing St George – even as the rope threatens to sever me at the waist. The guys who keep ripping each other's shirts try to explain that it's impossible to take pictures, but then shrug when they realise I'm an ignorant Yank.

'*Il ne comprend pas. Il ne parle pas français,*' one guy says.

'*Bon. Il comprendra dans cinq minutes,*' scoffs another ominously.

As the plaza fills to capacity, it's determined that I'm a danger to myself – if to no one else – and a policeman escorts me across the sand to the pavilion, where the TV cameras and journalists are stationed.

'*Avez-vous une accreditation?*'

Not again.

Had I known this quaint folk festival took itself as seriously as an EU summit, believe me, I would have sent in my notarised application form months in advance, along with photo ID, blood and stool samples. That said, the Lumeçon *is* big in Belgium: it's actually on the front cover this week of the Belgian equivalent of *Paris Match* (unbelievably) – with a *full-colour pullout* to boot.

But *still*. Fortunately, this time I manage to blag a pass by mentioning Madame So-and-So – I don't know her, but she must be one powerful woman – *et voilà*, I get a place on the kiosk, in front of the brass band that's already oompahing the 'Song of the *Doudou*' and will continue to do so for the next forty minutes, tirelessly looping the same few bars of music. The galumphing tune creates a circus-like atmosphere and goes something like this:

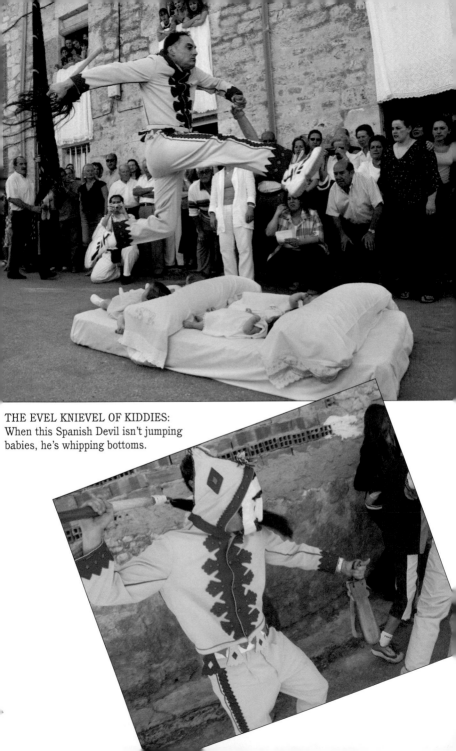

THE EVEL KNIEVEL OF KIDDIES:
When this Spanish Devil isn't jumping
babies, he's whipping bottoms.

WOULD YOU B-A-A-A-A-N IT? The 'good old days' of Spanish Goat Tossing – before British protesters helped put a stop to it.

THE COCK AND THE FOOL:
During the Rooster Run,
Spanish cadets recite odes to a dead
cockerel, and the 'Ugliest Man in
the Village' dresses up as a 'fool'–
David Beckham in Real Madrid kit.

KRAZY FOR KARNEVAL: The Rhineland's Washer Princess brandishes her wand as a warning to men on 'Dirty Thursday', while masked revellers in the Black Forest beat onlookers with inflated pigs' bladders.

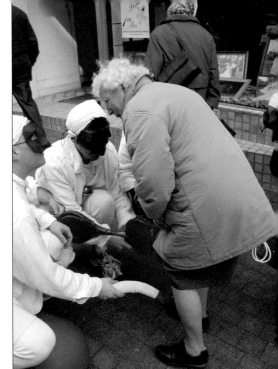

IT'LL HAVE TO BE HARDER THAN
THAT: An Arse Blower wilts as his
fellow fools pump air up a woman's
skirt and a happy couple demolishes
the myth of French sex appeal.

WHO SAYS BELGIUM
IS BORING?
Walloons wallow in
the sand before
St. George does battle
with the 'Doudou'
in the heart of the EU.

FOR GOD AND COUNTRY:
Catalonians celebrate St. George
with books and roses in Barcelona,
while Kefalonians lie in wait for
a miracle as the cadaver of
St. Gerasimos passes over them.

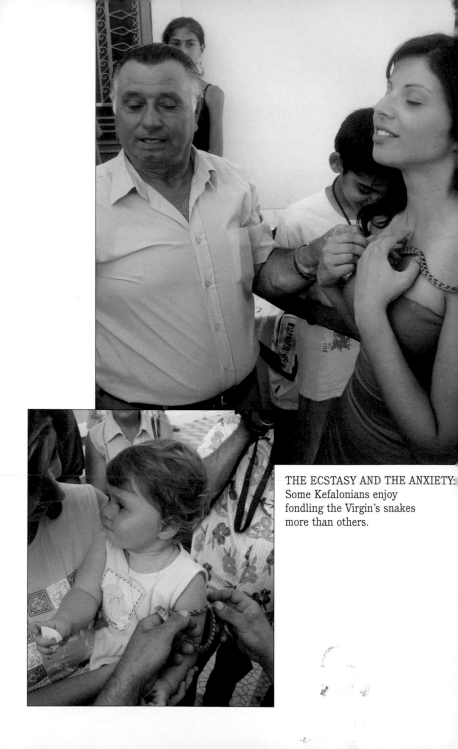

THE ECSTASY AND THE ANXIETY:
Some Kefalonians enjoy
fondling the Virgin's snakes
more than others.

da-duh, da-duh, da-DUH
da-duh, da-duh, da-DUH
da-duh, da-duh –

– You get the idea. Likewise, the 'doo-doo' is the not-very-scary nickname of the Dragon, one of the many idiosyncrasies that could have driven Magritte and other surrealists to snap their paintbrushes in half and throw away their canvases, unable to compete with the strangeness of truth versus fiction. To wit: the Belgian version of St George wears a yellow leather jacket with red trim, white tights and black boots, topped with a crested golden helmet that harks back to the time when Belgium was under Napoleon's thumb. The saint's sidekicks are a dozen 'Chinchins', men in flat cowboy hats and long, tartan coats who have spotted, fur-covered boxes strapped round their waists. If you didn't know that they're meant to represent big dogs, you'd think they were wannabe Belgian cowmen with some strange Scottish fixation. The enemies of St George and the Chinchins are eleven devils in black who taunt them with inflated pigs' bladders and have demon faces painted on their backs. Then there's the *Doudou* itself. Far from being fearsome, the green wickerwork could be an effigy of Snappy the Crocodile borrowed from a local playschool. It has a flat head, a swollen, toadlike body, and a long pole for a tail that's decorated with ribbons and . . . 'lucky' horsehair. Throughout the battle, the local oiks try to grab the tail and rip off tufts of hair; afterwards, they strut around, gifting strands to their families and friends. Although it looks like it's made of papier-mâché, the Dragon is over ten metres long and weighs more than 200 kilos, requiring eleven men in white to carry its body and eight guys in green foliage – the 'Men of Leaves' – to hold up its tail.

The final absurdist touch takes the form of about a billion Belgian policemen in old-fashioned blue uniforms and white domed helmets that match their big, white, patent-leather belts: *les Keystone Kops*. As a Machiavellian motivator, this is pure genius: forcing policemen to wear silly hats makes them work twice as hard at proving their masculinity. The police are in charge of keeping the hooligans at bay. Thousands of people have piled into the plaza, and the half-naked men at the front are bent over the rope, taking their punishment from the rear. To keep the pressure from slicing them in half, the police are pushing back against them, so the poor buggers are getting it from both ends. *And to think that coulda been me.* The battle hasn't even begun, and already the police are yanking people out of the crowd: some happily, others not so, being marched off in headlocks, all to the circus-like 'Song of the *Doudou*'. St George and his minions have barely entered the arena when a yob jumps onto the dragon's tail – *lucky hair, lucky hair!* – and half a dozen bouncers plus a few Leaf Men pile on top of him, battering him into submission and then shoving him into the arms of *les Keystones*.

At any one time inside the arena, at least a hundred people are hopping, dancing, running, punching, riding or wandering in a confused daze on the sand. The Chinchins are jumping around, waving their hats to the crowd, and the devils are slashing at the air with their inflated pigs' bladders, taunting their enemies in the arena, while the zombified masses on the other side of the rope are trying to grab the *Doudou*'s lucky hair. Occasionally, someone will bodysurf onto the pitch, grabbing the organic balloons and fighting a tug of war with the devils.

While all this is going on, St George is prancing on a black stallion, its mane braided with red-and-white ribbons. The guy who plays the role has the droopy face of a character actor, and he spends most of the time in an awkward *pas de deux* with the Dragon, endlessly circling without ever really engaging (Lumeçon comes from the word *limaçon* – snail – and refers to the spiral patterns of certain militia drills). For its part, the overgrown lizard has a hard time negotiating turns, let alone chasing anything. From time to time, the Dragon will lift its long tail and slam it down on the outstretched hands (and heads) of the crowd. Instead of scrambling to get away, the spectators actually surge forward, with everyone trying to grab a ribbon or horsehair, making life even more miserable for those on the rope. The Dragon's attendants immediately dive into the masses, fighting to extricate the tail, hammering and pounding at fingers with their fists. Meanwhile, a spectator is stretchered off the pitch, his nose gushing scarlet, and somewhere a volley of shots is being fired as the 'Song of the *Doudou*' plays on . . .

Compared with all this genuine drama – all the real battles out there in the audience – the play-acting in the arena seems *boring*. Every so often, a Chinchin will hand St George a comedy lance – the tip's blunt like a paddle – and the saint will prance around, twirling it like a slow-motion baton before poking the Dragon in the head, body and tail. Eventually the lance 'breaks', so he pulls out his sabre. That doesn't work either. More circling and ducking under the Dragon's tail – at one point it nearly knocks his helmet off – and then he tries the lance again. The whole shtick is repeated three times.

I'm obviously too sober to enjoy it. The problem isn't the Keystone Kops, or the Snappy the Crocodile Dragon, or the wonky St George, or the general corniness and the fact that

Doudou sounds like a synonym for crap. That's all suitably, and possibly even endearingly, surreal. What I object to is the denouement. Having failed to beat the Dragon, St George does the most unsaintly thing: he cheats. He whips out a *revolver* and *shoots* it. Even then, with superior firepower, the Walloon is such a wally it takes him *three shots* to kill the monster. So much for the Age of Chivalry. Rather than representing the victory of Good over Evil, the Belgian interpretation ends up symbolising the notoriously different notions of fair play that exist between England and the Continent. It almost makes you glad the English don't celebrate St George's Day.

Then again . . .

PART TWO:
AN IMMODEST PROPOSAL

Consider St George's Day in Barcelona.

Not only do the Catalonians get the date right, but they turn the palm-treed avenues of their capital into a massive book and rose festival, combining literature and romance in the springtime. Besides Catalonia's patron saint, *La Diada de Sant Jordi* pays homage to the high priest of Spanish literature, Cervantes, who died on 23 April (as did Shakespeare). It was even the inspiration for the UN's 'World Book Day', which is now observed in over a hundred countries on St George's Day (though bizarrely, England usually celebrates it in *March*).

For Catalonians, Sant Jordi serves as a national day and provides a potent rival to the commercialism of Valentine's Day. That said, Sant Jordi wouldn't be Catalonian if it weren't good for business. Barcelona outranks Madrid as the publishing capital of the Spanish-speaking world, and booksellers rake in roughly a tenth of their annual sales in just one day, shifting one and a half million books. Instead of chocolates, friends, lovers and family members exchange books and roses, the twinned symbols of their native tongue and St George. Traditionally, men receive the books and the women roses. Among younger generations, though, couples swap books and flowers as they see fit.

'It used to be a little *machista*, but not now. Now it's equal,' Narcís Sayrach assures me in a thick, gargling accent that I can barely keep up with. As the devout President of the Friends of St George (*Amics de Sant Jordi*), he says he normally speaks exclusively in Catalan; he's making a concession for me, translating constantly in his head to talk to me in Castilian Spanish, the Dragon's tongue.

Like Catalonia itself, Catalan lies halfway between French and Spanish but is distinctive in its own right: if you speak either language, you can understand just enough Catalan to realise that you don't understand it at all. Of course, Narcís could just be having me on – even in the mountain villages outside Barcelona, it would be rare to find someone who has trouble speaking Castilian, let alone in the middle of the region's cosmopolitan capital. Only 50 per cent of Catalans speak the language day in and day out. But Narcís, who takes his name from the self-obsessed youth of Greek mythology, is an exceptional character, a small, pale man with a colourful past as a rebel priest. His father, a contemporary of Gaudí, designed the apartment building where he lives, as well as the Modernist landmark next door, the Casa Sayrach. Both buildings bear the hallmarks of the elegant, phantasmagorical style of architecture that defies the hardness of stone and makes Barcelona truly unique among European cities.

As the breakaway capital of the Republicans during Spain's Civil War, Franco did his best to punish Barcelona and crush Catalonian culture, outlawing the language while looting the region's resources and encouraging Spaniards from other areas to relocate there. However, many of these Spanish 'immigrants' tried to fit in by naming their sons after Catalonia's patron saint, even though the soft 'j' sound doesn't exist in Castilian. 'They would say, I want to name my son "Chordi",' Narcís laughs. 'They couldn't even pronounce it correctly, but they wanted to show they were one of us.'

'So what was Sant Jordi's Day like under the Fascists?'

'Very grey,' he chuckles. It was illegal to sell books in Catalan unless they predated Franco's rule, so publishers would put old dates on new works to fool the authorities. Other booksellers would wander around the festival hiding Catalan books under their jackets. If Fascist officials heard you speaking in Catalan, the language of Communists and rebels, they would order you to 'Speak Christian' – Castilian being synonymous with Spanish Catholicism. As a priest, Narcís used to hide printing presses for Catalonian samizdat where no one would think to look: in the church, under the altar. He once got into trouble for keeping a portrait of Che Guevara in his study. 'Anything like that – even a book on the work of Karl Marx – could be labelled "subversive material". It was ridiculous! And it was like that until Franco died.'

I can understand his point about Marx – merely owning a

book doesn't make you a godless Communist – but what kinda priest puts a portrait of Che on display? Though infinitely more photogenic, and even Christ like in a clichéd kind of way, Guevara was just as totalitarian as Franco. I imagine Narcís trying to wear a hammer-and-sickle stole during Mass and then being outraged if his superiors told him off.

In reality, the inevitable schism came when he decided to get married. After quitting the priesthood, Narcís has now found his true calling in the service of St George. He and the other Friends of Sant Jordi are trying to raise funds to erect a statue of the saint in the entrance of Barcelona's Sagrada Familia cathedral. However, it's a difficult battle to raise funds. Many Spaniards still associate Catholicism with the Fascism of Franco, and Gaudí's masterpiece is still a long way from being finished, never mind the statues and assorted whatsits that will decorate the interior. Having sown dragon's teeth, the Church is reaping the rejection of the masses. 'Many people now don't believe in the official religion,' Narcís says.

What's more, the traditional symbolism of St George and the Dragon has been inverted. Some of the modern portraits on Narcís' walls picture the saint as a fey, vaguely effeminate boy holding a rod, without a dragon or spearhead in sight. 'I like interpretations of George as a friend; not as a warrior,' he says, opening another photo album by way of contrast. 'Look at this German image' – it's a stern man with a moustache and pointed helmet – 'There's nothing saintly about him. That's completely feudal.' The simple notion of St George representing Good and the Dragon Evil has gone out of fashion, just as Christian ideas of morality – what constitutes Good and Evil – have been widely rejected, as evidenced by the cod psychology surrounding the Battle of the Lumeçon. Strangely, though, the compassion of Christ survives as an atavistic trait, the source of Western humanism as preached by Erasmus and others; the twist in the tale – or tail, perhaps – is that this compassion now takes the form of a generalised sympathy for the Devil (not to mention ogres, witches and the other 'oppressed minorities' of fairytale lore). 'You know what?' a friend commented to Narcís. 'I kind of like the Dragon these days.' So much so that the roles of the characters have been reversed, or at least equalised. If you were to rewrite the story for current sensibilities, you'd need to point out that the Dragon wasn't inherently 'bad', or 'evil' – 'whatever *that* means' – it was simply misunderstood. A victim, even. *I blame society.* If the Dragon is female, she's a victim of male oppression. If it symbolises Sex, it's being repressed by an Uptight Christian. If it's a being of colour, it's a victim of the White Man. An endangered species, a victim of Western modernity. And so forth. And even if you accept that the Dragon was bad – it's hard to get round the whole killing-virgins thing – the poor beast didn't deserve to die; at most, it should have spent a few years in an open prison, with plenty of free rehab to help compensate for the failings of society. As ever, our perceptions of St George and the Dragon reflect the changes in Western society.

Catalonia's particular allegiance to the legend goes way back. The region's first mention of the name Jordi dates from the eighth century, while the Crusades abroad and the Reconquest at home popularised the saint's cult in the Christian heartland of northern Spain. The kings of Aragon – Narcís insists on calling them the Counts of Barcelona – soon adopted Sant Jordi as their patron. In the 1200s, King Jaume I, who had fought in the Crusades, credited his victories over the Moors in Mallorca and Valencia to Sant Jordi. (To this day, the townspeople of Alcoy just south of Valencia re-enact a battle of Moors vs Christians on 23 April, giving thanks to St George for putting in a heavenly appearance and saving them from the Saracens in another battle.)

Narcís shows me a photo from the V&A Museum in London of a Spanish altarpiece depicting the Reconquest of Valencia. Jaume wears the red Cross of St George over his armour, and his horse is draped in the striped red-and-gold flag of Catalonia. The king is in the middle of killing a Moor; meanwhile, in the foreground, a mirror image shows St George slaying the Dragon.

In one version of the myth, the overgrown lizard melts into the ground and a bunch of roses bloom on the spot; in another, the Dragon's head bounces off, and the drops of blood leave roses in their wake. The Catalonian custom of giving roses to women on Sant Jordi's Day stems from these chivalric tales. During the rebirth of Catalonian culture and patriotism of the nineteenth century, Sant Jordi's reputation as patron of Catalonia was confirmed. 'He was adopted as a symbol of a people who want to live in justice and in peace,' Narcís explains. 'The Dragon came to represent centralism.' In other words, the national government in Madrid. 'Here in Barcelona you won't see the Spanish flag because it represents submission and persecution.'

Instead, everywhere you go you see the flag of St George flying shoulder to shoulder with the horizontal red and gold stripes of Catalonia . . . and, occasionally, the dark-blue flag of the European Union. Maybe it's his affinity with St George, but unlike many on the Continent, Narcís says he respects Britain's stance towards the EU. 'They're not saying that they don't want to be a part of it. They want to be free to be themselves,' he says, a statement that could just as easily apply to

Catalonians' attitude towards Spain and the proposed European superstate. 'The EU shouldn't be a union of states – because they're artificial institutions imposed upon us – but a union of peoples.'

In the same way, Narcís views St George as a symbol of unity rather than division. He once had the opportunity to meet Václav Havel, the former Soviet dissident who became the first president of the Czech Republic. As a representative of Catalonia, Narcís presented him with a figurine of Sant Jordi.

Havel smiled. 'We've got off to a good start,' he said, explaining that he kept a figure of St George in his office in Prague.

That's typical of the reaction you get when you mention St George, Narcís claims. What's more, he says he's never had a bad experience when it comes to spreading the gospel of Sant Jordi. Well, apart from one time. He was organising an exhibit on Sant Jordi with a Catalan woman married to a Scotsman. 'Don't talk to me about St George,' the Scot said. 'When I think of that flag I think of imperialism and domination.' Narcís is still hurt by this smear on the saint's good name. 'Sant Jordi doesn't represent that,' he insists. 'He represents freedom – someone who broke chains. He's not an oppressor of anyone. He's a liberator. St George fights everything that impedes man from achieving his potential.'

Outside, the streets are flooded with books and roses. Barcelona is a romantic city at any time of the year, but on Sant Jordi's Day, it's even more swoon-worthy than usual. Imagine Paris in the springtime . . . *on the Med*. At its heart is La Rambla, the broad thoroughfare that's a cross-section of the city and life itself. At one end lies the port, with the palm trees and statue of a vindicated Columbus returning from America, and at the other the Plaça de Catalunya, boasting all the fruits of twenty-first-century globalisation (for better or worse): blue-chip banks, department stores and an outpost of the Hard Rock Café. Between these extremes, beneath the plane trees dappling the pavement, flows a lazy stream of humanity.

Pedro Amaya has been hawking roses on Sant Jordi's Day for more than thirty years, wrapping the blooms in the colours of Catalonia and St George along with a sprig of wheat. 'It symbolises bread, and the rose represents love – all the good things in life.' On a good Sant Jordi, he and his wife sell about 600 roses.

'The bad years are when it rains. You end up *eating* roses.'

'Do you save one back for your wife at the end of the day?'

'If I gave Esperanza a rose, she would throw it out the window,' he grumbles. 'At the end of Sant Jordi, she's sick of roses.'

But young love is alive and well. Drifting through the plaza in her own little bubble of *amor* is Silvia Sánchez, a twenty-three-year-old whose boyfriend has delivered a long-stemmed rose to her in person at the hospital where she works. In return, she has bought him a medical potboiler, the perfect gift from a nurse to an engineer. They're planning a romantic rendezvous this evening. 'We don't celebrate St Valentine's hardly at all, in comparison. That's nothing special – just chocolate. But Sant Jordi is the story – the history. Sant Jordi is Catalan.'

Perhaps it's not my place as a foreigner – much less as a writer – to suggest it. But just imagine if England were to do something similar, hosting a national literature and rose festival coinciding with St George's Day and the anniversary of the patron saint of the country's greatest contribution to world culture: the English language. A countrywide book fair on

23 April, the anniversary of Shakespeare's birth *and* death, could serve as the focal point for traditional celebrations, plus a whole range of concerts, plays, street parties and other activities showcasing England's diversity and accomplishments – maybe even with stands from other cultures that have St George in common. In fact, the event could act as a world literature festival, bringing England into sync with the rest of the globe on World Book Day. A touch of romance could be added by exchanging roses on the day, not only as symbols of St George but as the national flower. By celebrating Shakespeare and St George with blooms and tomes, the event could be both national and international, appealing to Europhobes and Europhiles alike, so that everyone could rally round the flag and drink a toast:

For England – and/or Europe – and St George!

CHAPTER FIVE

THAT OLD-TIME RELIGION
SNAKE HANDLING AND FIRE DANCING IN GREECE

PART ONE:

A SERPENT'S TALE

For the record, I never have, but if I had, I wouldn't brag about it.

I was at the Pagan Federation's annual convention in Croydon, the part of London where concrete goes to die, and a couple of witches were giving a talk on – wait for it – the 'Things We Don't Talk About!' The warlock was from the West Country and his partner was from the West Coast, a Californian of Middle American proportions. In another life, they might have been retro celebrity lookalikes: imagine if the guitarist from Slade – the one with the proto-mullet – had hooked up with Mama Cass of the Mamas and the Papas. In my line of work, identikit rebels are a kind of occupational hazard. Europe is brimming with ten-a-penny pagans and faux witches' 'sabbats', and Britain may very well be to blame: England has the dubious honour of being the birthplace of the movement known as neopaganism, Wicca, white witchcraft or simply 'The Craft'. Having come across so many of its practitioners over the years, I reckoned that I needed to find out more about this new 'old religion' – to learn the difference between, say, the Gardnerian and Alexandrian branches – so I went to the annual summit of pagans from the British Isles and beyond.

As witches go, the transatlantic duo were refreshingly candid – so much so that even some of their kindred spirits regarded them as controversial. Riffing on sex, drugs and magic, they criticised the 'sanitising' of modern witchcraft, mocked so-called white witches who claim they never curse their enemies ('Cursing is an everyday thing. It's something *we all do*') and ridiculed the twee lingo used to describe 'sex magick', a quirk that reflects the movement's Victorian roots. Neopagans are rarely naked, for instance; they prefer to be 'skyclad'. 'And why does everyone talk about *yoni* and *lingam*?' the American cracked, confessing that she often got the mystic terms for genitalia mixed up, a confusion that could presumably be quite painful when it came to following the instructions in a sex manual.

But it was when they started musing about blood sacrifice that the talk really turned interesting. 'There is ample – *ample* – evidence to suggest that pagans have sacrificed their fellow humans and animals to their gods,' the Slade lookalike said. 'We're now told that our gods no longer demand blood sacrifice. How do we know that? Or is it because social conventions have changed?'

His partner quickly pointed out that rather than murder, blood sacrifice might take the form of simply scattering the ground with fertiliser made from fish blood. She had a 'friend', she claimed, who even offered her own menstrual blood as a sacrifice to the gods. 'And I tell ya what – she's got a nice-lookin' garden this year!'

'I've had experience of women's periods,' the man piped up, apropos of spoiling our appetites. 'It's nothing nasty; it's nothing unpleasant.'

Mmm . . . tastes like chicken.

During another lecture, a grey-headed man gave a slideshow of rocks, henges and dolmens from around the world. He looked completely normal – respectable, even – the type of gent who might pass on to his grandchildren a passion for birdwatching or stamp collecting or – as it turned out – cock-and-fanny-spotting. To his eyes, every megalithic slit, hole or misshapen protuberance had deep sexual meaning. 'The tree itself is literally *fucking* the Earth Mother,' he'd say, or 'The stone has a female shape on account of it being a rhomboid.' At another juncture, he showed us a slide of a triangular rock with a hole at the bottom: 'Nature has kindly filled that for us with algae–*red* algae. That is obviously a vagina.'

Obviously? I'm no gynaecologist, mate, but . . .

Don't get me wrong: it would be fascinating to find a genuine, living relic of ancient paganism – some ritual or event that provides an unbroken link to antiquity – as proof that ephemeral beliefs can outlast the societies that produce them: *I want to believe.* But to do that, you'd have to travel to the pagan roots of European civilisation, the place where polytheism produced works of art, architecture, literature, science and philosophy so far ahead of their time that their rediscovery during the Renaissance provided the inspiration for the modern era right to the present day. Even Christian writers over the centuries have had a hard time squaring their prejudices against 'heathens' with the advances that the Greeks and Romans made thousands of years ago. Surely if any aspect of paganism has survived in Europe it would be among the ruins they left behind. Then again, I could be embarking on a wild-goose chase. At least it beats watching a bunch of robed neopagans flouncing around in a Ritual of Nature performed in a concrete bunker in Croydon. If I'm honest, it's also an excuse to go to Greece and witness two events I've always wanted to see, including a ceremony invoking Constantine, the first Christian Roman emperor, whose conversion from paganism may have been genuine – or not . . .

If the regions of Greece ever competed in an Olympics of myth and mystery, the island of Kefaloniá would surely be able to stand its own, thanks partly to the invaders who have shaped its history over the centuries: Romans, Byzantines, Franks, Normans, Turks, Venetians, British, Italians and Germans, followed now by masses of tourists from the UK and Italy who've read *Captain Corelli's Mandolin,* or at least seen the movie. According to legend, Kefaloniá's unique firs provided the timber for Odysseus' ships – Ithaca is just across the water – and the wild ponies on Mount Aenos, the highest point on the island, are descended from those left behind by Alexander the Great. The island's goats have silver teeth, possibly tinted by a special mineral in the soil, and a geological fluke causes sea water to disappear into holes on one coast and mysteriously reappear on the other. The remains of Kefaloniá's patron saint were miraculously preserved after his burial five centuries ago, and the faithful believe he walks the island at night, curing the insane; every year, the nuns who take care of his corpse replace the worn slippers on his feet. To mark the anniversary of St Gerasimos' death, the priests do the walking for him, carrying his desiccated cadaver upright in broad daylight over pilgrims who lie in the road, waiting for a miracle. The choice of a mental-health specialist as a patron is by no means co-incidental: even among their volatile countrymen, Kefalonians have something of a reputation for being as crazy as they are clever. If it hadn't been for the steady flow of conquerors, it's fair to say that Kefaloniá's gene pool would have been more paddling- than Olympic-sized.

As important as St Gerasimos is to the island's well-being – he's celebrated on two feast days – even he has to yield to the Mother of God. Throughout Greece, 15 August is a national holiday commemorating Mary's 'Dormition', the day that Christ's mother 'fell asleep' and ascended into heaven, according to Greek Orthodox and Roman Catholic theology. In Kefaloniá, several miracles mark the occasion. The villagers of Pastra on the southern part of the island believe that dead lilies bloom again when left under the Virgin's icon, while a couple of neighbouring villages up in the mountains lay claim to an equally mysterious phenomenon. From around 6 to 15 August, the tiny churches of Markópoulo and Arginia are invaded by snakes – animals that are most often associated with evil, if not Satan himself. Instead of removing or killing them, though, the locals celebrate the annual appearance of the 'Snakes of the Virgin' by mollycoddling and kissing them, even draping the holy reptiles over their children as a blessing. I should point out that, unlike the rattlers handled by holy rollers in Appalachia, the snakes that occupy the churches in Kefaloniá aren't dangerous.

Even so, I still wouldn't go out of my way to touch one, let alone kiss it. But Kefalonians view the snakes as a bona fide blessing.

'If there are many snakes, people feel it will be a good year. If there are no snakes, a bad year. If there are a few snakes, there will be . . . problems,' explains Kostas Zapantis, a native of the southern part of the island who built the hotel where I'm staying. To underline the importance of the snakes to the locals, he recites the story that attracted me here in the first place: the only times the serpents have failed to appear in living memory were in 1940 – the year the Nazis invaded – and in 1953 – the year an earthquake levelled Kefaloniá.

Not surprisingly, the origin of the serpents' tale is also intertwined with the island's cycle of invasion and destruction. Variations on the story range from the extremely vague – people can't agree on whether the setting was Markópoulo or Arginia – to the suspiciously specific, with exact dates supplied, despite the lack of any historical evidence. Here's the bells-and-whistles version: like many villages in Kefaloniá, Markópoulo faces the Ionian Sea but is actually built on a hillside, far removed from the coast. In theory, this provided some protection against murderers, rapists and pillagers who happened to be sailing by, though it hasn't always worked. During the Second World War, the Nazis accused Arginia, which is even higher up the slopes of Mount Aenos, of harbouring guerrillas. They massacred the entire village, save one person who escaped to tell the story. Centuries earlier, around 1600, Venetian pirates supposedly looted and raped their way through Markópoulo and a convent devoted to the Virgin Mary located on the site of the current church. When the same thing happened again in 1650, the convent was abandoned, but it eventually reopened. Then, in 1705, pirates struck a third time (three being a key number in many religions). The nuns prayed to an icon of the Virgin Mary, and this time she saw fit to deliver them by turning them into snakes. When the pirates broke into the church, all they found were serpents with the Sign of the Cross on their heads slithering around the icons. Scared witless, they burnt the convent to the ground. The only object to survive the inferno was the silver icon of the Virgin . . . supposedly the same one that attracts the snakes to this day.

Now, you might be thinking, not unreasonably, *If I had to choose between pirates and being turned into a snake, I'd take my chances with Long John Silver.* Why didn't the Virgin transform the nuns into, say, *birds* that could've flown away rather than reptiles whose legless locomotion gives most animals the creeps? Well, Mary moves in mysterious ways. In Judaeo-Christian culture, of course, snakes have had an image problem ever since the Garden of Eden. However, the ancient Greeks and Romans took a more nuanced view. Having snakes for hair was definitely a bad thing, but the blood from Medusa and the other Gorgons could also bring the dead back to life. Some of this magical blood supposedly found its way into the hands of Asclepius, who experimented with it and wound up becoming the ancient Greek god of medicine. His symbol – a staff with a snake coiled around it – is still used by doctors in the West today. Snakes were also linked to the spirits of the dead, a nifty parallel with the legend of the nuns. In Virgil's *Aeneid*, the Greek hero watches in awe as a serpent unwinds itself and eats the food he's left as an offering at his father's tomb; Aeneas assumes the snake is either the grave's guardian or the incarnation of his father's spirit. Similarly, when the philosopher Plotinus, the founder of Neoplatonism, shuffled off this mortal coil, a snake crawled out from under his deathbed and escaped through a hole in the wall.

When I first heard the legend about the snakes of Kefaloniá, I imagined a gilded sanctuary a-writhe with glistening serpents: I pictured dozens – no, *hundreds* – of snakes of different sizes and colours hissing across the floor, climbing up the walls and dripping from the ceiling. When I wasn't casting myself as a terrified Indiana Jones in *The Raiders of the Lost Ark*, I was wondering whether I would be able to tiptoe around the church without treading on one of the reptiles with my big feet. Knowing my luck, I'd accidentally squash one – tantamount to murdering a nun – and end up getting stomped to death by the Orthodox equivalent of the Christian Brothers.

Given that I've been expecting a Hollywood miracle, it's something of a letdown to hear that the word on the street and in the *kapheneions* is that only two itty-bitty snakes have been found in Markópoulo this year. Worryingly, this weekend is also the anniversary of the Big Ones of '53, the two back-to-back earthquakes that scored 6.7 and 7.2 on the Richter scale – equivalent to a large thermonuclear explosion.

I'm beginning to wonder if maybe I've picked the wrong year to visit.

Kostas assures me that all modern buildings, including his seaside hotel, have been built to withstand seismic shocks. 'Now if we have an earthquake, all we have to do is stay in our beds.' Whereas his ancestors would have attributed events like earthquakes and the Miracle of the Snakes to the whims of the gods, Kostas is a thoroughly modern man. His default assumption is that the annual epiphany of the serpents must have a rational explanation. 'The truth is that the snakes live in that area. Young people have to collect them.'

If it is a natural phenomenon, though, it's still got herpetologists stumped. The Virgin's serpents belong to a rare breed known as *Telescopus fallax*, or cat snakes (they have vertical pupils). Contrary to most reports, they are actually poisonous; the saving grace – apparently – is that the venom comes out of their back teeth, and their mouths aren't big enough to get a good grip on humans. What makes Kefaloniá's cat snakes 'holy' are the vaguely cross-shaped markings on their heads. Scientists' best guess as to why the snakes put in an annual appearance at Arginia and Markópoulo is that there must be a migratory path connecting the two villages. What's strange, though, is that snakes normally shy away from large groups of people, never mind noisy village fairs. Also, newborn serpents tend to be overly aggressive rather than docile and easy to handle like the ones that begin appearing in Kefaloniá in August.

Having declared his disbelief in the Markópoulo miracle, Kostas starts telling me a tall tale about the Battling Brescanis, two Venetian brothers who slew a dragon that terrorised the island in 1509. As he describes the beast's size – it was fifteen metres long! It could swallow a cow with one gulp! – Kostas is animated to the point of possession, his eyes two bloodshot, hazel orbs toggling in and out of his head. He's like Homer, with added eye contact; a reminder that the *Odyssey* was more like *Die Hard* at Delphi than *Ulysses* in Dublin. 'But the truth is,' he says, momentarily recovering from the excitement, 'it was a big snake, and when the farmers saw it, they were scared.'

Mind you, he adds, plenty of old-timers claim to have seen giant snakes, three or four metres long, with horns on their heads, that lived next to the ocean. A woman he knew swore she'd seen one thirty or forty years ago. 'She told me that she

139

had seen a snake run into the sea *screeeeeeaming!*' he says, jolting forward and mimicking a mouth with his fingers, moving it horizontally across an invisible beach.

I stare back at him, expecting him to wink, blink or crack a smile any second, but his eyes are bulging credulously, his open hand still suspended in the air like a finger puppet. He holds my gaze for a good ten seconds, intent on me taking him seriously or at least swallowing the story whole. As far as I can tell, he seems to believe the horned snake story or, perhaps more accurately, he realises it's one of the many strange phenomena on the island that will never fully be explained.

Like the Miracle of the Snakes. 'There's no explanation for it. It's the time they live here. But Christians think they see a cross on their heads. We make the stories according to what we believe.' He mentions the myth of Perseus slaying the dragon and parallels it with the story of St George, who, of course, is one of the patron saints of Greece (you can never have too many). 'The Christians made up a new religion. But all Christian saints have something to do with the ancient Greek gods.' Barely four hundred metres down the road from the hotel, overlooking the ocean, there's a bright-blue chapel of St George built next to the ruins of an ancient temple. 'The archaeologists say it's to Apollo, but it's really dedicated to Poseidon,' Kostas claims, noting its position next to the sea and the fact that Perseus was inextricably linked with the god of the sea: the dragon that Perseus killed belonged to Poseidon. 'We need someone to kill the dragon,' Kostas says, lurching forward and wagging his finger. '*Never* St George kill the dragon. *Never* Perseus kill the dragon. But *we* need to believe it.'

*

Before I head up to Markópoulo, Kostas gives me one of the best bits of travel advice I've ever received: when parking on a narrow road next to a precipitous drop at a Greek festival, always make sure your car is pointing in the direction in which you want to leave. This will save you from reversing straight into the arms of Hades while making a fifty-point turn in traffic so dense that even grandmothers hobbling along the roadside occasionally get thumped by passing cars.

If you spend enough time on Kefaloniá, it's said that you'll start having bad dreams because of all the atrocities committed here, such as the Nazis' slaughter of some 4,000 Italian solders during the Second World War. Well, I've just arrived, and the nightmares have started already. Only mine don't have anything to do with vicious Nazis or rampaging Turks; no, my horror is much more mundane. I keep dreaming about driving, negotiating the narrow curves cut into the mountains with nothing but oblivion on the other side. I wake up exhausted from the effort; I think I'm even waving my arms in the air while I sleep. As much as I love driving, here it feels like trying to run along a curvy ledge at the top of a skyscraper with a madman coming at you from the opposite direction. And just as you're inching your way around a hairpin bend on a one-lane ledge high up in the mountains just wide enough for one and a half cars, along comes a Kefalonian, hurtling towards you, eating a gyro with one hand, jabbering on his mobile with the other, sticking one foot out the window and balancing a bottle of Robola on his lap. I'm a nervous wreck. If I'm picking up any psychic vibes from a past life, I must have been an operatic Italian – à la Captain Corelli – who reversed his tank off a cliff.

Mercifully, Markópoulo is only about halfway up the southern slopes of Mount Aenos, a tiered hamlet of barely a hundred people carved into the side of the mountain. In the distance below, the resort town of Katelios lies in a bowl filled with the blue mist of the ocean. The sun is sinking behind the mountain and its last golden rays are retreating over the hillside, leaving Markópoulo in twilight, with the tommy-gun thrum of electric generators competing against the invisible construction work of the cicadas sawing away in the bushes. On the top tier of the village stands an illuminated bell tower linked by a zigzag pathway to the church below. The diagonal street connecting the two levels has been strung with festive lights and the stalls of a bazaar selling every knick-knack imaginable, as well as slabs of fly-catching gelatinous sweets and toilet-brush holders containing shells and other aquatica trapped in clear plastic. In the courtyard of the church, several vendors, including a man with a withered leg, are peddling devotional candles in sizes ranging from thin drinking straws to fat wrath-of-God staffs perfect for smiting Satan. Priests in beards and sweat-making black robes are flogging religious gewgaws, and little old ladies are jabbing silver-coloured stickers of the Virgin and Child on anything that moves.

From the outside, Markópoulo's church is a plain, cream-coloured box with a red-tiled roof and a terrace overlooking the rocky terrain of olive trees and conifers rolling down to the coast. Inside, though, the small, open-plan sanctuary has been decorated in colours bright and vibrant enough to withstand the dazzling sheen of Kefaloniá's sunlight: satiny gold backgrounds and rich tones of ruby, emerald and garnet. The altar screen at the front has been lacquered to the point that it could be made of dark butterscotch, and the walls around the room are painted with a parade of saints ranging from a Greek patriarch and a man in a fez and dervish-like skirts all the way back to John the Baptist, who's instantly recognisable by his eternal bad hair day. Overhead is a baby-blue sky studded with gold stars, low-hanging chandeliers and a large seal of the Virgin and Child keeping vigil over Markópoulo, two snakes twined around Mary's hands.

But where are the real things? The room is swarming with people wanting to kiss the silver flat-panel icon of the Virgin and Child – reputedly the original relic that delivered the nuns from the pirates – and the combined heat of their bodies and the candles and the residual sunlight intensify the aroma of incense and basil on the altar.

I go out onto the terrace in search of serpents. A movable mob of locals, outsiders and Kefalonians returned from abroad for the religious festival are clamouring around a man in a 'Rangers Chewing Gum' shirt with the words 'Michigan High' printed on the sleeve. In his hands is a single buff-coloured snake with dark markings, its slender body no more than eighteen inches long. Its head is the size of a pen cap, and its tiny tongue flickers in the air as men, women and children proffer up their hands to have it draped over them, the snake for the most part docile but occasionally trying to make a slither for it by darting up a hairy forearm or down a particularly deep crack of cleavage. To their credit, most of the babies and toddlers aren't entirely sure about this particular form of blessing, but their parents reward them with a hearty 'Bravo!' when they brave the serpent. Husbands photograph their wives with the snake and vice versa, and teenagers are transmitting snaps to their friends on their mobile phones. The more enthusiastic followers take the snake in both hands and kiss its wriggling, scaly body, thankful, no doubt, that the nuns weren't turned into asses.

I manage to stick my hand over the jostling shoulders and touch the velvety scales of the serpent. The snake handler is using his pinkie to point out the Sign of the Cross on its head. The Greeks nod appreciatively, but, frankly, I'll be damned if I can see it.

I'm not the only one who's disappointed. 'It's not much of a miracle this year,' scoffs a Greek Australian who's come here from Athens. She works in tourism and had to beg her employer for time off at the height of the season to see the famous Snakes of the Virgin. 'My boss told me, "You've got two days – and you better bring back pictures." I've wanted to see this for a long time. You see videos of the event from previous years and there are hundreds of snakes – *hundreds*.' Her face drops. 'This year there are two. And one of 'em's dead – probably from over-handling.'

The next morning, after two hours of standing in the sanctuary at Markópoulo, I duck out of the Sunday service early to make the skin-tingling, toe-clamming, bowel-loosening journey to Arginia, further up the mountain. Negotiating the two-way traffic wouldn't be so bad if it weren't a one-lane road, little more than a paved donkey path – a ledge with enough bends in it to give a snake a backache. The map shows it as a straight line merging into a bit where the cartographer obviously gave up trying to draw each curve accurately and just filled it in with a squiggle, grumbling *Why not? Nobody goes there anyway.* Ascending Kefaloniá's highest peak – the third tallest in Greece – it feels as though I'm puttering into the firmament. Out of the corner of my eye I can see the contours of the island and marvel at the varying colour scheme of blues, whites and greens. The sea couldn't decide which shade of blue to be, so it opted for all of them, with a few hues of green thrown in for good measure. At the same time, though, I'm all too aware of the sheer drop on the other side of the path, hundreds of feet into oblivion. The particularly perilous corners are adorned by crosses or sometimes miniature Orthodox churches: these domed death-markers and pray-for-your-life points are infinitely more effective than any tame sign warning that SPEED KILLS.

At Arginia my mountaineering is rewarded with a bumper crop of reptiles: ten snakes kept in glass jars. The man minding them lets one slither over my shoulder and, with the Virgin's blessing, I venture over to the village of Pastra, where the other miracle is meant to take place this weekend courtesy of the Mother of God: lilies that have been picked in June supposedly bloom to life once more when placed under the icon of the Madonna on 15 August. By the time I arrive, though, the church is locked. Next to the front door there's a small processional litter decorated with dried flowers: if they did bloom, they must have withered again very quickly.

Later, I ask Kostas if he believes in the Miracle of the Lilies. 'Who knows?' He shoots me a sly look. 'I don't know if somebody has to change them or not.'

We're sitting out on the terrace of his hotel next to the aqua pool overlooking the turquoise sea. I could stay here all day, but for Kostas, a local man who's built his resort from nothing, the view must provide a very profound sense of satisfaction indeed.

'What's the significance of having just a few snakes appear?'

'That means we'll have problems for this year,' he says – at least that's what the villagers believe. 'Listen, I don't believe in signs from God or anything like that. But for people who centre their lives around religion, it is very important.' He waves his hand in the air and mentions the notoriously obscure prophecies of the Oracle at Delphi. 'Greeks always try and translate signs from God. But you can translate signs many different ways. The same happens now, and the same will happen in the future.'

'Do you view superstitions as an impediment to progress?'

'It's nice to have superstitions. If you don't have superstitions and traditions, you would be the same as the British or the Swedish. But we also have to have a balance. We can't sit and do nothing this year because there are only a few snakes.'

In the same way, he views the annual pilgrimage of the mentally ill to Ayios Gerasimos on 16 August as a depressing ritual. 'It's a very sad day to see all the people hoping for something to change in their lives.' He shakes his head. 'Superstition is a problem if you decide your life by it. Now many people believe in Christ; before, they believed in Nature. People can't live without some form of belief.'

He laughs. 'But you know, if nothing happens this year after only a few snakes appeared, next year people will say God is great and has helped us.'

PART TWO:
FEET OF FAITH

So far so good for Kefaloniá, but for my purposes, the snakes of Markópoulo were a dead end. Fortunately, though, I've come across a ritual on the mainland that sounds even more mysterious. Every year in north-eastern Greece and southern

Bulgaria, villagers from the ancient region of Thrace sacrifice a lamb or a bull at a holy well and then pray themselves into a trance before walking – and even *dancing* – barefoot across burning coals. Although the fire-dancers swear they're devout Christians, the Greek Orthodox Church has repeatedly condemned the ritual of the *Anastenariá* as latter-day idolatry, a relic of 'the orgiastic worship of Dionysus'. What makes this pagan link promising is the ritual's location. Thrace was supposedly the birthplace of Dionysus, a son of Zeus, who lived just a lightning bolt away on Mount Olympus. Originally a naughty god of fertility, Dionysus was later rebranded Bacchus and became synonymous with full-blown hedonism, the god of wine, women and song. More intriguingly, he was also associated with fire.

Eureka! It's not really the done thing to strip off and streak through the reading room of the British Library, but in my mind, I'm only wearing sneakers. See, I've found this book by a Greek academic, and it's called *Dionysiaka: Aspects of the Popular Thracian Religion of To-Day*. Actually, it's more like 'Yester-Day'; the author, Dr Katerina Kakouri, began her research in 1951, and the English translation dates from 1965. The title page, just below Ye Olde Gyro Shoppe lettering, has a cut-out photo of a woman's head, like a portrait from a locket, ringed by the words: BACCHANTE OF THE 20th CENTURY. The Bacchantes were groupies of Dionysus who wandered around the woods in fawn skins and a continuous state of ecstasy. The middle-aged gal in the picture does have her eyes closed, but I can't tell if she's ecstatic or dead, and I wouldn't particularly want to see her cavorting in a fur bikini. However, Kakouri is adamant: 'The *Anastenariá* has preserved the ancient Dionysian ecstatic cult.'

And I'd like to believe her. After only a few pages, though, she's already dousing her case with cold water. While it's true that fire was probably a part of Dionysian worship, she admits that there's nothing to suggest his followers ever took part in fire-walking, let alone fire-dancing. *Oops*. In fact, it all happened so long ago, we don't even know exactly what Dionysian worship involved, apart from wine, dancing, some sort of sacrifice and possibly orgies. That's another problem: there's absolutely no sex, drinking or debauchery in the *Anastenariá*. On the contrary, the modern 'Bacchantes', as Kakouri insists on calling them, profess to be devoutly Orthodox. They even carry icons of St Constantine and St Helena – the archpatrons of Orthodoxy – across the coals, claiming that their feat commemorates a miracle. In fact, the opposition from the official Church seems to have more to do with control than spiritual matters: organised religions have always fought to keep nonconformists in line. Ironically, bishops' claims that the event is pagan were probably inspired by the selfsame folklorists who were hell-bent on finding something – anything – to 'prove' continuity with Greece's glorious past.

By far the best book on the ritual is *Firewalking and Religious Healing,* written by a Greek-speaking American anthropologist who visited and lived in one of the villages of the *Anastenariá* during the 1970s and 1980s. In fact, his work is so authoritative I think of it simply as The Book. Loring Danforth recounts stories of the devotees, known as *Anastenarides,* walking and dancing across the coals, slapping the embers, and even squeezing them in their fists without burning themselves. 'When I'm on the fire, I feel the warmth, but I don't feel any pain,' he quotes one fire-dancer as saying. 'It's as if I had tender feet and was walking barefoot on gravel for the first time.'

Danforth also explains that families have passed the icons of the saints down the generations: legend has it that the oldest icon – a portrait of St Constantine and his mother, Helena, painted on a rectangular panel of wood – incorporates a piece of fabric from the Roman emperor's clothes. The *Anastenarides* keep these typically Orthodox icons in their homes, elevated on ledges as makeshift shrines, and treat the images as if they were living beings capable of working miracles and curing illnesses but also – somewhat sinisterly – inflicting suffering on their owners.

Not surprisingly, then, people don't flock to become 'slaves' of St Constantine and St Helena. Many join the *Anastenarides* involuntarily, driven to dance on the coals because it's the only way to get the divine duo off their backs. Reports often claim that the ritual gets its name from the Greek verb 'to sigh' or 'groan', but Danforth points out that the dancers use a much stronger term to describe their experience: 'screaming' or 'shrieking'. In fact, the most likely root of *Anastenariá* (or *Nestinarstvo* in Bulgarian) is *asthenis*: a sick person. The Book describes initiates fainting, sobbing, tearing their hair, pounding their heads and beating themselves black and blue. Other symptoms of chronic Constantinitis range from sleeplessness and depression to dreams and visions, as well as pyromania and a loss of bladder control (which would be me if I had to walk across hot coals). Examining doctors typically conclude that the sufferers have nothing physically wrong with them; it's all in their minds. For the *Anastenarides*, this is proof of the limitations of science: modern medicine is powerless to cure initiates because they're simply 'suffering from the Saint'.

To be sure, Constantine the Great isn't just any old saint. As the first Roman emperor to convert to Christianity, his individual change of heart meant that most of Europe (and consequently a third of the world's population) has remained at least nominally Christian to this day. After his conversion in AD 312, Constantine ended the persecution of Christians and actively promoted the upstart religion. His rule split the Empire – and Europe – into the Latin-speaking West based in Rome and the Greek-speaking East centred in Constantinople (now Istanbul). For Greeks, then, Constantine is essentially the earthly founder of their Orthodox Church. What's more, he helped found the Byzantine Empire, the last time that Greece was a major player in world affairs. That's why half the country is still called Kostas, Dinos, Dina, Tina, Elena, Lena or any of a dozen variations on the two saints' names. In fact, 21 May – the joint feast day of Kostantinos and Eleni – is practically a public holiday because it's so many people's 'saint's day', traditionally more of an occasion than a person's birthday.

21 May is also the first day of the *Anastenariá* festivals in the border territories between Greece and Bulgaria. Dancers on both sides of the border trace their roots back to the area around Kostí, a village in the dense forests of the Strandzha Mountains near the Black Sea. Now part of south-eastern Bulgaria, Kostí also belonged to ancient Thrace, the eternal battleground between Europe and Asia overlapping the current borders of Bulgaria, Greece and Turkey. Regional wars in the early twentieth century forced the Greek-speaking Thracians to flee to northern Greece, and by the 1920s, most of the *Anastenarides* had settled in five villages in Greek Macedonia. For years, the *Anastenarides* maintained their strange, foreign custom in private, fearing a repeat of the persecution they had suffered back home. One of the first records of the *Anastenariá*

– from the late nineteenth century – mentions that it had survived despite the Church's attempts to stop it 'with axe, fire and whip'.

The most common story of fire-walking's origins is set in Kostí centuries ago, when the local church of St Constantine and St Helena caught fire. The villagers heard cries coming from the sanctuary and rushed in to find the saints calling out to be saved. A brave few rescued the icons from the inferno and emerged unscathed, thanks to the miraculous protection of the saints (a story that echoes the Virgin's miracle in Markópoulo). Variations on the legend contend that the church had been built by Constantine or that the retreating Turks burnt the building and Constantine's soldiers saved the icons. One version even transplants the legend to siege-stricken Constantinople. The Turks have set fire to the city, so Constantine rushes into his palace to rescue the True Cross. Holding the relic high, he strides through the conflagration, forming a flame-free path that allows the Christians to escape the city unharmed. But the most ingenious adaptation manages to combine elements of all of the above, while underlining Constantine's status as a hero not just of Christianity but of Greece. The future saint is chasing infidels back from whence they came (read: Turkey), when his retreating enemies try to slow him down by torching Kostí and the surrounding villages. At that point, though, Constantine has his famous vision of a cross in the sky – 'In this sign you will be the victor' – and gallops through the flames to victory. The date, so they say, was 21 May . . .

In all of the versions, fire-walking is depicted as a bona fide miracle, incontrovertible proof of the saints' unique protection of the *Anastenarides*. In recent decades, though, similar rituals around the world have become so well known that fire-walking in the West has become almost passé – pedestrian, even. Rather than a mysterious feat of faith rooted in an ancient culture, fire-walking has been ripped out of context by hippie-hucksters and commercialised as the spiritual equivalent of an extreme sport for the type of people who most of us wish would spontaneously combust anyway. However, these can-do fire-walking 'workshops' don't always go to plan. The godfather of the global fire-walking movement admits to having learnt the hard way that (contrary to the American credo) when it comes to pits of burning coals, bigger isn't necessarily better. In an event run by another empowerment group, a dozen marketing executives flame-grilled their feet during a bonding exercise in Florida a few years back. Aptly enough, they worked for Burger King. Then there were the seven (out of ten) employees of a British insurance company who were burnt on a motiv-ational course – though presumably they were covered for accidents. Not so the New Zealanders who tried to set a world fire-walking record in 2004 by sending 341 people across a twelve-foot bed of coals, all in the name of charity. Not only were they disqualified on a technicality, but twenty-eight of them required emergency treatment. They wound up spending more on their medical care than the funds they raised for their local hospital.

Even when would-be fire-walkers burn themselves, though, they tend to explain it away with the same logic as the faithful on Kefaloniá. 'Yeah, I got massive third-degree burns, I had to have skin grafts taken from my backside and I spent months in hospital with my face in a pillow, but I really got a lot out of it. It was a real learning experience.'

The lesson being: don't walk barefoot on burning coals.

While it's easy to be sniffy about fire-walking, the truth is scientists still don't know why it's possible. As with the Virgin's snakes, the default assumption is that Nature must have an explanation; the thing is, we still don't know what it is. One theory is that fear makes people's feet sweat – like me driving in Kefaloniá – and the heat then turns the moisture into a thin buffer of steam. A more common hypothesis is that the ash forms a buffer over the coals, allowing people to walk across quickly without actually touching the burning embers. One scientist even strapped raw steaks to his feet and trod on a bed of coals for a TV crew, arguing that the feat wouldn't work if he switched the coals with, say, a red-hot grill. However, a group of experienced fire-walkers immediately proved him wrong, even leaving footprints in the glowing red grill.

As for fire-*dancing*, teams of Greek and German scientists have studied the *Anastenariá* over the years, running all the obvious tests and even taking samples of the skin on the dancers' feet. Still, no one can explain why they're able to linger barefoot on the coals. To my relief, the *Anastenarides* frown on outsiders taking part; if you don't have the protection of the saints, you're destined to get burnt.

And I don't start off on the best foot. Of the five villages in north-eastern Greece that celebrate the *Anastenariá*, I've decided to travel to Ayia Eleni, the setting for Danforth's book. Arriving on the eve of the 21st, I stop at the church, hoping that someone might point me in the direction of the *Anastenarides*. Despite past frictions, both groups profess to be Christian: the church is even dedicated to Saints Constantine and Helena, who of course do double duty as the fire-dancers' patrons.

At first, the old gent sitting on the bench outside goes out of his way to try to welcome me; he's lived in Belgium and speaks French.

But then I ask. '*Anastenariá*?'

'Me? No – *Orthodoxos.*'

Just in time, my guardian angel of an interpreter, Evangelia, pulls up and explains that we're looking for the *konaki*, the place where the *Anastenarides* worship. Not coincidentally, it's located on the other side of the village, almost as far as possible from the official House of God. The small, purpose-built 'chapel' stands just across the way from a grass arena, complete with floodlights, a metal ring fence and benches around the perimeter, plus a tin-roofed section for VIPs and a sloped mound in the middle. The fire site is flanked by the town's water tower (*that could come in handy*) and – surreally – a funfair. In fact, a tilt-a-whirl, or waltzer, has been set up right next to the mini-arena. Flashing bulbs spell out the name of the ride in English: CRAZY DANCE.

The *konaki* itself is a rectangular building as plain as the local Orthodox church is gaudy. The private meeting room of the *Anastenarides* has pale, grey walls and a hard-wearing parquet floor, with photos of past leaders at the back of the room and a makeshift shrine at the front. A couple of golden incense holders hang above a ledge full of icons, and the chimney hearth has a small square space in front of it covered in cracked, red clay to protect the floorboards underneath. That's where the *Anastenarides* dance indoors on the coals during another religious festival in January.

I've come here with Eva to try to make contact with the dancers. I'm expecting to encounter some reluctance – after all, it is a spiritual matter – but I'm hoping to show them that I'm not just parachuting into town for the big finale; I've tried to go that little bit further. However, that doesn't get me very far at all.

As we enter the *konaki*, an old man is holding forth about the history of the event with some women from Athens, particularly the story of the two local priests who had confiscated the icons back in the Seventies and wound up paying the price.

'They dropped dead,' he grimaces, using a word that Greeks normally reserve for the death of an animal.

On that note, he goes to sit with a fellow musician on a bench at the front of the room. I approach with Eva to ask if he might spare us some time, too.

The man narrows his eyes at Eva. 'But he doesn't even speak Greek!'

'I'm here to translate for him.'

A dismissive wave. 'Tell him if he wants to learn about the *Anastenariá*, he should go away and read the book written by Danny. He's an American who lived here for months – and *he* spoke Greek!'

'You mean Loring Danforth?' I ask. 'I've got his book in my car.'

'I don't know any Danforth; the name of the man I'm talking about is Danny.'

In bad dreams, I end up trapped in dead-end conversations like this. There's not much I can do but actually go and fetch the book, sensing that it's pointless anyway. After more stonewalling, the man concedes that we're talking about the same person.

'So what does he want to know?' he asks Eva.

What I'd really like to know is why the *Anastenarides* dance on the coals, how one becomes a member of the group, what it feels like to be in a trance and whether they've ever been burned, but the truth is, The Book covers all that pretty comprehensively. Plus, I'm so flustered by this point that the only neutral way I can see into a conversation is this: 'I – I'd like to know whether the event has changed over the years, especially in the past couple of decades since the book was published.'

'It hasn't changed at all!' the man barks. 'It's exactly the same!'

Maybe I'll have better luck with the leader of the *Anastenarides*. When he's not acting as Chief *Anastenaris*, Tasos works as a psychiatrist in Thessaloníki, and it would be fascinating (in theory, at least) to find out his views about the link between faith and mental health. Trouble is, he's not talking. According to The Book, Tasos' choice as leader of the *Anastenariá* in 1983 was somewhat controversial: unlike his predecessors, he never actually danced or walked on the coals. It seems the dancers weren't spoilt for choice at the time, however, and any doubts about a non-fire-walker's suitability to be Chief Fire-walker were glossed over by stories of visions in which the saints revealed Tasos to be their chosen one. The dancers also attributed his reticence to the fact that he was a 'scientist'; presumably, though, they didn't give up hope that one day he might lead them across the fire.

More than twenty years later, Tasos still seems to lead by exhortation rather than example. Tall and stooped, he has a thick moustache and longish pewter hair that's combed straight back into a learned bob, making him look something like a Mediterranean Marx. However, given his size and countenance (he appears permanently hacked off), you could easily mistake him for a bailiff or repo man – someone who chucks people onto the streets for a living – rather than a doctor specialising in the intricacies of the human mind. No doubt Tasos is a fine psychiatrist, but I reckon I'd have to be crazy to see him.

'All he needs to know is in The Book,' he tells Eva outside the *konaki* as a small crowd gathers around to witness my humiliation.

I point out that I've read The Book – I've even called Maine to talk to the guy who wrote it. I've dug up other stuff in the British Library, too, and hired an interpreter who's tried to contact people in advance. I've flown 1,300 miles and then driven another 200 to the middle of Macedonia to witness the event. Could he at least see fit to speak to me?

I'm practically whimpering. 'I . . . I'd like to know how the tradition has changed in recent years.'

'It hasn't changed at all.'

If that's the case, I could have stayed at home.

'God – that was worse than an audit!' Eva groans afterwards. She's a city girl from Thessaloníki, and some of her most difficult assignments involve interpreting for executives from multinationals who come to Greece to make sure their local operations aren't doing anything dodgy or downright illegal. As you might imagine, these encounters can become rather heated. Sometimes the local subsidiaries even bar the doors. 'But that's nothing compared to the reaction here!'

With time to kill before the evening rituals, we take a stroll around Ayia Eleni, a flat farming village of boxy modern houses and green fields planted right up to the roadside. The local church is decked out with blue-and-white Greek flags alongside the gold banners of Orthodoxy, their emblematic two-headed eagles reflecting the Church's quandary between East and

West. The building has a red roof, a foyer encased in stained-glass panels and whitewashed walls painted unconvincingly at the edges to look like grey cornerstones. It's a reminder that Mediterranean palettes have probably always been more exuberant than the artworks they inspired during the Renaissance. Rather than a restrained white-marble place of worship, for instance, the Parthenon was originally a Technicolor temple, throbbing with gaudy hues and flesh tones as bright as the Mediterranean sunlight. If Michelangelo had presented his *David* to the man behind the Parthenon, no doubt Pericles would have taken one look and said, 'Nice statue. But when are you going to slap some paint on it and put in the copper eyelashes?'

In that vein, I decide to ask Eva a question that's potentially just as offensive. When I first visited Greece, not that long ago, I'd been shocked by how little of the country's ancient culture had survived. Of course, much of modern Greek (and English) has its roots in the ancient language, but apart from that, how is it possible that a civilisation spanning two millennia left behind little more than some lurid tall tales and crumbling edifices? (The subtext of the question being: Could the same happen to Western civilisation today?) Admittedly, I'm something of an innocent abroad in this respect: I didn't grow up with cheap island holidays, ouzo and plate-smashing or dancing around the pool to the bouzouki. When I went to my first 'Greek Night', I half expected at least one of the costume changes to involve diaphanous robes and olive-leaf laurels; even something as corny as an actor in a robe strumming a lyre and hamming it up with the *Iliad*. As long as it wasn't too drawn out, even the bucket-holiday crowd would enjoy the novelty and melodrama: *it's Greece, innit?* But there was nothing: no trace of ancient Greece in the national songs, dances or 'traditional' costumes. On the contrary, to my untrained and ignorant eye, it seemed the overwhelming influence on Greek culture was – and here's the potentially offensive bit – *Turkish*.

So what happened?

Ask the Greeks, and they'll give the obvious answer: 'The Turks. The Turks are what happened.' While Western Europe was sunning itself in the reflected glory of Graeco-Roman civilisation – the advances that inspired the Renaissance, the Enlightenment, the Industrial Revolution and Western empire-building – Greece itself was under the thumb of the Ottoman Empire. The hemlock-bitter irony is that the ancient Greeks gave the West a leg up while their descendants spent the same crucial four centuries falling behind under the rule of Eastern conquerors.

'You know, sometimes I think that we Greeks have adopted only the bad traits of the societies that have ruled us,' Eva muses.

'But isn't there anything left of ancient Greece in contemporary culture?'

She scoffs. 'There's nothing left!' She had to field similar questions when she was a student in Germany. History buffs would try to strike up a conversation in ancient Greek – 'and in an Erasmian accent!' – and be disappointed when she couldn't understand them. If Greek students do learn about their ancient past at school, she says, the history lessons tend to be confined to boring lists of names and dates. In fairness, though, it must be hard to teach schoolchildren about the ancients without incurring the wrath of parents and the Church. Forget sex ed. Greek mythology would be a million times more controversial, encompassing bestiality, bloodlust, voyeurism, murder, suicide and just about every other '-icide' you can think of.

'There's a real clash between the Orthodox Church and ancient Greece,' Eva continues, pointing out the difficulty of explaining the pagan past in a country where 98 per cent of the population is still nominally Orthodox. Were the ancestors of modern Greeks idolaters and therefore condemned to hell? Or were they blameless practitioners of an imperfect religion centuries before the advent of Christianity? This is complicated by the irony that much of the Christian Word of God was originally written in the everyday language of pagan Greece: the word 'Bible' itself is derived from ancient Greek. In recent years, the once all-powerful Orthodox Church has had to stoop to bickering with secularists over issues such as the censorship of 'blasphemous' books and attempts to remove the cross from the national flag. Historically, of course, it could be argued that the Orthodox Church (and its Catholic counterpart) have tried to weed out dissent to prevent their roots from undermining them. That's partly why the Orthodox Church has always been sceptical of sects like the fire-dancers.

Eva also has her doubts about the *Anastenariá*, especially after consulting a friend who practises alternative medicine in Thessaloníki. 'He says it's a trick. He didn't tell me how they do it, but he says it's a trick.'

Back in the *konaki*, the drum and lyre players have struck up a sinuous, insistent melody that sounds more Eastern than Western, and Tasos leads the *Anastenarides* on a night-time procession through the village to collect the icons from the homes where they're kept. The final stretch takes us through the heart of the funfair, and the incense of the *Anastenariá* is subsumed by the greasy smoke from the gyro and souvlaki stands. Tasos descends into the small, domed chapel outside the *konaki* that houses the sacred well and re-emerges with a bucketful of water. Without warning, he sloshes it in an arc across the crowd, doing this three times. A little old man gets hit full in the face, Buster Keaton-style. Tasos then brings up more holy water for the people to bless themselves with, and the troupe spends the rest of the evening dancing with the icons before carrying them over the coals the following night.

Now, this was meant to be the big finale, the all-singing, all-dancing conclusion to my search for a living remnant of the ancient past. Just think – people actually *dancing* on *fire*! Not walking; *dancing*. Regardless of whether it has anything to do with Dionysus, it must be pretty impressive. All the accounts I've read play up the mystery of the ritual, painting images of incense wafting through the air, golden sparks flying into the heavens and exotic music enticing the dancers onto the coals.

Truth is, if I knew what was good for me, I'd follow their lead, romanticising it, simply because that's what sells. Ever since the birth of travel writing, people have yearned for the picturesque. And when the facts don't fit the clichés, plenty of hacks fill the gaps with fiction. But I just can't do it. It may be I'm too literal-minded – or that I have an overactive imagination – or that my imagination has been overwritten by a standard-issue, twenty-first-century, plug-'n'-play model straight from Hollywood. Having read about 'fire-dancing', though, I'm expecting the *Anastenarides* to actually *dance* across a bed of burning coals. They don't have to do the cha-cha, tango or Charleston. I'm not asking for some kind of Ultimate Greek Night, with a pit barbecue followed by Zorba the Greek and 'Never on Sunday' on the embers. But when I hear the term 'fire-dancing', I'm expecting the practitioners to linger on the coals rather than hotfoot it across. Rightly or wrongly, I'm hoping to witness something transcendent, something beyond the rural Greek Orthodox equivalent of a corporate-teambuilding-outward-bounding-are-you-hard-enough exercise. What I really want to see is a feat of faith.

The first hint that it may not be all I imagined comes when I return to Ayia Eleni on the night of the 21st. It's been raining on and off all day – the gutters are overflowing – and the wood for the bonfire has been sheathed in plastic. About thirty logs have been propped up against each other to form a cone some five feet high on the grassy mound next to the funfair. That may sound big enough, but the little lumber tepee is dwarfed by the size of the pitch itself. What's more, the eerie lyre and drum music emanating from the *konaki* has to do battle with the Greek Eurovision anthem (sung in English) and the noise of the carnival rides and the waltzer flashing CRAZY DANCE.

Eva has managed to track down someone who will speak to us, a cousin of Tasos' who's an official of the local folklore society and something of a substitute *Anastenaris*. Georgios tells me some of the lore surrounding the event, such as how the *Anastenarides* used to dance on coals in private during the Second World War and how, although Bulgarian troops could hear the music, they could never find the dancers. He also explains that the *Anastenarides* sacrificed a black lamb this morning, slitting its throat so that the blood gushes into a hole dug near the holy well.

'The lamb has to be a virgin,' he stresses.

I don't how the farmers ascertain that, but I'm too sheepish to ask.

However, I do bring up the remarkable change in the *Anastenariá*'s status, having gone from a private ritual of refugees to the main attraction at a public spectacle featuring their very own custom-made *konaki* and fire-dancing pitch. Georgios says the rest of the village has become more accepting of fire-dancing over the years. 'They like it because more outsiders come here.'

'Do any of the outsiders ever take part?'

'Occasionally we have some foreigners who walk on the fire.' He savours a grin. 'Afterwards, we take them to hospital.'

Like his cousin, Georgios steers clear of the coals and maintains the line that the Chief *Anastenaris* doesn't need to lead the group across the fire. 'It's not necessary. It's a personal calling whether someone walks on the fire. But everyone who participates is a member of the *Anastenarides*.'

At the moment, Tasos is overseeing the pre-fire-dancing inside the *konaki*. He and the others are dressed in normal streetclothes, though if he donned a black robe and suitable headwear, he could easily pass for an Orthodox patriarch. He's standing amid the candles and incense at the makeshift shrine in the corner of the room, and several dancers kiss his hands as he distributes the icons of the saints and the sacred red kerchiefs known as *simadia*. The music that's looping around the room sounds vaguely ancient and Eastern, partly because of its structure and partly because of the instruments producing it. Insistent and trancelike, it's similar to a snake-charmer's melody. There's no clear beginning or end to the songs and no typically Western progression from verse to bridge to chorus and back again. Instead, the music twists and turns in on itself and occasionally merges into another melody, all the while driven by the syncopation of the baritone drums and the plaintive whine of the Thracian *lira*, which looks more like a fiddle than an ancient harp.

Around fifteen dancers – men and women aged thirty and upwards – are winding through the incense-filled room as minders keep the public from blocking their path. The dancers circulate anticlockwise along a narrow path between the onlookers from the front of the room to the photographs of past *Anastenarides* at the back. They dance individually, seemingly without any fixed steps, hopping back and forth from one foot to the other, as if they were trotting across hot coals. Some of the men hold one arm in front and the other behind their backs, as if to take a deep bow, and the blessed few who carry the icons dance with them lovingly, as if the flat-panel images of St Constantine and St Helen were flesh-and-blood partners.

Most dancers wear neutral expressions – you might think they're just going through the motions – but one guy's in agony. His face is thin and pale, the perspiration highlighting his features as he dances around, clutching a red carnation to his chest, his mouth open in a silent cry. You'd think he's being eviscerated by an invisible beast.

'He's obviously psychotic,' mutters an onlooker from Athens. Eva agrees: the man can't be right in the head. Perversely, though, he's just what I was expecting to see; the kind of behaviour The Book describes. If anything, I was hoping to witness more religious ecstasy up close and personal – *so that's what faith looks like*. It takes me a while to remember where I've seen that expression before – the open mouth; the pale, drawn face of suffering – it's in the portraits of the saints by the Spanish painter El Greco – who was of course . . . a native of Greece.

The Book tells how the saints torment many prospective *Anastenarides* into joining the dance; it's the only way to relieve their mental suffering. So far, though, the man in the tan T-shirt and corduroys is the only dancer to show any outward sign of an altered state. Sure, there's a potbellied little woman who's clapping and whooping it up, but you don't have to be a fire-dancer to realise she's doing it for attention. She's the over-emotive type who wails so much at funerals she practically jumps into the coffin with the dearly departed.

Tasos receives the suffering man at the shrine and then leads him through the onlookers, swinging an incense burner as they go. The faithful reach out and waft the holy smoke towards themselves. As the doctor and his patient return to the shrine, the happy clapper is blocking their path.

'Get out of the way, woman!' Tasos shouts.

She storms out of the room, but the dance continues until he gives the order to light the bonfire. To my surprise, the dancers and musicians take a break (if it were me, I'd want to be all tranced up before facing the coals), but over the next couple of hours, they dance three times with lengthy intervals for smoking and relaxing in between.

While we're waiting, Eva and I grab a ringside bench outside. The rain has turned the night air cool and the sky clear except for a slight shadow on the face of the moon. Shortly after ten thirty, a couple of men use long sticks to spread the remnants of the bonfire in a circle barely two metres across and probably an inch thick. They're still levelling off the steaming bed of embers and ash as Tasos leads the *Anastenarides* slowly around the floodlit field three times. As the music grows more insistent, two men carrying the main icons begin the fire-dance. Rather than dance, though, the *Anastenarides* hotfoot it across, followed by other barefoot 'dancers' who either walk or run, clearing the bed of coals in four or five steps.

'That's not a trick; that's a deceit!' Eva says.

And if you arrived at the event without any prior knowledge of it, you could easily get that impression. Then I remember a Greek newspaper article from 1984 quoted in The Book: 'From now on the spectator is obliged to experience the entire ceremony from a distance,' it said, 'like a spectator who watches a magician or a charlatan performing onstage . . . The ritual has died.'

And that was without any mention of the funfair. I was so excited about coming here, I must have blocked it out. Cynics always try to be the first to pronounce old traditions dead if they don't conform to their preconceptions. The reality, though, is that traditions evolve. Just because something has changed doesn't mean it's deteriorated. On the other hand, as I'm realising, it doesn't guarantee improvement, either.

After a few minutes, the floodlights are switched off (all the better to see the red embers beneath the ashes), and the fire-walkers crisscross the coals, sometimes kicking up sparks, while the carnival continues uninterrupted: the swing boat, the two dodgem car rides (one just wasn't enough) and the tilt-a-whirl flashing CRAZY DANCE.

The man who was suffering so much in the *konaki* is being led around the fire by Tasos. He's holding a *simadia* this time, with his trousers rolled up to his ankles, and he looks – well, he looks like a guy who's about to walk on fire for the first time.

'Why doesn't the Chief *Anastenaris* go into the fire?' asks a man on the sidelines.

'Must be because he's a psychiatrist,' cracks his friend.

The pale initiate eventually takes the leap of faith, his mouth open and head thrown back, and quicksteps across the coals, reaching the other side apparently unscathed. In fact, he's soon bounding back and forth.

Now that's just showing off.

After twelve minutes of fire-walking and running, the event does end in a dance, but this takes place on the damp grass, with the *Anastenarides* joining hands and jigging around the pool of fire. As they return to the *konaki*, the crowd rushes forward to test the coals. No doubt about it, they're still hot: in fact, they'd be too hot for a barbecue.

However, with the carnival in full swing right next to us, the act of faith that we've witnessed seems like just another sideshow: *Step right up! See the Dancing Dionysians and the Field of Fire!* And as with so many of these attractions – the 'Incredible Three-Headed Man', etcetera – the fire 'dance' doesn't live up to its billing. It could be that the 'dancing' has been exaggerated over the years. But any sense of mystery, let alone spirituality, is obliterated by the lights and noise from the mechanical rides nearby.

Tasos eventually agrees to grant me an audience days later, but by now, my money's run out – Eva's already gone out of her way to help – and I don't relish a couple of hours of being glowered at. If I'm going to gaze at stony exteriors, I'd rather go to Mount Olympus, south of Thessaloníki. And anyway, I reckon the *Anastenarides* kept referring back to The Book – 'the dance hasn't changed!' – because Danforth's magnum opus, written roughly two decades ago, has frozen it at a crucial point in time, as they'd like to remember the tradition rather than the reality of what it's become. I'm no psychiatrist, but no matter how much they insist that the leader of the fire-walkers doesn't need to walk on fire, it can't do much for morale. Maybe that's why they're reluctant to talk to outsiders . . . their personal experience is the only mystery they have left.

*

Then, where I'm least expecting it, I find what I've been looking for.

The *Anastenarides* of Ayia Eleni take a break from the coals on the second night of the festival, so I've decided to visit another group of fire-walkers in the meantime. In truth, I've already written off the event at Langadás, mainly because my *Crusty Rucksack* guidebook mentions an admission charge and recommends arriving early 'to get a good seat', advice that makes it sound like even more of a circus than last night's event. Langadás is also much bigger than Ayia Eleni and barely twenty kilometres from Thessaloníki, Greece's second-largest city; I based my initial decision to visit Ayia Eleni on the assumption that the smaller and more remote a place, the more traditional it must be – for what it's worth, Dionysus was originally a god of the countryside. Still, the event at Langadás can't be any more disappointing, and maybe if it's a real commercial desecration, with a big stadium and ticket vendors hawking plastic binoculars over loudspeakers, I can cast Ayia Eleni in a better light, or at least put it into context.

It's around seven o'clock when I arrive in Langadás – well past the guide-recommended time – and I spend another half-hour driving around its leafy streets and surprisingly trendy pavement cafés searching for the Fire-Walking Festival. In Ayia Eleni, you couldn't miss it: the funfair blocked off the main road into the village. But there's no sign of a street carnival here – not even the jackhammer noise of generators. I've arrived interpreter-less (I'm skint by now) and it suddenly occurs to me that despite my surface fascination with the Greek alphabet and etymology, when it comes to actually speaking the language, I don't even know the basics. This is the first country I've ever been to where I'm completely tongue-tied

– it would take me years to comprehend a language in which the word for 'yes' sounds like 'nay'. But that's just a side-thought. The overriding realisation while I'm driving aimlessly around a sizeable Greek town in search of an obscure festival is that this is definitely not the best time to conclude, 'Hang on, I don't know a word of Greek!'

Well, I do know *one* word. I stop at a park full of families on the main road into town and approach a mother who's sitting in her car.

'*Anastenariá*?' I ask, pointing at the group in the park like a halfwit.

'No,' she responds hesitantly. 'Eh . . . one moment.' She climbs out of her car and hollers in the direction of the trees: '*ODISEA!*'

I'm so surprised to hear the name being used for a living person that I echo it out loud before I can stop myself: 'Odisea.'

'Yes – in English, Ulysses.'

I thought that was Latin, but I'm amazed (and humbled) that she would even bother translating it for me. Not only that, but she leaves her baby in the car and troops all the way over to the wooded area at the back of the park to find her husband, who then leads me to a café-bar to ask directions on my behalf. After several more wrong turns, I eventually come across a fun-fair that's much smaller than the one at Ayia Eleni, with only a couple of food stands and rides that look as rickety as oversized cereal-box toys. I'm on the very edge of Langadás, in a neigh-bourhood of newcomers whose bungalows have been spruced up and expanded over the years. However, there's not a *konaki* or bonfire in sight. A policeman directs me up the street and around a corner, using his finger to write '300m' in the dust on his car window. I still can't find what I'm looking for – much further and I'll be in farmland – but a kindly family sitting out on their porch points me the rest of the way. I take a right, and smell the scent of burning pine. I turn again at a little domed church on the corner, and there it is – a cone of logs, just like the bonfire last night, only this is framed by a couple of bungalows in the middle of a narrow residential street roped off on both sides. Barely two dozen people are gathered, all but a few of them locals from the surrounding neighbourhood of Thracian immigrants.

One of the outsiders is an elderly man from Athens, an English-speaker named Kostas who takes it upon himself to intercede on my behalf. He shows me the pavement leading through a small front garden to the *konaki*, which appears to be part of a typical red-tiled house rather than a purpose-built hall like the one in Ayia Eleni. The outside is as roughly finished as the other homes on the block, the corner bricks left exposed by a slapdash coat of paint. On the porch, the night air is cool, but the moment I step into the small foyer, the warmth and incense are overpowering, intensified by the hypnotic rhythm and repetitive melody emanating from the next room. Photos of *Anastenarides* past and present hang on the wall of the foyer, though here they form more of a family album than an ancestral shrine. I peer into the room next door, where the dozen or so dancers and musicians are in the middle of their second set of the evening. The dancers serpentine continuously around the room, approaching and retreating from the icons and incense at the front, and a couple of them are dancing with the icons. The melody is slightly different to that at Ayia Eleni – faster and higher-pitched – with the addition of a bagpipe made of animal skin, but it has the same sinuous Eastern sound to it, the tune winding in and out of itself, constantly coiling and uncoiling;

before coming here, if I had heard it on its own, I would have placed it much further East than the cradle of Western civilisation. The room's decoration adds to this Eastern feel, with a patterned carpet and handwoven textiles and embroidered wall hangings, all in rich, dark tones that somehow mesh together to create a sense of accumulated history as opposed to an empty, modern space waiting to be filled.

Outside, as dusk turns to darkness, Kostas tells me the familiar story about the dance's origins – in his version, Bulgarian soldiers torched the church containing the icon of his namesake saint, Constantine. I mention that the atmosphere here feels much more intimate than at Ayia Eleni, and he relays my impression to a couple of local men. They nod with satisfaction. 'Ayia Eleni is more touristic. This is more traditional.' When Kostas last came here, about fifteen years ago, the event was much more of a public spectacle. Since then, though, the *Anastenarides* have split into three separate groups for reasons that probably have to do with the fractiousness of human nature. Each has its own *konaki* and holds a backstreet firedance on one of the three nights of the festival. The ritual has reverted to its roots – so there may be hope yet for Ayia Eleni.

The moon has shed the remnants of last night's shadow, and the coals have been spread into a glowing circle in the middle of the street. Around 200 men, women and children have gathered by now, and a few policemen are standing by just in case, but the setting still feels intimate, like a spiritual street party. The *Anastenarides* are dancing one last time in the *konaki*, and by the time they emerge onto the street, the coals have burnt themselves into a greyish-black mass, red embers lurking underneath. With the full moon overhead, and the music circling around them, the men and women dance across the coals, repeating the same quick step as in the *konaki* but also taking their time to stamp out the fire. The *Anastenarides* here seem to spend longer on the coals, crisscrossing the fire until they've all but extinguished it, consciously or subconsciously re-enacting the story of the ritual's origins. One old man with a kerchief around his neck and an icon cradled in his arms trudges across as if he were crushing grapes to make wine. An elderly woman dances across the coals and then bends over to pound them with her palms. Some of the younger men and women cross the fire in couples, linking arms, while others waiting on the sidelines use their feet to kick embers back into the fire. Of course, it could be that the fire isn't as hot as the one in Ayia Eleni – they may have waited for it to die down before beginning the dance – but it doesn't matter to me. The *Anastenarides* are actually *dancing* on the coals and ashes, while a small crowd of mostly friends and family gathers round on a quiet suburban street in the moonlight. I may be imagining it, but the spirit of the dance here feels like more of a celebration than an obligation, a victory over the flames rather than a trial by fire. I may not have found a relic of the ancient world in Langadás, but I have encountered something mysterious and magical: a ritual that's survived miraculously on the backstreets of a Greek suburb.

CHAPTER SIX

NO GREEK LOVE ALLOWED
OIL WRESTLING IN TURKEY

PART ONE:

A BEAR-WRESTLING CIRCUS

You can't blame the gay fans, really. What with all the swarthy young men in black leather breeches lubricating their half-naked opponents with olive oil and then wrestling them to their knees and ramming their hands down their pants, well, it was only a matter of time before Turkey's national sport found a camp following on the international scene. Yet devotees of Oil Wrestling were horrified when photos of glistening, hard-bodied Turks wound up on homoerotic websites around the world. A gay group calling itself the Bears of Turkey even started advertising a bus tour for foreigners to drool over the Kirkpinar Oil Wrestling Championships, a semi-sacred event that dates back to the very foundations of Turkey.

As if Oil Wrestling didn't have enough problems already. In recent years, Islamic hardliners have objected to the flesh-baring spectacle – particularly the 'hands-down-the-pants' hold – while doping scandals have undermined the sport's ultra-macho image – *surely* Turkish wrestlers don't need to boost their sky-high testosterone levels! Not to mention the occasional brawls – dozens of oiled-up Turks punching it out on the field – or, even worse, the lingering rumours (perpetuated by know-nothing outsiders) that the most Turkish of sports may have actually been invented by the Greeks as part of their ancient Olympic Games. Throw in the fact that all this takes place on the cusp of the European Union, in a border town that used to be the Ottoman capital, against the current backdrop of Turkey's attempts to join the EU, and, well, there's only one reaction I could have: *I've gotta go.*

Trouble is, I know next to nothing about Turkey. In fact, I know so little, I haven't even seen *Midnight Express*. Which is probably a good thing. While boning up on Oil Wrestling, though, I realise that my destination is the same as the train's in the movie: Edirne (that's uh-DEER-nay), Turkey's 'Gateway to Europe', the last stop before the Greek and Bulgarian checkpoints, more than 200 kilometres west of Istanbul. Edirne is actually part of the ancient region of Thrace, just over the border from the original homeland of the *Anastenariá*. However, the legend of Kirkpinar roots Oil Wrestling firmly in Turkish history, dating it from the period over six centuries ago when the first Turks swept in from Asia and invaded Europe. One of their leaders, Suleiman Pasha, dreamt of uniting the two continents under Islam, fulfilling the vision of his grandfather, Osman, who bequeathed his name to the Ottoman Empire.

The story goes that Suleiman crossed over from Anatolia

(the Asian part of Turkey) around 1354 to venture deep into Rumelia (the European side) with forty of his best warriors. When they weren't fighting the Greeks and Bulgarians, the Turks would fight each other in wrestling matches to keep from getting bored. During one impromptu tournament, the two youths left standing at the end were so evenly matched they ended up wrestling to the death: both died of exhaustion. Their comrades buried them where they fell and continued their raids in the Balkans. Years later, the Turks found that forty springs had spouted forth from the spot where the original wrestlers who crossed into Europe had fought. They called the place Kirkpinar – literally, 'forty springs' (a recurrent number in Islam, as well as Judaism and Christianity). Alas, due to the give-and-take of territorialism, the original site now lies inside Greece. And given that most Greeks aren't overly fond of Turks, much less their oleaginous customs, Kirkpinar was forced to up sticks to Edirne in 1924, shortly after the Turkish Republic was formed from the rump of the Ottoman Empire.

For more than six centuries, then, Oil Wrestling, or *yagli gures* (YAH-luh GOO-resh), has provided an unlikely continuity for Turkey. The country has plenty of other traditional pastimes – camel-wrestling, for instance, pitting two horny humpbacks against each other – but Oil Wrestling exemplifies the ideals of bravery, strength, camaraderie and cunning that transformed a ragtag bunch of nomads into one of the world's biggest empires, stretching from Arabia to North Africa and Eastern Europe. A former sponsor of the event hails Kirkpinar as 'a deep-rooted legend about how the great Turkish nation left Central Asia and took Anatolia and Rumelia as the homeland'. And even when the Ottoman Empire fell into decline and was humiliated by the West, Turkey's Oil Wrestlers served as a source of pride for their countrymen, travelling throughout Europe and America, thrashing foreign champions and returning home heroes. Today the sport reflects the battle between Turkey's ancient roots and its modern aspirations, the clash between the way Turks see themselves and the reality of how they're perceived by the West. Whereas aficionados argue that Oil Wrestling is as aesthetic as it is athletic, requiring brains as well as brawn, the first instinct of many outsiders is to snigger about it being homoerotic. So you can understand why devotees might take offence at their tradition being turned into an attraction for sex tourists. More specifically, you could understand why they might be wary of a lone, gay-bait Westerner who turns up with a camera asking questions about Oil Wrestling . . .

Akif takes his umpteenth drag on a Marlboro and touches his Turkish–English dictionary for reassurance. 'I'm a little nervous,' he says, his voice tiptoeing across the syllables like eggshells. 'This is my first interview with a foreigner.'

'Don't worry,' I assure him. 'This is my first interview with a Turkish Bear.'

Not to mention my first time in a gay bar in Istanbul. If I knew next to nothing about Turkey before coming here, I lived in completely blissful ignorance of the alternative animal kingdom that thrives in our midst. For Akif and his e-pals, a 'bear' isn't a club mascot in the traditional sense. No, a gay bear is kinkier than your average bear. On the international scene, bears, or *ayilar* in Turkish, don't conform to the usual stereotypes of the effeminate queen or the buns-of-steel bodybuilder. Gay bears are typically fat/beefy, hairy chested and heavily bearded (with or without the corresponding baldness). Most importantly, they're straight-acting. They're the butchers and bakers and candlestickmakers among us, 'top blokes' in every sense of the term who have a fetish for hirsute fatties. Along with 'otters' and 'seals', they inhabit a parallel world served by magazines like *American Grizzly* and videos with similarly innocuous titles such as *The Three Bears*. (A word of warning: if you don't want to have your fond associations with the term warped for ever, don't go Google-ogling 'bear' on the Internet. If you're straight, it could put you off sex for life. For me, it will be a long time before I'm able to hear someone described as 'a bear of a man' without cracking up. And I doubt I'll ever think of Yogi, Baloo or Pooh Bear in quite the same way again.)

Within the species of *Ursus homosexualus*, Akif is a fine specimen of a Chubby Bear: short and barrel-bodied, with thick dark hair, plus a goatee and stubble that could etch glass. You wouldn't necessarily think he's gay; just happier than the norm. He does wear two earrings – a diamond stud on one side and a gold hoop on the other – and he works as a promoter/manager in the music industry. Not exactly a butcher or baker, I know, but the acts he manages play *halk muzigi*: traditional Turkish music. And there's nothing desperately trendy about him: no erectile hairgel or ironic-geek eyewear. He's wearing blue jeans and a simple, open-necked shirt.

The café-bar, on the other hand, is gagging to be in Soho or Greenwich Village. Due to the tyranny of geography, though, it's in the gay epicentre of Turkey, on the European side of Istanbul. The area around Taksim Square is a modern shopping and business district that's just scruffy enough to feel bohemian. The moment you enter the G-Box, you're assaulted by eyesore psychedelia – walls of wavy pink, orange and red lines – with three clocks on the wall telling the time in Istanbul and two other gay capitals: Berlin and London. The back room where Akif and I are sipping our *frappés* is decorated with another retro-Sixties print and a de rigueur disco ball suspended from the ceiling. I wouldn't even know I'm in Istanbul, except for the Turkish pop on the stereo – intercut with Gwen Stefani – and the woman in a shawl in the kitchen dishing up food to the whippet-thin waiters. God knows what she must make of all this.

Firing up another cigarette, Akif says he doesn't go around waving a rainbow flag, but if someone asks whether he's gay, he'll tell them. He also makes a point of informing clients upfront. 'But artists don't care who you are.' And anyway, in his case, the clue's in his surname: it happens to end in the letters G-A-Y.

'Many people comment on that,' he laughs.

Though he reckons he's known he was gay since the age of three, Akif didn't come out until he moved to England for a couple of years after school. 'When I went to London, I found the gay lifestyle.' Like the rest of the world, homosexuals in Turkey have imported the term 'gay' (or *gey/lezbiyen*) from English to describe themselves, in addition to the formal Turkish word, *esçinsel*. However, Akif prefers to call himself an *ibne*, embracing the epithet in the same way that some gays in the West proudly call themselves 'queer'.

Alas, not all concepts translate internationally. 'Bear is not a nice word in Turkish,' he explains. 'People will say, why did you do that, you *ayi*?' He thumbs through his dictionary for the definition: a clumsy, awkward person; an oaf. As with so many trends, though, the Bears of Turkey took their inspiration from America (I'm so proud). And the local bear clan might not even exist if it weren't for the Internet. Around 1997, way back in the early days of the World Wide Web, the founder of the group began cruising the Net for men who shared his sexual proclivity. Eventually, he started a website (ayilar.net since you ask, but remember: I warned you) and adopted the movement's netiquette, right down to the international mating call that bears use to hit on each other. Rather than growling Grrrrr, they say Woof! – or *Vuf!* in Turkish – for reasons unknown. Also, gay bears don't necessarily mate with other bears. According to Akif, the site's founder is actually very thin. He's what's known as a 'Bear Lover': a man who likes his beefcakes with a thick coat of hair.

In contrast, Akif is a Bear who doesn't like bearish types.

'So what is your type?' I ask.

He giggles bashfully. 'Maybe you should look in the mirror . . . Though normally I go for someone a bit slimmer.'

I've come all the way to Turkey to be called fat by a gay bear.

In a sop to my ego, Akif explains that his ideal pin-up is Brad Pitt *à la Troy,* while many Bear Lovers lust after Russell Crowe in *Gladiator.*

Now, I'd sworn to myself ahead of time that I wouldn't stoop to the whole awkward-straight thing of loudly declaring my heterosexuality or trying to work it into the conversation – there's such a thing as protesting too much. To my surprise, though, Akif had established the fact right from the beginning. 'You're not gay, are you,' he'd said, more as a statement than a question.

So I don't think he's hitting on me. Besides, he's already spoken for . . . well, sort of. Akif just broke up with his long-distance Basque boyfriend, but he has another lover who he met years ago in Turkey through the webring. At the time, Akif was living in Ankara, his hometown, and his friend was logged on to the chatroom with the username *Şişmanşever*, or Chubby Lover.

For a laugh, Akif wrote: 'I'm chubby, come and love me!'

The guy emailed for specifics, and Akif told him his weight and height.

'Woof!'

So they made a date to meet at the local McDonald's. Unfortunately, they missed each other that time, but they eventually hooked up and have been friends ever since. 'He helps me to see the good side of my belly. If we go to a restaurant, and I order a salad, he'll ask me, "Why did you order a salad instead of something like pasta?" Before, I didn't like my belly. But now I do.'

In the same way, the group has provided an alternative for gays in Turkey. The webring had been running for several years when the Bears were profiled in one of the country's biggest newspapers, *Hürriyet*. After that, membership shot from thirty men to over a hundred from all over Turkey. The reaction from the new members was ' "Thank you very much. Now I know I'm not alone",' Akif recalls. 'In Turkey, many gays, especially in the countryside, still think they're alone and there's only one role model in their life. They think, *If I'm gay, I have to be a drag queen or a transsexual*. The media shows only the flashy side of homosexuality. The queens are funny and flamboyant, but I think it's a very bad image for us.'

Or at least a very clichéd one. The subject of homosexuality in Turkey is as slippery as Oil Wrestling itself. Just when you think you've got a grip on it, a new fact will knock you flat. First, you have to understand that unlike 'civilised' European nations, Turkey has never banned gay sex, despite the psychological pull on the country from Islam and the Middle East. That's in contrast to, say, England, where gay sex was a crime until 1967, and Scotland, which didn't decriminalise homosexuality until 1980.

However, it's hard to tell how much can be read into Turkey's official tolerance: the lack of a ban on buggery may have been a judicial oversight, or lawmakers may have decided to leave sex to the realm of religion. Although the Turkish Republic is a dogmatically secular state, 99.8 per cent of the population is at least nominally Muslim. After the war in Iraq (which borders Turkey for 352 kilometres), religious extremists have become more vocal, with some calling for the creation of an Islamic state similar to Iran. 'If the fundamentalists gain momentum, they might try to outlaw homosexuality,' Akif says. 'Homosexuality is a really big sin in Islam.' Gay rights campaigners will debate that particular theological point to the death – they argue that the divine destruction of Sodom, for instance, had nothing to do with sodomy. At the popular level, though – particularly among those too afraid to ask – the common assumption among Turkish Muslims is that gay sex is so wrong in the eyes of Allah that it must be illegal, too. 'Lots of people don't know that homosexuality is legal in Turkey,' Akif says. This creates plenty of scope for the police to abuse their authority, ensuring that the local gay and lesbian movement isn't as loud and proud as it might be.

Another hot topic is the extent of homosexuality in Turkey, past and present. The now pseudo-conventional view holds that, like the ancient Greeks, the Ottomans were more than happy to have men lie on them. Gay rights campaigners often highlight the sultans who dressed their male lovers as women or murdered families for refusing to let them have their way with their sons. Apparently, young men from conquered territories were forced to work in Anatolia before being sent to the frontline to service soldiers. There's also an old guide to Istanbul's hamams that details the talent at local bathhouses, rating the male attendants on their beauty and how often they could make their customers come. However, most of these examples focus on a minuscule portion of the population. And murderous sultans and male sex slaves hardly qualify as Great Homosexual Role Models From History. Even today, most of Turkey's overtly gay bars, discos, bathhouses and cinemas are concentrated in just a few districts of Istanbul.

Before coming here, I contacted a Turkish guide who advertises tours of gay Istanbul. (Unfortunately, 'Ahmet' is out of town this week – in Iran, of all places.) His website categorises the clientele at different bars – 'mostly old gay man with moustache going there' or 'Istanbul transvestis . . . don't go there alone' – and gives the likelihood of getting laid at different bathhouses: at one hamam, 'sex is possible but little dirty', whereas another under-punctuated listing advises that 'not clean sex is possible'.

I can't tell whether that's good or bad.

I'm also a bit stiff, so to speak, when it comes to kissing another man. In Turkey, you're liable to see just as many public displays of affection between males as between men and women. Many men kiss each other on both cheeks to say hello or goodbye, and it's also customary for young men to kiss their elders' hands out of respect. The Gay Istanbul site goes even further, making the highly controversial claim that in Turkey, 'like most Islamic countries, almost every man would have sex with another man. In Turkish culture, actually in Muslim culture, if two men are having sex with each other, that does not mean that they are gay, it is just part of the hidden culture.'

Akif agrees, estimating that 70 per cent of Turkish men have had some sort of homosexual experience, be it masturbation, fellatio or full-on sex. Most of them, though, would be 'top guys' who insist they're straight. 'Lots of men think it's just a hole to fuck, and if they do, they think, *I'm not gay, I'm just a fucker.*'

I can see the T-shirts now.

For the record, Akif's not exclusively top or bottom, but 'versatile'. 'In Turkey, if you're gay, you're expected to be effeminate. That's more accepted. If you're not, people ask, "How is it possible? You have lots of hair and you act like a man!"'

Around the same time that the *Ayilar* 'came out' in the Turkish media, they hit on the idea of organising a bus tour to see Oil Wrestling at Kirkpinar as a way of coming out to their ursine brethren overseas. 'We thought it would be a great show for men who like bears,' Akif shrugs. 'It's a very erotic show – men hugging each other and sticking their hands down each other's pants. I'm not interested in bears, but when I saw Oil Wrestling, I *was* interested.'

The *Woofs!* came flooding in, especially from Germany, England and Spain. But then the Turkish media got wind of the story and whipped it into a maelstrom, with commentators thundering about the loss of Turkey's traditional values and the desecration of its most venerable sport. 'It's immoral,' spluttered the head of the Traditional Sports Federation. 'We shall pass this matter on to the interior, foreign and other ministries to ask for this disgusting business to be stopped.' A foreign news agency highlighted the controversy as a 'bright' – a filler story about funny foreigners – and it soon made headlines around the world. Meanwhile, the emails to the Bears turned nasty, warning, 'We will kill you if you come.'

To avoid any bloodshed, the Turkish Bears cancelled the trip. 'Turkish nationalists don't like us because they want to keep Oil Wrestling traditional. They think it's very masculine, but it's not – it's totally homoerotic,' Akif says, admitting that his interest in Oil Wrestling is essentially skin-deep, give or take a few inches. 'It is a very sexy thing. However, I would never add anything dirty to it because I'm not going to try to touch the wrestlers or wank when I watch it.'

That's a relief. In the country as a whole, Oil Wrestling does have a hardcore fanbase, with at least 350 tournaments held throughout the year on both the European and Asian sides of Turkey. For Westernised city-dwellers, though, Oil Wrestling is about as yuppie-friendly as trading in your car for a camel. Far from an admirable tradition symbolising what makes the nation great, it's seen as a risible pastime representing everything that holds Turkey back from becoming a truly modern European country. However, Akif reckons a makeover could be just what the sport needs: where the gay vanguard leads, mainstream culture often follows. 'It would be a very good advertisement for the country.'

Unlike the path to the EU, Turkey's road to Europe is remarkably smooth and clear, a motorway so modern it puts Germany's *autobahn* to shame. My guru of *yagli gures* is cruising along the highway that links Asia to Europe, connecting Istanbul to Edirne 200 kilometres away on the Greek and Bulgarian borders. Driving through the wheat and sunflower fields of Turkish Thrace, Aydemir Ay tells me that his family settled in Edirne in the 1930s, having upped sticks from Thessaloníki – Atatürk's hometown – not long after it reverted to Greek ownership. Within a generation, his family was so well connected that Aydemir's father was elected mayor. I ask him if it's common for outsiders to be accepted so readily, and he points out that one of the top officials at the University of Thrace in Edirne is a Turkish Bulgarian. 'In Anatolia, that would be a problem, but here it isn't, because we're part of Europe.'

'You mean you're more progressive?'

'No, more educated.'

Edirne is also more attractive than your average border town, probably because the Turks never intended it to be a mere frontier city. Originally named Hadrianopolis, after the Roman wall-builder, the Turks nabbed it from the Byzantines in 1361 – the reputed starting date of the Kirkpinar Championships. For nearly a century, until the Ottomans finally captured Constantinople and turned it into Istanbul, Edirne served as their capital. And even after it lost that honour, Edirne was a favourite summer playground for the sultans and a crucial staging post for military campaigns.

Superficially at least, modern Edirne looks much like any other mid-sized European city, corner kebab shops included. Instead of cathedrals and churches at its heart, though, it has mosques. And they aren't just ordinary dome-and-minaret jobs, either. Edirne's centrepiece is widely regarded as the country's finest mosque, built in the sixteenth century by the Ottomans' greatest architect, Mimar Sinan, a Greek Christian convert obsessed with honouring Allah by outdoing the Byzantine Ayia Sofia Cathedral in Constantinople. The culmination of his life's work was Selimiye Mosque, which stands elevated above the city, its magnificent dome mirroring the heavens like a moonstone guarded by the four pointed spears of its minarets. At night, when the mosque is illuminated, hundreds of birds circle and swoop in the ethereal floodlights like angels, or the souls of the dead. Unfortunately, the truth is much more prosaic: they're feeding off the insects suckered in by the light. In fact, the two rivers that make Edirne 'the city where waters meet' may be the reason why Turkish wrestlers began splashing on olive oil in the first place: it's a natural mosquito repellent.

When it comes to our dinner, I ask Aydemir for the full-on Turkish experience, so he takes me to a little boozer with beads hanging in the doorway and sticks of wood lining the walls, as if we were in a rustic bamboo hut rather than a pub on one of the city's main thoroughfares. We order a round of *mezes* including fried liver cubes, a bright-red dip of pureed raw heart mixed with chilli and a cross-section of boiled sheep's brain floating in water and lemon juice. 'You're going to think we're a bunch of barbarians!' he says, grinning self-consciously.

I certainly don't think I'd ever get the munchies for sheep's brain, even though it's as smooth and creamy as the softest cheese. I eat several squares of it – a feeble attempt at machismo – but it's hard to get past the Petri dish presentation and the furled worms of the cerebral lobes. The mixed grill is much more appealing, featuring beef sausages and lamb *köfte* meatballs to die for.

I've read in the *Turkish Daily News* that Turks consume a kilo of olive oil each year compared to twenty times that amount for the average Greek. The disparity probably has something to do with the fact that sunflower oil is cheaper, and most of Turkey's sunflowers are grown in Thrace. In that case, though, it seems strange to me that the locals would ship in up to two tonnes of premium olive oil for Kirkpinar.

'It doesn't make much sense, does it?' Aydemir laughs.

'Is it true that the olive oil is extra-virgin?'

'Yes, because it has less than one per cent acidity.'

For the wrestlers, or *pehlivans*, the sweat is bad enough without having to contend with cheap olive oil stinging their eyes.

Practically every account of Oil Wrestling refers to the fact that the combatants can ram their hands down each other's pants. However, none of them actually explains why. I'm determined to get to the bottom of it, so to speak.

'What exactly are they trying to grab hold of?' I ask.

'They're trying to grab their *kasnak*.'

Now that's a new word for it.

'Not their nuts. Their *kasnak*.' Or waistband. The wrestlers wear form-fitting black trousers known as *kisbets*, which are tailor-made from six layers of water-buffalo hide and heavily embroidered around the groin and backside to keep them from tearing when their opponents take hold. Besides the decorative stitching, most wrestlers also have their sponsors' names stamped in silver studs across their butts, completing the whole fancy-pants effect. Dripping wet, the *kisbets* weigh up to thirteen kilos and are tied tight at the waist. Opponents try to pry their fists down each other's *kisbets* purely for leverage, Aydemir assures me. 'Because once they grab your *kasnak*, it's match over. They can play with you like a child.' Slips of the hand are tolerated, but if a wrestler grabs his opponent by the short and curlies – let alone anything more substantial – he's immediately penalised.

Running from the waist to the middle of the calf, the *kisbet* is designed to conform with Muslim dress codes for men. However, the ol' hands-down-the-pants technique did draw a complaint from some fundamentalists a few years back. 'But the Society of Traditional Sports wrote back to them and said

Mohammed was a wrestler,' Aydemir shrugs. 'After that, they were silent.'

From the corner of my eye, I notice a gaggle of drag queens on the TV in the bar. This year a camp celebrity told *Hürriyet* newspaper that he might try to become the Aga, or Lord of Kirkpinar, a position open to the highest bidder. But Aydemir reckons it's a publicity stunt. 'He's a singer – he's a *gay* singer,' he says by way of explanation. 'I doubt he has enough money.'

PART TWO:
GODS OF TESTOSTERONE

When I decided to get stuck into Oil Wrestling, I grandly imagined that I might actually grease up to experience the sport firsthand. However, I've begun to reconsider after grave warnings from a couple of Turkish friends and practically everyone else I've met here. Aydemir assures me it's easy to find wrestlers who will show me the tricks; I can hire them for about fifty euros, or thirty-five pounds. Given the whole gay-tourist controversy, though, it strikes me as vaguely seedy to turn up at Kirkpinar as a lone Western man and hire a muscular Turk as a wrestling partner (*it's for research, honest!*). Also, paying fifty euros to have my butt kicked seems a bit steep, particularly when I could have it done for free. No doubt there are hundreds of Turks who would queue up for a chance at real, live Yankee-bashing: '*This* is for the Iraq War!' THWOCK! 'And *that's* for *Midnight Express!*'

Frankly, Aydemir thinks it would be suicide. 'If you're facing an Oil Wrestler, you have ten seconds to run,' he laughs. 'If you don't run, you'll soon be in the air – or on the ground.' A few years ago, a Korean bodybuilding champ came here to try his luck at Turkish Oil Wrestling. 'He went flying through the air. Then, ten seconds later, he was on the ground.' He wound up being thrown half a dozen times in one minute, reconfirming the old maxim: whereas Oil Wrestlers often win at other styles of wrestling – such as Kenan Simsek, who won silver in freestyle wrestling at the 1992 Olympics – no foreigners will ever be champions at Kirkpinar.

I have plenty of time to contemplate my folly as we go for a stroll on Friday around the river isle where the championships take place. Sarayici Island feels big enough to be a peninsula in its own right, with plenty of space for the Kirkpinar stadium, a fun fair, loads of market stalls, a cemetery and the ruins of the so-called New Castle destroyed by the Turks in 1878 to keep the Russians from seizing their munitions. Aydemir takes me through a wooded area called Tavuk Ormani: aptly enough, Chicken Forest. The story goes that the Ottomans used to keep thousands of fowls on the island to feed their troops. Apparently the whites of the eggs also helped bind the mortar in Selemiye Mosque. Nowadays, all I can see is a lone rooster strutting among the plastic chairs and tables of the place where we stop for tea. The café's centrepiece is an airy stone building that seems far too ornate to have been a mere hunting box, but it was designed for Mehmet IV, a huntin'-and-ridin' sultan who died in Edirne in 1693 after being dethroned and kept under house arrest for several years with two concubines as his literal cellmates. We sit at the small table inside, surrounded by carved arches and cushioned window seats, and a trio of strangers soon joins us: two elderly men from Edirne and a middle-aged engineer who's Turkish but visiting from Germany. We're soon chatting like old friends about the issue that's the focus of seemingly every corner-shop conversation in the land now that the EU has agreed to start talking about talks to hold talks to someday, in the future, let Turkey join the club.

Certainly, the economic benefits of joining the euro aren't what they once were. 'The only strong, dynamic country in Europe is Britain,' says the factory worker from Stuttgart. 'Germany is dead. The economy is terrible.' It's so bad, in fact, he's actually thinking about moving back to Turkey – an example of reverse migration that would have been unthinkable less than a decade ago.

Whereas Germany's opposition to Turkey joining the EU is pretty much expected, what really galls the Turks is Gallic rejection. As Aydemir puts it, 'We can't understand why the French don't love us.'

One of the old men asks me point blank: 'Why do the British support us and the French don't?'

Hmmm. How to answer that one? Two reasons come to mind: first, the British are genuinely more tolerant and fair-minded than many of their European counterparts; second, and less nobly, I reckon it's a political manoeuvre to weaken the old guard of the Franco-German alliance within the EU.

What I *don't* say is this: given Europe's existing problems with ethnic integration and Islamic terrorism, it's no wonder the French and Germans are nervous. It doesn't help, either, when the Turkish prime minister keeps calling the EU a 'Christian club'. With a population of seventy million, Turkey would rank as the biggest nation in the EU after Germany – provided, of course, that its population stayed put. Akif, for one, estimated that fifteen million Turks would emigrate to Europe tomorrow if their country were allowed to join the EU. That's probably an overstatement – and a deeply contentious one at that – but in broad, sweep-of-history terms, Turkey's entry into the EU could very well mark the culmination of centuries of westward migration. Turkey still has a long way to go to qualify for EU membership, but to my mind, it's already passed one of the most important tests – winning the Eurovision Song Contest in 2003. Whether intentionally or not, Turkey's victorious pop anthem mirrored the country's efforts to win over Europe, as a spurned woman vows to gain her lover's affection 'Every Way That I Can'.

After we're done talking Turkey, the conversation turns to Kirkpinar. This afternoon the wrestlers will lay a wreath and pray at a grave commemorating the sport's legends, some of whom are immortalised in statues outside the stadium. The unrivalled master of Oil Wrestling was Kel (The Bald) Aliço, whose more ominous moniker was 'The Cruel', reflecting his merciless wrestling style. In the nineteenth century, the moustachioed slaphead won the championship twenty-six times, occasionally without even having to wrestle. Legend has it that he would simply hang up his *kisbet* in the stadium to scare off any young pretenders: whether they were frightened by his technique or his tackle is unclear. During the Golden Age of Oil Wrestling, Sultan Abdülaziz invited the country's top fighters to live in his palace in Istanbul. Abdülaziz fancied himself a dab hand at Oil Wrestling, and there's a story that he once challenged Kel Aliço to a bout, ordering the master wrestler not to cut him any slack just because he was sultan. 'If you lose,' he warned Aliço, 'I will cut off your head.' The match ended the only tactful way possible: in a tie.

The sultan of Oil Wrestling was messily deposed in 1876, and the *pehlivans* suddenly found themselves turfed out of the palace and forced to make their way in the world at a time when wrestling in general was very much in vogue. Turkey's musclemen toured Europe and America, competing against other 'exotics' from India and Japan and perpetuating many of the stereotypes that persist to this day. While their French manager billed them as 'The Sultan's Lions', 'The Amazing Turks' and so on, they played into the Western view of Turkey as a nation of barely civilised barbarians. Koca Yusuf, whose turbaned statue stands next to Aliço's in front of Kirkpinar stadium, earnt the nickname 'The Terrible Turk', demolishing all comers. In one match against a fellow *pehlivan* in Paris, Yusuf 'tore his opponent's nostrils, broke his ribs and twisted his arms'. It took the ref plus half a dozen policemen to break up the fight. In New York's Madison Square Garden, organisers pitted the Terrible Turk against a local Greek nicknamed 'Little Hercules' in a match 'animated by a race feud as well as personal antagonism', according to the *New York World*. 'If the fervent prayers of all the Greek flower peddlers in New York avail, the Cross will wave above the Crescent when their countryman has finished with the follower of the Prophet.' True to form, though, the Greek lost. 'He made as if he wanted to kill a few thousand Turks at one blow. But he saw Yusuf in his corner and got over his hostility.'

Although Yusuf's name is still invoked in the opening speeches at Kirkpinar, the Terrible Turk's brutality undermined his popularity abroad. Ever-suspicious of being ripped off – and chances are he was – Yusuf demanded to be paid in gold, wearing some $10,000 of bullion in a belt everywhere he went. Like many *pehlivans*, he planned to return home after earning his fortune in the West. However, the steamship he boarded in New York in 1898 collided with a British ship and sank in the North Atlantic. Aydemir and the old-timers glide over the details, but the survivors' accounts I've read claim that Yusuf was one of the foreign 'fiends' in steerage who used their knives to cut their way through the crowds. Nearly 600 – or three out of every four – passengers died at sea, and only one of the seventy women on board survived. One version contends that the 250-pound wrestler forced his way to the front and jumped into a lifeboat that was already full, catapulting everyone into the sea. Another account claims that Yusuf was swimming in the water and grabbed on to a boat, but the passengers chopped off his hands to keep him from drowning them. Either way, his forty-pound gold belt probably helped drag him to his death.

Perhaps a much better role model for Oil Wrestlers is Kurtdereli Mehmet, whose statue also stands on a pedestal in front of the stadium. Mehmet defended Turkey's honour in France, Britain and America during the last days of the Ottoman Empire. Near the end of his career, in 1931, the undefeated champion declared: 'In every wrestling match, I picture the Turkish nation supporting me, and I think of our national honour.' Atatürk liked that so much he sent Mehmet 1,000 lire and a letter declaring that his statement should be 'a professional maxim for all Turkish sportsmen'.

Since its Golden Age, though, Turkey's national sport has increasingly become the preserve of hardcore aficionados like Aydemir and the dozens of men and boys who sleep rough in the fields surrounding the stadium to see the championship. One of our tablemates, a balding man with trousers stretched tight around his belly, jumps up to act out famous encounters from the past few decades, such as the wrestler who weighed

150 kilos and had arms so long 'they could reach across this room', and the David-and-Goliath battle between a 90-kilo wrestler and a giant weighing 140 kilos. Thanks to the oil, the little guy wound up on top, but there was no way he was going to be able to flip his opponent, so he started scraping his forearm up and down the big guy's spine. After an hour of torture, the giant surrendered.

Aydemir mentions my interest in the hands-down-the-pants hold, and the man regales us with the story of a match from the Sixties involving a former champ who had let himself run to fat. Most heavyweights have some sort of paunch – a gut helps protect them from literal invasions of their privacy – but this guy also had chicken-thin legs, so when his rival did shove his hands down his breeches, the ex-champ's *kisbet* fell down around his ankles, leaving him with his hands cupped over his privates and his bare white butt exposed to thousands of laughing spectators. *Kisbet* slippage results in instant disqualification; and in his case, years of mortification.

None of this is making me any more confident. On our return through Chicken Forest, I have plenty of time to weigh up my chances of emerging from Oil Wrestling with what little dignity I have intact. The man from Stuttgart invites us to meet a *pehlivan* friend who's waiting for this afternoon's ceremonies to begin. Ismail Gül is sitting with his son, Sefa, on a shady patch of grass next to the wrestlers' entrance. After making our introductions, Aydemir challenges Sefa to a warm-up bout. He doesn't stand a chance. Before he's barely stooped forward, the kid lunges for his right leg, grabs his thigh and latches his ankle with his foot, tipping him on his backside.

'JR, you try!' Aydemir laughs.

Determined to avoid the same fate, I keep my right leg far

back. Of course, I could just pick the kid up and hurl him to the ground, but knowing my clumsiness, he'd probably break something or end up crippled for life, and that wouldn't endear me to his dad or the other thousand wrestlers who are milling around. Before I know it, though, Sefa scampers forward and latches my left ankle. I fall in slow motion, landing flat on my butt, with my stomach 'facing the stars'. So much for my Oil Wrestling career: I've just been whipped by an eleven-year-old.

Sprawled on the grass, I try to work out how I'm going to spin this to my friends back home: *He may have been eleven, but I'm tellin' ya – he was big for his age!*

In reality, Sefa barely comes up to my belly button.

He was packed with muscle!

He weighs all of 32 kilos.

He had fangs for teeth!

Yeah, but that snaggletooth grin gives him all the fearsomeness of a chipmunk.

However, his father has no doubts about his potential. 'You will read about him one day. He's a future champion,' he says, slinging his arm around his son's neck.

Sefa grins some more. 'I will be a *başpehlivan*' – a master wrestler – 'when I am twenty-two years old.'

So give it a decade or so, and I might have a claim to fame.

Ismail couldn't be prouder. He's the typical sports-mad father who's risen up the ranks and won a few regional titles but never broken through at the national level. With the benefit of his knowledge and experience, though, he's determined that his son will be able to hit the big time. Just to be here, wrestling at Kirkpinar as father and son, is a huge accomplishment, he tells me.

'This is the Olympia of Oil Wrestling.'

*

People keep saying that, but to my mind, the constant references to the ancient Olympics raise awkward questions about the true origin of 'the heirloom of the Turks'. 'Oil Wrestling was not transmitted to the Turks from any other nation,' harrumphs the government-sponsored guide to Kirkpinar. 'It is completely peculiar to the Turks.' That may be, but the booklet then goes on to admit that the nomadic tribes adapted their peculiar pastime from the ancient Greek practice of getting oiled up to wrestle.

I try to raise the subject as delicately as possible over dinner on Friday night with a Turkish wrestling official, and he starts thumping the table. 'Kirkpinar is older than Olympia!'

By that, he means that Kirkpinar is the world's oldest continuous annual sporting event; the Olympian Games were held every four years. Given Turkey's history of victories and defeats, though, it's hard to believe that the championships have continued for more than 600 years without a single interruption.

'It's in *The Guinness Book of Records!*' Aydemir exclaims as we cross the bridge to the island on Saturday morning.

Then it must be true.

The Kirkpinar stadium is an overwhelmingly orange rectangle – the colour's meant to represent the sun – decorated with balloons, Turkish flags and a big banner across the judges' tribunal that declares it ER MEYDANI: 'THE MEN'S FIELD'. From the moment I enter the arena, a couple of things hit me – well, almost. I've barely stepped through the gate of the press pen and onto the grass when two wrestlers come brawling towards me, spraying sweat and olive oil, their eyes red-rimmed and furious. One is missing a chunk of skin from his ribs; the other is in the midst of thudding to the ground. I have to scuttle back to keep from getting greased.

What's inescapable, though, is the overpowering smell. The stadium reeks of olive oil. Up until this very moment, I'd never thought of olive oil as having a scent; or if it does, it's like salt or rice – so faint as to be non-existent. I know gourmands say you can tell extra-virgin *olio d'oliva* from the more promiscuous stuff by its 'bitter', 'fruity' or 'spicy' scent, but I've always suspected they're bluffing, like the poseurs who claim that a wine has a 'manure nose' while still pronouncing it 'eminently quaffable'.

However, with two tonnes of olive oil sloshing around the place, even I can smell the stuff. The stadium is one great big bowl of macerated grass salad, the oil turning the long blades a greasy green. It's not that it stinks; it's just that you can't get away from it. The olivey odour invades your nostrils and saturates every membrane in your skull. Even after you've had time to get used to it, a sudden gust of air will send a new blast wafting past and you notice the smell all over again. You'd get a similar effect if you walked around with a couple of olives stuffed up your nose.

The font of all this oliveness lies on the far side of the field, roughly where the waterboys and benches would be if this were a typical field-based sport. This being Oil Wrestling, however, the site is occupied by a crew of 'Oil Men' in white baseball caps who are pouring gallons of gourmet olive oil into long-necked tin and copper decanters. While they keep the oil flowing, the musicians next to them keep up a constant racket of military music from the Ottoman Empire, half of them banging on bass drums and the other half blowing on traditional reed instruments. The *zurna* looks like a clarinet but sounds like an oboe crossed with a bagpipe; it makes a noise like an angry wasp trying to cut through cellophane to sting you. As a boy, Aydemir used to beg his father to let him leave early; the music gave him a headache. Apparently the wrestlers find it stirring. One of the many unique aspects of Oil Wrestling is that the band adjusts its performance according to the play on the field. The musicians start the matches with stately marches but will quickly pick up the tempo to prod the men into fighting if the wrestling flags.

The wrestlers are warming up in the bright sunlight at the end of the field, below a couple of Turkish flags flanking a portrait I don't immediately recognise.

I (stupidly) ask Aydemir who it is, realising instantly that this is a very quick way to lose whatever credibility I have.

It's Atatürk, of course, but in one of his less common poses. Practically everywhere you go in Turkey, you find statues and portraits of the many Faces of Atatürk, the founder of the modern Republic who's idolised as nothing less than the Saviour of the Turkish People. The flesh-and-blood version visited Edirne for all of five days back in 1930, and ever since, the room where he stayed in the town hall has been preserved as a mini-museum to his greatness. Most government-issue portraits I've seen depict him as a military strongman in a fez or a matinée idol in formalwear staring seductively straight out at you – think Omar Sharif with a touch of Bela Lugosi – but this profile dates from his later years, some time in the 1930s. Rather than the proud 'Father of the Turks', he's more like a wise grandfather in a natty suit and tie, with a trim moustache and silver hair, a kindly old gent – maybe a family physician – more accustomed to dandling babies on his knee than ruthlessly crushing opponents.

Under this benevolent image of the national patriarch, roughly 1,800 men and boys have come from around the country to wrestle this year, ranging from preteens to forty-somethings and divided into nine categories based on a combination of weight, height and skill. All the diversity of Turkey is here, from the legions of dark, moustachioed stereotypes who are naturally olive-skinned to the palefaced exceptions like a strawberry blond whose back is turning red despite the copious application of nature's suntan oil. Some are Turkish Adonises (if that's not a cross-border contradiction in terms), while others are downright scary, like the guy whose face looks as if it's been hammered flat to fit the contours of a perfectly spherical head, which in itself is barely half as wide as his neck, the excess folds of skin gathering at the base of his skull like a pup's – only if you wanted to pick him up, you'd need to use a crane. I've seen some of these guys ploughing through the breakfast bar at my hotel, and it's occurred to me (while wishing they would have left me just one egg to go with my olives and cucumbers) that the oil-wrestling Ottoman soldiers would have been very fearsome indeed, especially for Tommies, who must have thanked God for the invention of the gun, just so they didn't have to fight hand-to-hand against these behemoths – let alone endure the humiliation of Lawrence of Arabia, who was gang-raped by some of the sultan's minions.

During the elimination rounds, a multitude of physiques are on display: scrawny boys and athletic twentysomethings, as well as men who are completely smooth and sowbellied, with pink flesh and soft teats (*squeal, piggy, squeal!*), and others whose bodies are covered in great tectonic plates of hair. If it weren't for the oil, the latter would lose every match; their opponents could grab a fistful of body hair and throw them any way they pleased. Perhaps that's why most of the wrestlers are no strangers to shaving and waxing, their follicle-free pecs glistening in the sunshine. And some of these guys are absolutely ripped – jacked – buff – whatever you want to call it, with every muscle striated, defined and delineated as if they were walking anatomical models: caricatures of masculinity come to life. *Behold, ye Gods of Testosterone!*

Gawping, I point to one titan of anatomy and ask Aydemir who he is.

'He's stupid. He loses every year.'

Before each match, the wrestlers get oiled up in what is theoretically a well-defined ritual, using their right hands to grease their left shoulders, chests, arms and *kisbets*, then reversing the process with their other hand. When that's done, their opponents are meant to ceremoniously smear oil on their backs. In reality, though, the scene at the end of the field is an oily free-for-all, with dozens of men in tight leather trousers in various stages of either lubricating themselves or being lubricated. The Oil Men can't pour the stuff fast enough, dispensing great green-gold slicks that ooze down the wrestlers' torsos and sluice off their trousers, gushing onto the ground. The combatants splash on the oil as if it were water, and when they've finished basting their upper bodies, they get the Oil Men to point their nozzles down their trousers, bending over and waggling their embroidered butts to get good and greasy all over or lifting their studded waistbands and thrusting their groins under the golden showers.

Needless to say, the assembled photographers are loving all this, clicking and buzzing around the men until the officials have to step in and shoo them away. For professional snappers, Oil Wrestling works not only as sport but as *art* – a chance to fulfil their creative aspirations by capturing images that could've come straight off an ancient vase – with a lucrative after-market as soft porn. Practically every shot is a money shot. And the wrestlers tolerate the close-ups and suspicious camera angles more than you might expect. Then again, maybe they're media-savvy enough to realise that if they're ever going to become rich and famous from Oil Wrestling, it doesn't hurt to have an international following, much like the master wrestlers of old. And if some of those foreign fans want to see oil trickling down their backsides, well, that's the price of fame.

Once they've got their greasy shots, the photographers tend to hang out around the water pumps in the corner of the field, a row of eight green spigots where the wrestlers go to rinse themselves before and after matches. The resulting photos work on at least two levels, particularly in monochrome, with their torrents of white spume splashing over hard-bodied warriors, ricocheting off their lips and cascading down their cobbled abs to follow the treasure trail south. Images like these feature heavily in an exhibit outside the stadium, as well as any number of books produced over the years. Aydemir's father showed me one that consisted of grainy black-and-white photos of half-naked men grappling with each other. Flipping through the pages, he said proudly, without any unseemly overtones, 'Very artistic.'

It's certainly unlike anything I've ever seen.

For starters, it's one of the few sports in the world that has musical accompaniment. What's more, each match begins with a dance. Not by cheerleaders or entertainers, you understand, but the wrestlers themselves. The dance known as the *peshrev* is a very manly, *muy*-macho ritual, giving the wrestlers a chance to puff out their chests and size up their opponents while also making a token show of humility. An official called a *cazgir* stands on the sidelines and bellows the roll-call of wrestlers, mixing in jokes and puns but ending with a high-pitched exhortation in Arabic that's reminiscent of the calls to prayer that echo from the mosques five times daily:

> *Allah! Allah! Illahlah!*
> *Mohammed-is-the-Prophet-of-God*
> *Young Turkish lions – go!*

With that, the drums and *zurnas* grind into gear and the wrestlers stride across the field in a line, high-stepping in stilted slow motion, swinging their arms, clapping their hands and slapping their thighs. On their first approach to the VIP box, the men kneel to touch the grass and their hearts in a sign of respect. Then it's back to more clapping and thigh-slapping as they pair off against their opponents and strut back and forth across the ankle-deep grass. Each time they pass each other, the wrestlers pause to perform different ceremonial checks: swinging their arms, fingering their *kisbets* or hugging and rubbing their backs. Most wrestlers go through the motions with bored solemnity, but a couple of high-spirited dancers bound across the field to the crowd's applause, swinging their arms and slapping their thighs, obviously gunning for the Best Dancer Prize awarded at the end of the competition.

The actual wrestling starts with the forty or so men squaring off in pairs spread out around the field, circling and bitch-slapping each other into headlocks. The wrestlers can't use their fists or smack their rivals in the face – that would be punching – but the men *are* free to soften up their opponents by bashing them repeatedly about the neck, head and cervical vertebrae with the karate-chop edge of their hands and the hard, bony ridge of their forearms. These skull-juddering impacts send the oil and sweat flying and must sting, to say the least: to train, the 200- to 300-pound gorillas hone their barehanded hammering technique by hitting tree trunks. Aydemir swears you can identify an Oil Wrestler by his ears: after years of getting clobbered, they stay swollen and misshapen like belligerent, gnarled cauliflowers.

Once the men have a good grip on each other's necks, the butt- and groin-grabbing begins. They immediately start probing each other's pants while trying to keep their own legs at a distance. One wrestler will usually try to slip out of the headlock and clinch his partner from behind, forcing him to his hands and knees so he can attempt to flip his opponent on his back. The problem is, he can't get a proper hold because of the oil. What's more, the bottom guy is using the long tufts of grass to his advantage, gripping it to keep from getting rolled.

With no other option, then, the top man will invariably start rooting around in the bottom guy's drawers. Not only that, but he'll lean on his opponent's neck with one arm – *down, bitch!* as I think they say in prison – so that the bottom man's bottom juts into the air: all the better for the top man to ram his hand down his pants, either by groping around the front and diving down his crotch or inserting his fist along the gulley in his backside. Sometimes – and I apologise if this sounds like a Turkish version of the *Kama Sutra* – the top wrestler will wind up straddling his opponent from the front, so that the bottom guy's head is stuck between his knees. Either way, the top Turk will go for a crotch- or bum-hold, stuffing his arm down his opponent's *kisbet* all the way to the elbow, as if he were performing an impromptu proctology exam: *Just hold still, and I'll have this gerbil out in a jiffy.* It's the kind of deep-cushion sofa-fishing that people do when they're searching for loose change down the back of a settee, only here the top guy seems to be saying, 'Pardon me, but I've dropped some change – *down your ass.*' I can't claim firsthand experience, so to speak, but it looks for all the world like the practice known as 'fisting'. What makes the scene even more bizarre is that although the men on the bottom invariably grit their teeth and scowl, they yield to the indignity without a struggle: they're passive and prostrate while the top men finger their prostates.

'Why don't the wrestlers on the bottom try to fight?' I ask Aydemir, so slackjawed and aghast that my lips barely make contact on the consonants.

'They're resting.'

In that case, wrestlers are 'resting' all over the field. At any given point throughout the afternoon, at least half a dozen men – if not many, many more – are dotted around the field, bent over on their hands and knees, gripping the grass . . . and being fisted. Most of the Oil Wrestling matches seem to end up like this: two men in the grass hunkered down doggie style, with nothing but a fist, some black leather and lashings of gourmet olive oil between them.

I can't imagine what the gay fans see in it.

As with any duel, though, what's fascinating about Oil Wrestling is how a moment of strength can simultaneously create a moment of weakness. When two men are crouched on the field, for instance, the wrestler on top has the obvious advantage: if he can flip his opponent on his back, it's game over. If he's not careful, though, the guy on the bottom can roll him so that – because he's on top – his back hits the ground first. From potential victory comes defeat. And oil is a great leveller. On the other side of the field, a big bruiser has hoisted his opponent in the air sideways. If the giant can carry him for just a few steps, he wins. As he's starting to walk, though, he slips on the oily grass and falls backward, landing on his butt and – crucially – his back. His dreams of winning Kirkpinar have ended in a pratfall.

Aydemir's mobile rings. His father has arranged for us to speak with a couple of former Kirkpinar Agas. I'm particularly keen because one of them is also the chairman of the Traditional Sports Federation, the group that protested against the Bears of Turkey visiting Kirkpinar. Sitting side by side in the VIP section, the two men present such an obvious contrast that even I can tell one is European and the other Anatolian. Mehmet Iris is clean-shaven, with light-brown eyes and a pinkish complexion, his plump frame contained within a cream-coloured suit and matching poly-blend tie. His opposite number, Alper Yazoğlu, wears a dark jacket, sitting so still and stern-faced during the wrestling that you'd think he was posing for a daguerreotype. But the real giveaway is his moustache. It's so bushy he could hide small animals in it. Sure enough, Mr Iris is a businessman here in Edirne, while Mr Yazoğlu hails from Bayburt, a town in north-eastern Turkey that's closer to Iran than Istanbul.

We sit behind them, and I run through my questions with Aydemir. 'Let's not forget to ask about the gay singer who wants to be Aga.'

'That is not a nice question for them.'

Still, it's gotta be asked. Of course, that's easy for me to say – I don't have to ask it in Turkish, let alone in public to a couple of my father's associates.

First, though, we ask them why they paid for the privilege in the first place.

'You bid to become Aga out of respect for your fathers and your grandfathers and for our customs,' Mr Iris says. 'If someone is successful and earns a lot of money, he should do this out of respect for Edirne and for a love of Oil Wrestling.' Presumably it's not bad for business, either. In the Kirkpinar guide, there's an ad for his chain of appliance stores featuring a photo of him as the youngest-ever Aga in 1981.

A decade later Mr Yazoğlu, the owner of a holding company, was the first person to sponsor the championships for three years in a row, from 1991 to 1993, simply because no one else would bid for the honour. 'Kirkpinar is legendary,' he says. 'This is our tradition. As soon as we can walk as children, we begin wrestling with our fathers.' As Aga, not only did he help pay for the Kirkpinar contest, but he also helped fund the Balkan Cemetery Memorial outside the stadium, built a public school in Edirne, improved the local water supply and donated money for sports. Mr Yazoğlu won't divulge how much the honour cost him, but Mr Iris is happy to spill the beans: he reckons he spent twenty-five kilos of gold to host the event.

'Gold?' I whisper to Aydemir. 'Because of inflation?'

He nods.

Give or take a few doubloons, that's a cool £200,000.

'And what does he think about a gay singer being Aga?' I nudge Aydemir.

Mr Iris shoots him a look that says, *I can't believe you're asking me that.* 'In our culture, there's only women and men. There are no others. It makes us sad that a gay singer wants to be Aga. This is a traditional sport.'

Mr Yazoğlu is equally dismissive. 'This is a unique sport that includes prayer. No other sport in Europe includes prayer.' He also cites a statute in the Kirkpinar rulebook that forbids Agas from bringing the game into disrepute. 'Money cannot buy everything. You need to be a respected person *and* you need to have money to be Aga. Frauds and whorehouse owners, for instance, can't be Agas. Homosexuals cannot be Agas.'

As someone with a vested interest in tourism, Aydemir's attitude towards gays is much more laissez-faire. 'I have lots of gay friends,' he says with a shrug afterwards.

I brace myself for a big, almighty BUT – something along the lines of 'I think they should be dragged through the streets and horsewhipped'. However, Aydemir claims he's all for gay tourists visiting his hometown. 'There are lots of gays in Edirne. But it's not a problem. They are humans, too.' When the controversy over the Bears broke out, he was among the younger generation that argued in favour of welcoming them. 'An old mayor said "Don't come here", but that is stupid. I said, "They're tourists and they're big spenders. And they won't fuck us."'

. . . *over*, I think he means.

It's been a long day, and much as I'd like to visit the real thing, the closest I'm going to get to a Turkish bath is a restaurant called Hamam, just opposite my hotel. Despite the tacky kebab-shop signs outside, it's actually an upscale eaterie hidden away in a former bathhouse. The intricately decorated tiles on the walls have been left intact and you can see the old central-heating stone through illuminated blocks of green glass set in the middle of the floor. I can't help but notice the artificial Christmas tree in one of the windows. Aydemir explains that it's yet another Western custom that's catching on in Turkey;

evidently the owners like Christmas trees so much, they've decided to keep one up all year round. Likewise, there's no escaping television. A state-of-the-art projector has turned the smooth, white wall next to us into a giant TV screen, displaying a late-night variety show featuring a Kurdish crooner in a virulently yellow shirt.

Given that we're the only customers left, Aydemir asks the waiters to switch to the news channel. A panel of talking heads is debating the latest clash between the government and practising Muslims: a couple of women in shawls tried to enter a public building but were stopped by the police.

'In Turkey, women with veils aren't allowed in public buildings or schools,' Aydemir explains.

'Is that because of Islamic law?'

He laughs. 'No, the government.'

Turkey's secularism is enforced with near-religious zeal. As Aydemir tells it, Atatürk had three options in 1923: Turkey could become a Soviet satellite, an Islamic regime like its Middle Eastern neighbours, or something truly unique – a modern, Westernised republic with a predominantly Muslim population. For Atatürk, the decision was obvious. Although he ruled as a dictator, he laid the foundations for a democracy, adopting European legal and administrative systems and particularly the French model of dogmatic secularism to keep Islam from meddling in affairs of state.

'So that's why France's rejection of Turkey in the EU stings so much.'

'Exactly.'

He notices some new images flashing up on the wall and starts laughing. It's an end-of-show segment, a 'bright' about funny foreigners, only the objects of ridicule are mostly English:

they're the dozens of men – and some women – who fling themselves down a grassy cliff in Gloucestershire each year in pursuit of a cheese.

'Stupid idiots!' Aydemir cackles as one of the casualties is stretchered off clutching his prize Double Gloucester cheese.

I happen to know a thing or two about the Cooper's Hill Cheese Roll, having featured it in my first book, *True Brits*. Come to think of it, it's one of the traditions that started me off on this dubious career. Now I'm here in an old hamam, in a part of Turkey frequented by few Westerners, talking to a guy about Oil Wrestling – and *he's* making fun of the Cheese Rolling footage that's just happened to pop up on the wall.

'An American once asked me what kind of stupid people cover themselves in oil and wrestle at the hottest time of the year.' Aydemir grins. 'But I'll always remember you as the man who wrote a book about Cheese Rolling.'

There's far less fisting and much more hugging on Sunday, perversely making the finals infinitely less entertaining. In keeping with the original legend, the matches at Kirkpinar used to go on for hours – as long as it took for the wrestlers to toss each other, so to speak. However, in recent decades the officials have tried to update the sport by introducing time limits and other rule changes to appeal to modern attention spans. If neither wrestler wins outright within forty minutes, the match goes into extra time, with the men still trying to flatten one another but also competing for points. A victory on points tends to be profoundly anticlimactic, though, so the referees can also penalise the men for failing to fight: three strikes and they're out.

Even so, many finals amount to little more than two giants hugging and leaning against each other for forty minutes and only really starting to wrestle during the final ten. By the third day of grappling under the broiling sun, most of the athletes are exhausted – wrung out – the sweat, grease and body fat dripping off them. During the breaks, the referees dole out bits of gauze for the men to daub their eyes, dispensing more than a kilometre of the stuff during the championships. It's a good thirty-five degrees in the shade – I'm sweating just sitting here in the press box – and judging from the smell, the heat and humidity have begun to turn the olive oil rancid. While finalists have been competing all day in various categories, the real glory is reserved for the heavyweight *başpehlivan,* or 'master wrestler', division.

Meanwhile, there's a bidding war echoing over the loud-speaker for The Most Expensive Sheep in the World – a jocular superlative that means nothing to little ol' citified me; I have no idea what the going rate is for a Turkish sheep (now, if you asked me about a Spanish *goat* . . .). By bidding for the animal, men are competing to be next year's Aga. Eventually, the auctioneer drives the price to 182,000 lire, just over £76,000.

Sold! – to the current Aga, a businessman from Anatolia.

But Aydemir's disgusted. 'Last year he paid 300,000!' he exclaims, making no attempt to hide his dislike for the pint-sized figure in the VIP box. 'Maybe it's because I cannot accept that such a stupid Anatolian can come here and become Aga of our tradition.' To be fair, though, the man will probably end up spending much more than 182,000 lire, and his knockout bid last year was reportedly triple the previous amount, so he's probably still paying above average. Also, it's not as if any rich locals were fighting to outbid him. What irks Aydemir is the man's comportment. Agas are supposed to be dignified, he says; this guy wouldn't recognise Dignity if it were wearing a fez and riding a camel. In his fancy-dress Otto-wear, the Aga's been hamming it up and strutting around in shiny black boots that make him look even shorter than he is.

While two wrestlers are still slogging it out in the semi-final, the Aga grabs the microphone and starts gabbling in an increasingly high-pitched voice over the loudspeaker, virtually hyperventilating with happiness: *Thankyouthankyouthankyou!* and pledging all sorts of things to make next year the best competition ever.

Aydemir frowns. 'It's not really clear what he's saying. He's making a real show, though. He's forcing himself to speak with an Anatolian accent. He can probably speak like me, with an Istanbul accent, but I'll bet he's putting it on. He's like a kid. I think the crowd might boo him,' he adds hopefully.

But my friend's definitely in the minority. The band hustles over to the Aga to *zurn* in his honour as he's carried around the field on people's shoulders, waving and cheesing to the crowd, who respond in kind – though many of them are probably hoping in vain that he'll repeat last year's stunt and scatter handfuls of banknotes in the air.

At some point, amid all this commotion, a wrestler named Şaban Yilmaz trumps his opponent to compete for the title of *başpehlivan* in an hour's time.

Meanwhile, Aydemir informs me that we are in the presence of a living legend right here in the press box, the former champion who's been immortalised this year with his very own statue outside the stadium, alongside the larger-than-life figures from the Golden Age of Oil Wrestling.

Rather than posing heroically like his statue, at this moment Ahmet Tasci is crammed into a plastic seat in his *kisbet*, wearing what looks like a hotel towel around his neck. He's hunched over a clipboard signing a form certifying that he's given the officials a post-match urine sample. This is particularly poignant in his case – not the peeing per se (though it's surprising the wrestlers have any moisture left, let alone enough to urinate on demand) but the fact that he's had to battle in the past to beat false allegations of doping. In 2000, he was stripped of his ninth title for allegedly testing positive for a banned substance. He appealed and won – Aydemir reckons someone had switched his urine sample. Tasci was vindicated, but the scandal interrupted his winning streak and possibly cost him his third gold Kirkpinar belt. As it is, Tasci is the only man to have won two gold Kirkpinar belts: *başpehlivans* who notch up three consecutive victories get to keep the 1.4-kilo belt, worth around £12,000. He also competed in the Sumo Wrestling World Championship in Japan and won third place in 1995. Now forty-five, he's well past his prime, but he's still built like a minotaur, with a bull-like head, neck and shoulders balanced atop a squat, beefy frame and pneumatic calves the size of softballs. Sweat is dripping down his nose, and one of his ears is practically swollen shut, the cartilage ballooned with blood and fluid.

I'm not going to say a *word* about the hotel towel.

Instead, we ask him his view on the younger generation of wrestlers. 'Their condition is lower,' he says thoughtfully. 'I'm half as fit as I used to be, but I made it to one of the final rounds. And I'm old. If they were in good condition, I wouldn't have almost made it into the final eight.'

'So are you worried about the future of the sport?'

He grimaces. 'We need a star.'

'Like you?'

'No, no, not me,' he avers, with a humility that would have

been unheard of in his prime. 'I am not a star.' Nowadays, he says, a lot of men win the *başpehlivan* for one year, but they aren't able to keep it. 'Training alone isn't enough to be a star. You need to have patience and the will to win.'

Aydemir thanks Tasci for his time with a traditional show of respect, urging me to do the same – 'Kiss his hand! Kiss his hand!' – but I beg off as politely as possible. I barely know the man, and I dread to think where that hand's been.

Down below, a couple of middleweight Oil Wrestlers are still locked in hand-to-hand combat, though hardly anyone's watching. The real focus is the upcoming heavyweight final between Şaban Yilmaz and Ekrem Yavuz. The latter is first out on the field, but despite repeated summonses over the loudspeaker, Şaban is AWOL.

The crowd starts to whistle and boo.

After at least ten minutes, Şaban finally emerges from the wrestlers' tunnel, surrounded by a retinue of cheering fans. The rest of the audience is still pelting him with scorn, but he simply ignores the hecklers and upstages his rival. Of course, Ekrem is no fifty-pound weakling, but from a distance, the most noticeable thing about him is his coat of all-over body fur – I would call him a bear of a man, but I wouldn't want it to be misconstrued. Şaban, in contrast, exudes physical charisma. For someone who regularly gets clobbered on the head, he's photogenic enough, and the rest of him is like a statue made flesh; *David* come down from his pedestal. The guy must bathe in testosterone. He's probably not much taller than me, but his muscles are denser to the nth; magnified by at least a factor of three. And by swanning in at the last minute, he's made his rival look like a shmuck, an over-eager amateur rather than the conscientious athlete that he is. Even now, having arrived late, Şaban's taking his time.

He's sitting on the grass, cinching up his *kisbet* and giving an interview to some guy with a microphone. The drum-and-*zurna* band has filed onto the back of the field for the *peshrev*, and both men start parading back and forth across the field for the ritual dance. Again, though, Şaban milks it, wading through the musicians to wave to his supporters, seemingly oblivious to the boos and whistles. *We need a star*, Tasci had said. And in Şaban, it seems, a star is born.

If only he'd wrestle. Like a lot of would-be celebrity athletes, he keeps half an eye on the grandstand, concentrating as much on his image as the match itself. Most of the final consists of Şaban and Ekrem circling in a headlock and leaning against each other. Every so often, to liven things up, Şaban will bash Ekrem around the head, spraying the air with sweat and grease. When Ekrem slaps him back in much the same way, Şaban huffs to the judges, pretending that he's been punched. Ekrem, however, is an old-fashioned sportsman, a workhorse who baulks only when his opponent palms his skull and just happens to smudge his fingers all over his face, including his eyes. But of course Şaban isn't gouging him intentionally; his hand slipped: *it's the oil, innit?*

The whistles are raining down like ice water.

'This is too boring,' Aydemir says with a frown.

An old-timer next to us laughs. 'We'll fall asleep!'

As the stadium's shadows encroach on the field, the bout moves into overtime. The band is doing its best to ratchet up the tension, but the main drama so far has come from the ref, who's been dishing out penalties in a vain attempt to get the men to fight. During the last ten minutes, he evens it up to 2–2. One more strike, and the match is over. After all the hoopla, it looks like Kirkpinar will be decided on points.

With just a minute left, though, Şaban lunges at Ekrem, grabbing the calf of his *kisbet* and lifting his leg so that he has to hop backwards. It's no use: Şaban follows through and dumps him on his backside.

The ref doesn't look convinced; he's staring up at the tribunal – did Ekrem's back really hit the ground? – but Şaban is already off and sprinting around the field, claiming victory. For their part, the spectators are so relieved to see some action they cheer ecstatically as Şaban skids around on his knees and pumps his fists in the air. His portable fanbase hoists him on its shoulders for a celebratory lap, and a woman in a shawl invades the pitch. Apart from a few female photographers, Şaban's mother is the only woman on The Men's Field. The champ jumps down and runs to greet her, throwing his arms open for a Hollywood embrace that will soon be beamed around the country in slow motion on the national news. The reporters clamour around as the crush carries him towards the winner's platform. Clutching his mother to his side, Şaban pays tribute to his supporters, his sponsors and his parents. 'And I'd like to give special thanks to my fiancée!' he gushes. Turkey's new Oil Wrestling champion may be a mama's boy, but make no mistake: he's a man's man.

OUR PATRON OF PILES AND PENISES

HAILING BLOOD, DEATH AND PHALLUSES IN ITALY, SPAIN AND PORTUGAL

PART ONE:

IS THAT A PASTRY IN YOUR POCKET . . . ?

Call me a sceptic, but I've never had much faith in academics who explain away ancient mysteries with vague theories about religion and sex magic. However, even I'm not so hard-headed as to dismiss a big, fat fertility symbol when it's staring me in the face, particularly a freshly baked, three-foot-long penis cake dripping with white goo.

Actually, it's more like a thick stick of bread, but its shape – testicles intact – is unmistakable. In fact, the words 'penis' and 'phallus' are far too prim to describe it; it's a dick . . . a cock . . . a *schlong* – a priapic pastry that puts the 'dough' into dildo – apparently the product of some X-rated bakery that also specialises in vagina tarts, sphincter doughnuts and buttock-shaped cinnamon buns. It's the kind of image you'd expect to see scrawled on a toilet stall, not baked and sold as a delicacy at a religious festival in a country as deeply conservative as Portugal.

As you'll have gathered by now (if you didn't suspect it already), many of Europe's most venerably surreal events have been perpetuated by religion, itself a bastion of human idiosyncrasy. Whether acknowledged or not, thousands of celebrations across the Continent (and the UK) commemorate the miraculous feats of saints and prophets. Whereas people once automatically attributed the inexplicable to God, it's only relatively recently that we've begun to assume that sooner or later, all things great and small will be explained by Science, the modern god. Even so, millions of people still believe in divine intervention.

Take Portugal's São Gonçalo, a saint who can supposedly cure whatever ails you, though the payback can be a bit embarrassing, to say the least. Gonçalo is also renowned as a marrying – and partying – saint: he's specifically associated with phalluses . . . and fish. On the first weekend of June, the romantic town of Amarante, less than an hour from Porto, throws a festival in his honour, with people strewing red carnations in the plaza to thank St Gonzalo for delivering them from illness. At the same time, so the guidebooks say, young swains woo their loved ones by presenting them with pastries known as *Doces Fálicos* – Phallic Sweets.

Now, you could view this as a refreshingly candid celebration of lovemaking, a relic of prehistoric sexual liberation before the uptight Christians took over. As the father of two daughters, though, I can say that any suitor who offered them a pastry in the shape of a penis could expect to have it stuffed somewhere that would make him question his own sexuality. It's ironic, too, that if you were to approach your average priest today and say, 'We're holding a street party for Saint So-and-So and, as part of it, we're going to sell giant edible penises,' he'd probably condemn you to hell on the spot. Even if they did sell like hotcakes.

But the surprisingly young priest at the Church of São Gonçalo relishes his namesake's earthy image. Father Ferreira Lopez comes from one of the countless villages in the area with a chapel dedicated to the saint, and his family has always called him by his second name, Gonçalo. At thirty-nine, he still has a youthful countenance, accentuated by some extra pound-age that's a testament to Portuguese gastronomy; there's such an abundance of good food in the north that most locals simply don't have big enough bodies to hang it on. It could be all the grilled meats and rich stews and seafood dishes drenched in garlic and olive oil, balanced with the sharp tang of the local *vinho verde* and followed by creamy desserts and pastries, topped off with strong coffee and *digestifs* of port. But I reckon the people of Amarante suffer from the same run-of-the-mill ills as the rest of us; the difference is the way they deal with them. The very respectable store just across the plaza from the Church of São Gonçalo, right next to the Café de São Gonçalo, sells newspapers, books, games and magazines such as *Vogue* and a Portuguese title outlining Fifteen Steps to Orgasm – after the first dozen, who's counting? – plus make-up, perfume, jewellery, an array of icons and . . . wax body parts. The four shelves of a glass-and-wood cabinet are stacked with hollow, disembodied arms, legs, hands and heads, as well as hearts, kidneys, intestines and breasts, alongside full-body figurines of men, women and children, all of them moulded from a yellowish-brown wax that's close enough to flesh-coloured to give me the creeps. It's a display that wouldn't look out of place in a voodoo shop. Here, though, instead of curses for their enemies, the faithful come in search of cures for their loved ones. For anything from £1.70 for a wax kidney to £4.00 for a child's effigy, they buy a replica of affliction and place it in the church, in the window of the crypt where St Gonzalo lies.

The red-domed sanctuary of São Gonçalo guards the heart of Amarante, towering over the stone bridge across the gorge of the river Támega. For me, Amarante is one of the real 'finds' of Europe, a place where I've arrived without knowing what to expect and immediately found myself overwhelmed by the beauty of the place and the warmth of the people. I could go on and on about Amarante: the riverside cafés and restaurant terraces overhanging the water, the blue-and-white tiles adorning the stone monuments, the terraced banks planted with vineyards, the cobbled lovers' walk and leafy trees tracing the river and the red tile roofs of the houses bleached white by the early summer sun. And then, of course, there's the centre of festivities this weekend: the cosy plaza tucked into the small triangle between the riverfront and the church.

Not wanting to be rude – even though I'm the one who's turned up unannounced – Father Gonçalo is giving me an impromptu tour of the church. He apologises that he can't take longer, but this is one of his busiest weekends of the year. The sanctuary's towering altarpiece is so dense with decoration, so heavy with gold and other precious metals that it's a wonder the church hasn't sunk into the riverbed. The walk-on, four-storey altar-stage houses life-sized statues of saints and contains two roofed tableaux supported by thick, twisted gold columns. These mini-temples frame a wind-down painting of St Gonzalo on bended knee, borne aloft by angels bearing red carnations as he beseeches Mary on behalf of us sinners. That's just one of at least half a dozen images of the church's namesake in the sanctuary compared to just a few crucified Christs, a token Santiago de Compostela (Amarante was a stopover on the Portuguese leg of the pilgrimage) and St Gonzalo's southern rival, St Anthony of Lisbon, who's relegated to the back.

The favourite saint of the north, in contrast, enjoys pride of place at the front of the sanctuary, with two chapels on the ground-floor level of the altar-juggernaut. The nook on the right is a little white-walled room containing a statue of the resurrected saint, plus some old paintings of his miracles, while the dark cranny on the left is actually the saint's crypt. Flowery Portuguese tilework grows around the lower half of the room, surmounted by fading wood panels and an embossed ceiling, with a blackened oil painting and small altar at the end framed by two vases of carnations and a plastic box of burning votive candles. The only natural light comes from a mullioned half-window where the sick and suffering place their grisly wax replicas. Gonçalo's life-sized effigy lies on a plinth in the centre, identifiable by his black Dominican robes, hooked pilgrim's staff and red itinerant preacher's book. Much of his painted plaster 'skin' has been worn away, his forehead rubbed smooth and white and his chin and cheekbones reduced to coarse, grey stone, corroded by the chemicals on people's hands over the centuries: an acid bath of love and affection.

Dressed in a short-sleeved shirt, Father Gonçalo leans proprietarily across the statue of his namesake saint. 'This is where people come to seek healing from the saint. So if your head hurts, you rub his forehead' – Gonçalo gives Gonçalo a rub on the noggin – 'and if your hand hurts, you rub his hand' – he kisses the eroded fingers. 'The tradition is that you rub or kiss the affected part of the body.'

Presumably if you're suffering from haemorrhoids, you're flat out of luck.

'People also leave effigies of body parts in the window: arms, legs – even vaginas, penises and testicles,' the priest continues, patting the stone windowsill.

I didn't see any of the latter on sale in the bookstore, but maybe tallow genitalia are strictly top-shelf, only-on-request material.

'And many people believe the saint has cured them.'

'Do you believe it?'

Father Gonçalo blows a long sigh, as if to say, *In a word, no.* Or, more likely, *Even if I do, I'm not going to risk being portrayed as a superstitious hick priest by a writer from London who I've only just met and who's probably agnostic anyway (aren't they all?).* So he gives me a qualified answer that's broadly affirmative, mentioning scientific studies that suggest having some form of religious belief can help cure illnesses. 'We know that many cures are psychological. It's difficult to say whether something is a miracle or a coincidence. The important thing is that people need faith. They can't live . . . they can't live by bread alone.'

Having vaulted that neatly – even finishing with a quote from Christ – he confirms the bare bones of Gonçalo's life: born around 1187 near Amarante, the future saint was among the first to join the newly established order of Dominican monks, the Friar Preachers who travelled around in their distinctive black robes and tonsures, embracing poverty and denouncing heresy. Having built the bridge at Amarante – and performed a piscine miracle that established him as a fisherman's friend – Gonçalo left the running of the church to his nephew while he went on a pilgrimage to the Holy Land. By the time he returned years later, his dissolute nephew refused to recognise him, and Gonçalo spent the last years of his life wandering around northern Portugal preaching the Gospel. Legend has it that he died at the doors of the old church on this site around 1259.

The Portuguese soon began to commemorate his saint's day on 10 January, and Gonçalo eventually gained a bit of a reputation as a musician, boozehound and even a consort of prostitutes: in short, a patron of wine, women and song – a development that no doubt would have horrified the evangelical friar. 'We can assume that the people attributed these qualities to Gonçalo and used it as a justification for the things that the peasants themselves were doing, saying, "The saint also did it, so it's all right for me as well." It's all part of the process of humanisation of the saint,' Father Gonçalo says. 'The liturgy of the Church has always been something dry and remote, and saints like Gonçalo humanise it.'

By the late sixteenth century, Gonçalo had become so popular the Dominicans built the new-improved sanctuary and an adjoining convent to receive all the pilgrims who came to pay their respects, particularly as he came to be known as *un santo casamenteiro*: a marrying saint. Father Gonçalo leads me to the cloisters next door and the room where he changes into his vestments before Mass. Overhead on a ledge in the corner is another effigy of Gonçalo, a gormless torso that dates from the fourteenth century: 'the oldest image we have of the saint'. A long, pale linen sash hangs down the front of the mannequin – an innovation that allowed crowds to touch the hem of the saint's garment without tearing off the effigy's clothes when it was being processed through the streets. Today, the cord serves another purpose. Women who are desperate to get married come here and have a quiet word with the saint. After tugging on the cord three times, the story goes, they're sure to snag a husband within a year.

No doubt some cod-psychologists would project deep sexual significance onto the act of pulling a saint's tail. But Gonçalo's posthumous fame as a matchmaker, with an emphasis on old maids, may simply stem from a misunderstanding. A village just outside Amarante is called Ovelha, and when outsiders heard tales of the local marrying saint, they may have misheard the name as *velha*, or 'old woman'. Legend has it that the original spinster was 'as poor as Job and as ugly as Medusa'. However, Father Gonçalo reckons this aspect of the saint's legend stems from Portugal's former colony across the Atlantic. 'I think it has more to do with life in Brazil. The cult of São Gonçalo is huge there. Brazilians have always had a reputation for being happy and carefree, and the Portuguese who returned here probably brought back the story of the marrying saint.'

And the rest. The Brazilians embellished the saint's legend so that he became famous for singing and dancing with prostitutes – purely to convert them, of course; the saint wore nails inside his shoes to keep from falling into temptation. Brazilians still show their gratitude to the saint by doing the *Dança de São Gonçalo* in his honour, a performance that can be spiritual or sensual – or downright surreal. In the version performed in the colonial town of Laranjeiras in the north-east of Brazil, eight men dress up as female prostitutes and dance while a lone woman called 'Butterfly' totes the saint's icon around in a little boat. Interestingly, Gonçalo's devotees in Amarante also used to dance around his effigy in the crypt before officials finally put a stop to it in the nineteenth century.

'But the Church hasn't been able to control the saint's cult completely,' Father Gonçalo notes, citing the Phallic Cakes, which are also found in some parts of north-eastern Brazil. He thinks the pastries originally had something to do with a pagan fertility cult practised by the Celtic tribes who occupied this part of Portugal and Galicia, north of the border. Alternatively, they might be related to the Roman fertility festival of Saturnalia that took place in midwinter, around the same time as Gonçalo's saint's day. 'We know that many elements of the Church are Christianisations of pagan cults.'

The snag is that Gonçalo's fame as a patron saint of fertility didn't develop until the eighteenth century, more than a thousand years after the Celts and Romans had been Christianised. In fact, Gonçalo's revamp coincided with the Counter-Reformation, when the Dominicans served as the enforcers of the Inquisition.

If anything, I would have expected the Counter-Reformation to try to stamp out the carnal aspects of the saint's cult.

'The Church has always tried to purify the cult, but it doesn't work,' Father Gonçalo says. 'It's not always possible to separate the religious from the profane. Faith doesn't exist in the abstract; it's always part of a culture.' As the defenders of orthodoxy, it also suited the Dominicans to have a popular saint among their ranks, especially one who was on intimate terms with the masses thanks to his sexual associations. 'People can open up and share their intimate lives with him. It's easier to relate to São Gonçalo than to a very remote saint up in heaven. He's a down-to-earth saint.'

*

224

Still, padre – have you *seen* the size of those pastries? As with flesh-and-blood models, pastry penises come in a range of shapes and sizes, from the aforementioned phallus of elephantine proportions to the more modestly (dare I say realistically) endowed, from little wee shooters to cannon-sized jobs that must hold a good pint of icing.

If the Phallic Sweets are pagan in origin, though, you would expect them to be more widespread. Of course, the fact that penis cakes are edible would make it that much harder to find archaeological evidence, but there should at least be some historical record to bridge the thousand-year gap in the pagan-to-Christian chronology. As it is, Amarante seems to be the only place to have cooked up phallic pastries, creating scope for a unique slogan: 'Come to Amarante: Home of the Penis Cake!'

To my mind, the best theory for Gonçalo's sex-god status has to do with Portugal's imperial decline. In the eighteenth century, the Portuguese empire stretched from Asia to Africa and South America. But the Portuguese found it difficult to compete against the Spanish, French and English because they simply couldn't produce enough people to defend their interests overseas. As a result, it's probably no coincidence that St Anthony of Lisbon – the only Portuguese saint more beloved than Gonçalo – is also famous for matchmaking. Although critics often caricature the Church as being opposed to sex, the reality is that Catholicism is all for it – provided it takes place within marriage and produces results, in accordance with the biblical diktat: 'go forth and multiply'. Whereas we tend to view sex as being about love and pleasure, for our ancestors, it was just as importantly a means to an end. A minuscule elite did have the resources to indulge in the pleasures of the flesh without fear of the consequences, but for the overall population, the purpose of sex was to create children to farm fields and fight wars. So having an annual Phallus Festival might have been a form of rustic sex education, with edible sex aids, at a time when manuals weren't easily to hand.

Alternatively, I reckon the anatomical breadsticks could just as easily have started out as a joke by a local baker. *Amarantinos* have long been more outrageous than most in their phallic obsession. Until 1809, the sacristy that now houses São Gonçalo of the Long Tail used to contain a couple of Eastern devils brought back from India by Portuguese adventurers. Despite the statues' pagan origins and obviously sexual characteristics, it's said the monks used them as fear-of-God props to scare confessions (and tithes) out of people. When Napoleon's troops invaded, they burnt them along with the church's Catholic trappings; after the French reverted to retreat mode, though, the Dominicans commissioned an artist to sculpt two new horned devils, supposedly with sexy features intact. However, King Pedro V was deeply unamused by the sight of a couple of horny black devils and ordered the monks to put them away. In 1870, the archbishop went even further and demanded that the sacrileges be destroyed. Instead, the head of the convent had the he-devil castrated.

And here's where the story turns even stranger, thanks to a visit by an English tycoon. 'Alberto' Sandeman promptly bought the devils to publicise his family's port-wine empire – there's still a Sandeman's port lodge in Porto. Despite official protests in Portugal, Sandeman exported the devils to his headquarters in London and exhibited them at the World Expo in Paris in 1889. However, the Portuguese never gave up the fight for their satanic sex symbols. Eventually, Sandeman agreed to return them, and upon their arrival back home in

Amarante, the he-devil and she-devil were received with speeches and a triumphant parade.

Today, it's hard to see what all the fuss was about. The *Diabos de Amarante* sit side by side, tucked away on an upper floor of the convent that has been converted into a sleek art gallery. The black devils stand about three feet high, with horns and thick red lips. The male is topless and the female is spilling out of her dress, but that's about as risqué as it gets. If it's true that the he-devil was mutilated – I reckon it may be a case of misunderstood euphemisms – I can't for the life of me work out where his phallus went. Unless it slotted into that crack in the wood there . . .

The other thing I'm dying to know is whether, as the guidebooks claim, Portuguese men actually get away with exposing their deepest desires to women by giving them a Phallic Sweet. And if they do, what's the etiquette of presenting someone with a penis cake? Would you try to impress a girl by buying the biggest one you could find? Or would you purchase a tiddler so as not to be upstaged by a pastry?

I've made a date to meet an *amarantina* who works in the communications department of the ultra-modern town hall next door. Célia Azevedo is a sweet twentysomething with short, dark hair who speaks good enough English to fill in the gaps in my Spani-guese. She loads me up with books, pamphlets and magazines about the area, as well as a list of culinary delights, including *Bolos de São Gonçalo*.

I wouldn't be the first foreigner to mistranslate these as St Gonzalo's Balls, but *bolo* means 'cake' in Portuguese, and there's nothing sexual about *Bolos de São Gonçalo*, even if they are small, round and consist of eggs.

'You can find St Gonçalo's Cakes all year round, but you only see the *Doce Fálico* at this time of year,' Célia explains. 'And some of them are really big! Like this—'

She measures an imaginary footlong with her hands.

I shrivel to think. We've only just met, but I have to ask.

'What's it taste like?'

'You know,' she smiles, 'I have never had it in my mouth.'

Years of newsroom banter come cackling to mind, but I bite my tongue.

'Really? Why's that?'

'People say it is very . . . how do you say it? *Duro?*'

Oh, God. 'Hard? Surely that's the point.'

Her face glows red and she laughs, blushing too much to talk. Nevertheless, she agrees to meet me later for a quick drink on the terrace of the Confeitaria da Ponte, with its view to the bridge, the church and the paddleboats on the river.

I ask Célia if it's true lovers exchange Phallic Sweets as tokens of affection. She looks at me as if I've just informed her that *amarantinos* are actually Martians.

'Maybe people coming from out of town, they buy it and take it home to their families because it's traditional or they think it's funny, but if a boyfriend gave me one of those, I wouldn't think it was funny at all!' She laughs. 'Everybody knows about it, it's a tradition. But it's not important, certainly not for my generation.'

Nor her parents', it seems.

'It's something that you see only at this time of year, and the people who've tried it have told me that it's not very good.'

I might as well jump in the river.

'And what about São Gonçalo being a marrying saint?'

She brightens, happy to tell me something I want to hear.

'Oh, that – yes. Sooner or later, most women go to pull on the saint's cord. And I'm one of them!'

'So how often do you go?'

'Oh, only once.' She blinks, as if to add, *I'm not desperate.*

Célia has to photograph the children's parade this evening, and I take a stroll through the streetmarket along the river, past a kerbside condom machine outside one of the pharmacies, until I find a stall selling *Bolos de Amor*. The woman selling them is sheathing a mound of iced, white-bread willies in plastic wrap, positioning one vertically so that they literally make a tent, with a red laundry peg attached to the tip. As I approach to buy one, the peg pops off.

Not sure if that's a good omen or not.

I plump for a thick eight-incher, and she charges me five euros – the going rate for a wax head, by the way – though I think that included the price of the photo. For a woman who earns her daily bread from dough dildos, she didn't seem overly pleased to pose with one (funny, that), pinching it at the tip and holding it at arm's length. She puts my iced phallus in a bag so I can sample it in the privacy of my hotel room.

No sooner have I purchased my phallus, though, than I'm hit with a bad case of penis envy. The vendor across the way tells me I could've bought an eigh*teen*-incher from her for the same price.

I've been screwed.

On the way up to my room, I ask the girl at the desk the old chestnut about penis-swapping. 'I read that couples exchange *Doces Fálicos* . . .'

'*Sí.*' She smiles and starts chatting in Portuguese about São Gonçalo while jerking her fist up and down in the air.

I do a doubletake. *Surely they don't wank the blessed pastry!*

But she's talking about the saint's sash, and how you have to yank it to find a man. 'And some say it works, too. I know a girl who came here from Porto, and she went in and pulled the saint's cord three times one year, and the following year she came back and she was married!'

'Have you done it, too?'

'No. I don't believe in it.'

'And what about the *Doce Fálico*?' – I'm not gonna let this go.

'I've already bought mine this year!' she beams, explaining that she buys it for her family and they eat it just as they would any other type of pastry. There's no sense of ceremony; it's just a tradition at this time of the year.

'But I've read that lovers exchange it as a sign of love.'

She shrugs.

'I've never heard of that. There are so many legends surrounding Gonçalo that no one knows them all.' Unfailingly polite, she doesn't want to tell me I'm crazy. 'You've probably read more of the legends than I have.'

More likely, the books got it wrong.

In writing this book, I've faced some unusual predicaments: should I frolic with the Arse Blowers? Dare I grapple with an Oil Wrestler? And now: how do I go about sticking a pastry penis in my mouth?

Like the body part it's modelled after, the Phallic Sweet doesn't look particularly appetising, even smeared with icing. The underlying pastry is so dry it's cracked on the sides, and the whole thing has enough heft to it you could turn it around and use it as a hammer. In fact, this could be a leftover phallus from last year, and I couldn't tell.

Sitting on my bed, I reckon I've got three options: the head, the shaft or the testicles. Call me a prude, but I can't quite bring myself to lock my lips around the tip, much less suck off the icing. I suppose the macho approach would be to take a manly chomp out of the middle. But I'm feeling a bit adventurous, so I do what in retrospect is probably the most dubious thing possible: I nibble the invisible doughboy's balls.

One bite's enough for me. It tastes like month-old white bread coated with sugar. The hard truth, it seems, is that baked genitalia are best enjoyed if you've grown up sucking on them all your life.

On TV, a man with sculpted eyebrows is promising that we're about to see 'The Most Polemical Programme in Portugal!' *Faithful or Unfaithful: The Test of Infidelity* mixes entrapment with the routine exploitation of reality TV. A ponytailed guy named Gonçalo (honest) 'wants to take his relationship with his girlfriend further'. God knows what that entails in his case: probably some light petting.

Our hero is stooped in front of a studio audience that's watching him both in the flesh and on split-screen so they can see every twitch of pain in close-up as his snaggletoothed girlfriend, an estate agent, shows a 'prospective client' around a mansion. The actor is billed as 'a powerful, rich, handsome, successful man' – by implication, everything that Gonçalo is not. This is a wild guess – I'll bet you didn't see this coming – but I reckon *The Test of Infidelity* involves Sr Suave making a pass at poor, unwitting Irini. Will she slap him or shag him? Will Gonçalo get to first base with Irini or get a gun and kill her before turning it on himself? Is hell deep enough and hot enough to incinerate all the makers of this trash?

After a long day of bollocks, I drift off before finding out, wondering if I should throw the sugar-frosted dildo out of the window in case I die in my sleep.

*

Amarante's *Festas de Junho* are three days of street fairs, religious processions, kiddies' parades, night drumming, fireworks, open-air concerts and samba, sermons and pop music echoing through the warm but cool early-summer air. The spiritual high point comes on Sunday afternoon, when the statue of São Gonçalo is paraded onto the plaza amid the throngs of Amarante, and Father Gonçalo and the choristers stand on the balcony at the top of the church, raining down red carnations on their patron saint. As picturesque as this is, the reason for their choice of flower is less appealing. In Portuguese, the word for 'carnation' – *cravo* – can also mean 'wart', the clustered petals looking not unlike the variegated flesh of a particularly nasty verruca.

And if Gonçalo can cure warts, why not acne and haemorrhoids? Two hours south of Amarante, villagers have an unorthodox cure for these afflictions: dropping their trousers in front of the saint. The village of Bunheiro, near the beach resort of Torreira, supposedly has a population of three thousand, but that must be counting every last cow and chicken. Driving into town, I pass as many tractors as cars, plus a few overstuffed hayricks and even a woman balancing a sack of grain on her head. The sea air from the Atlantic wrestles with the rich smell of manure from the fields planted right in town; a farmhouse with cattle out back is the next-door neighbour of the main church. And down the street is a small white building with a scalloped façade: the Chapel of São Gonçalo.

Inside, the saint's icon occupies the central alcove above the altar. Appropriately enough, his painted face – all wide eyes and raised eyebrows – looks vaguely shocked, as if, well, as if someone's just flashed their arse at him.

'People here say the saint is naughty – a prankster,' laughs António Amador, a spry, lively man who likes a joke himself. 'They say he *likes* to see backsides!'

In other words, round these parts, São Gonçalo is a bit of a dirty bugger. Strangely, though, Bunheiro doesn't have a tradition of *Doces Fálicos*. Like most places in the area, it celebrates Gonçalo's saint's day in January, but Dr Amador has opened the chapel out of season so I can see the saint for myself. A member of the church committee, he's also a physician, so he's the perfect person to clear up a burning question for me: what is it with the Portuguese and warts? How common are verrucas – not to mention piles and acne – that they have a saint devoted to their eradication?

He laughs. 'It used to be very common to get warts because people used to walk around barefoot all the time.' Dr Amador explains how the 'cure' works: the afflicted promise the saint that if they're healed, they'll then go to the chapel and drop their trousers out of gratitude. Back in the day, the chapel used to get hundreds of sufferers baring their butts in public; now it's more like eighty to a hundred per year.

Pardon the pun, but this seems arse-about-face. Surely believers should show their faith first, then wait for God to cure them.

The good doctor shakes his head waggishly. 'People say to the saint, "I'll give, but you give first." It's the same with Fatima' – the famous Marian shrine ninety miles south of here – 'people say, "I'll walk to Fatima on my knees or whatever, if God cures me first." If God doesn't cure them, they won't do it!' He cackles with delight. 'But people also say São Gonçalo's vengeful. If he cures a wart, and you don't fulfil your vow, he'll put it back in the same place it was!'

As vows go, I could think of easier ones to live up to. During the *Festa de São Gonçalinho* in the nearby town of Aveiro, people who've had their wishes granted by 'Gonzalito' stand on the church and throw bread to the crowd. Something similar happens here, Dr Amador says: people throw carnations or candy. 'But one of the other things that people do is come and show their *rabo*' – or tail – 'to the saint.'

He jumps up and darts into the sacristy. 'There's also a little icon in here. I can't find it now, it's about this high' – ten inches – 'and if people are too embarrassed to show their *rabo* in public, they can go into the back room with the icon. Otherwise, sometimes people will ask the congregation during Mass, "Could everyone go out, please, I need to show my butt to the saint."

'But other times,' he continues, 'there are too many people here for them to all go out, so they just drop their trousers quickly.'

'And what does the rest of the congregation do?'

'Oh, they laugh. I was here not long ago and a fifteen-year-old boy, a kid, announced that he had promised to show his penis to the saint if he cured a wart. He was so embarrassed, I couldn't help but laugh.'

The current priest also sees the joke: 'It's a tradition of the people here. It's a belief of the people' – but one of his predecessors didn't view it as a laughing matter, Dr Amador says. 'He was a little conservative. He wouldn't let people come in and show their backsides to the saint.' Some time ago, a woman who was covered in warts – or was it acne? – asked the priest if she could pray stark naked inside the sanctuary. He refused, so she wrapped herself in a sheet and stood outside.

'So as a doctor, do you think Gonçalo can cure warts?'

He leans back in his chair and grins. 'I think it's a superstition. People put it into their heads that the saint cures them. But we do know that warts are caused by a virus – a very weak one – and if you're strong mentally, it probably helps defeat the virus.'

PART TWO:
DAY OF THE LIVING DEAD

The principle of divine quid pro quo is also alive and well north of Portugal, in the Spanish province of Galicia. Folks in the backwoods village of San Xosé de Ribarteme believe that St Martha, the hard-working sister of Lazarus, can bring the dead back to life – or, more accurately, bring the living back from the brink of death. After all, it was while talking to Martha that Jesus declared: 'I am the resurrection and the life. He that believeth in me, though he were dead, yet shall he live.' So on her feast day – 29 July – this mountain hamlet hosts a very special event known as the Festival of the Near-Death Experience or simply the Procession of Rigor Mortis. Thankfully, this doesn't involve a bunch of stiffs testifying about tunnels of light; what it *does* involve is truly unique. People who've had a near-miss – a real life-or-death illness or accident – give thanks by donning a funeral shroud and lying in an open casket to be carried around the village in the annual Procession of the Coffins.

Now, leaving aside the everlasting logic-buster – why do religious folks pray to be spared death when they've got heaven waiting on the other side? – most people at some point make a wits-end supplication to the Supreme Being: 'Dear God, I don't know if you're up there/I've never been very religious (the modern yadda yadda), but if You help me pass this exam/cure my father/get me out of this mess/save me from alcohol poisoning/don't let me me die in Orkney (maybe that's just me), I promise I'll study hard next time/be a dutiful son/clean up my act/stop drinking/never fly in a toy plane over the North Sea again.' However, it wouldn't occur to most people to make a vow like 'Dear God, if You spare my life, I'll play dead and go coffin-surfing in Your honour.'

Then again, like Gonzalo, perhaps the Iberian God has a more colourful sense of humour. Rather than sombre spiritual undertakings, many *promesas* have all the fun of a dare between friends: *Sure, I'll cure your warts,* St Gonzalo says, *but then – I wanna see your ass.* And no matter how difficult or embarrassing the payback, at least it's fixed and finite. What's more, it must allow you to bank some credit in heaven: it's the kind of penance you should be able to sin off for a long time.

However, the woman at the Spanish tourist office – an hour away in Pontevedra – bristles at any association between death and Galicia. 'I'm sure the festival is very pretty, very folkloric, but it's an old-fashioned image of Galicia compared to the one we want to promote.' In truth, not all locals are that keen on the tradition, either. I'm staying a few kilometres down the mountain, and the newsagent confesses that she's never been to the procession. 'It gives me the creeps. A couple of years ago, a young man rode inside one of the coffins, but' – she stifles a giggle – 'it was so hot, he . . . he got ill.'

Which isn't that uncommon, according to one of the pallbearers. 'People have to be careful, because it's a short procession, it doesn't go very far, but it moves slowly, so they could be in the coffin for an hour.'

It's mercifully cool this year, thanks to the showers of the past few days, but every so often the sun comes out to remind us of its power. Even at the height of summer, this corner of the Iberian peninsula is an open-air greenhouse, as lush and green as other parts of Spain are dry and golden. Everywhere along the hills and valleys, something is growing: if not trees or grapevines, then ferns, grass or fields. Any human infringements – roads, houses and stone walls – are merely temporary.

The tiny hamlet that's home to the Coffin Procession is named after St Joseph, but its heart belongs to St Martha. The Patroness of the Resurrected gets the biggest icon in the small, lichen-spattered Church of San Xosé, plus a newly carved statue across the street, where Martha is surrounded by flickering votive candles with a view to the souls who got away: the hillside cemetery of graves built above ground, the corpses stacked in stone filing cabinets.

By eleven a.m., the football pitch-turned-car park is already full, and two outdoor *pulperías* on the fairground are packed, though it's a bit early for me to be indulging in the traditional pleasures of boiled octopus. The scene outside the church is strikingly similar to that at the Miracle of the Snakes in Kefaloniá: the liturgy droning over the loudspeaker, the thickets of candles and souvenir icons and a beggar with a withered leg. A couple of street vendors are also selling wax effigies; compared to the store in Amarante, their body parts are a steal. Mind you, they don't have the overheads.

Inside the gate, next to a neglected tombstone and the lame man, a father and son are wearing white-mesh tunics over their clothes and standing guard with tall candles. Manuel Pereira tells me that twenty years ago, just after David was born, the doctors told him that a birth defect meant his son would never have the use of one arm. 'They told me it was impossible to cure.' But as soon as he started praying to St Martha for a cure, a miracle occurred. Today David is healthy and a head taller than his dad – and handsome to boot. Still, it's taken his dad nearly two decades to live up to his side of the Marthian bargain by walking as a penitent in the procession. The fact that he himself is now ill with a disease he'd rather not talk about doesn't have anything to do with it, he claims. 'Every year I just kept letting it go, but I decided we had to come eventually.'

As midday Mass draws to a close, a lidless, rectangular coffin with white lining materialises next to the door of the sanctuary.

But where's the corpse?

Time was when the event attracted a good number of living dead, but these days, you just can't get the zombies. The guy minding the coffin says there are about ten caskets in storage. The church doesn't actually rent them for the occasion, but donations are gratefully received.

With the nearly departed nowhere in sight, the procession begins with an impromptu near-death experience: *if we can't find a corpse, we'll make one instead.* The icon of St Joseph is first out of the church, followed by a five-foot statue of Mary holding the Infant Jesus, both wearing big starred crowns and carried by a squadron of women, including a girl in a navel-revealing T-shirt emblazoned with the words *'Female Team*: THE PENITENTS'. As the group tries to negotiate the turn coming out of the door, the litter begins to tilt, and suddenly the Queen of Heaven comes crashing down on a middle-aged lady on the sidelines who's not much taller than the statue itself. The icon knocks her back, but not out. She's standing there, rubbing the bump on her noggin where Baby Jesus clobbered her (even the Son of God could be a holy terror), as the other matrons huddle around her, clucking and squawking exclamations of the bloody-obvious variety:

'It's not tied on properly!'

'You have to balance it!'

Mary and Jesus are duly returned to their pedestal, but the Mother of God's crown is all wobbly. There's no way the Queen of the Universe can go around looking like that, so the icon is quietly retired to the back of the church.

Last out is the star of today's procession, the soulful statue of St Martha, her eyes rolled heavenward as she crushes the Devil underfoot. Meanwhile, a stout woman with short orange hair has stepped into the dark-wood coffin. She's wearing a striped blouse beneath a mesh burial shroud and a much less common accessory for corpses: sunglasses. Never mind the fold-up fan in her hands. The pallbearers lift her into horizontal position, and a half-dozen atonal mourners bring up the rear, praising Santa Marta and hitting the notes with all the delicacy of a hammer pounding nails.

As religious processions go, though, this one's refreshingly short, making a circuit around the village: along the stone-walled road where vendors are hawking traditional delicacies, up through the forest clearing to the fairground, past the shoot-'em-up games and fluffy toy prizes, the bars and octopus joints, and the bouncy castle with the ginormous head of Bart Simpson, down a pine-needle path fragrant with acacia and eucalyptus trees, and then back to the church. The priests, pallbearers and mourners give the procession all the appearances of a real funeral cortège, an illusion broken only when the 'deceased' lifts her arm to scratch her nose or shift her shades. Some of the followers in her wake are barefoot, and the expression on the spectators' faces as they peer inside the coffin is the visual definition of 'morbid curiosity', their features contorted by fear, revulsion and wonder – *What's she in for?* –

tempered by a glimpse of their own mortality and what their own funeral procession might look like. 'It makes the hairs on your arms stand on end,' a woman gasps. But just as quickly, the fear's gone, banished by a joke or a Sign of the Cross.

The pallbearers carry the living corpse around the churchyard, taunting death one last time by taking her through the corridor of filing-box tombs and then into the sanctuary, where they present her, upright, to the icon of St Martha. The woman steps from the casket, hugging her loved ones and weeping, drying her tears on her burial shroud. After keeping a respectful distance, I ask her why she rode in the coffin.

'My husband had open-heart surgery last November.'

'And he survived?'

'Sí, gracias a Dios.'

'So why didn't he come and lie in a coffin?'

'Because I was the one who made the promise to Santa Marta.'

Understandably, she doesn't want to go into the details, so I thank her and leave. It wasn't much of a chat, but it's more than you get out of most corpses.

PART THREE:
BLOOD AND *BACI*

On this leg of my journey, I've seen more relics than I care to remember, but so far, for all the deified bones, I've yet to see a bona fide miracle. For that, I need to go to Italy – specifically, Naples and the Festival of San Gennaro.

'Neapolitans are *crazy*,' warned an Italian friend. 'In Napoli, be careful crossing the street. A red light doesn't mean anything, in fact, drivers will *stop* at a green light because they know other drivers will drive through on red. And be careful of pickpockets. And don't buy anything on the street. Other than that – they've got good pizza.'

And countless superstitions. Considering the city's proximity to Pompeii, the 'Fields of Fire' and the intersection of Italy's two main seismic faults, you can't blame Neapolitans for trying to grab as much luck as they can. The key to understanding the city is all in its name, arguably more so than any other place I know. Forget 'Naples'; a prim Anglo moniker is far too genteel a term for the turbo-charged scrum that is *Napoli*, a city that would make Babel look like a pinnacle of law and order. Goethe famously declared that a man who'd seen Naples could never be sad; I'd say you leave the place just happy to be alive. It's no wonder that Neapolitans are crazy; in a catch-22 kind of way, it proves they're sane. There's no way you could live in such a nerve-shattering environment without going a bit *pazzo*, and you couldn't stay there if you weren't a little touched in the head – or gifted with some superhuman resistance. Neapolitans are born with *carpe diem* encoded into their very DNA. They seize the day by grabbing its lapels, giving it a good shake, rolling it over, picking its wallet and selling it back at a profit. With Vesuvius looming like a once-and-future tombstone, they're hell-bent on cramming every last bit of humanity into the moment, determined to die laughing, shouting, eating, drinking, dancing, singing, farting and fornicating. *Fanculo* to whimpers, these people are going out with a bang.

But – and it's a big one – if you can raise your head above the hubbub and gaze beyond the mazy rabble besieging you –

the kamikaze traffic, the dark eyes and gambolling curves, the scent of the sea and the fury of the shouty man who grabs you at the train station – if you can ignore all that, you'll soon realise that this is San Gennaro's town. The cathedral houses the bones of the fourth-century martyr, and his kindly visage smiles down on Napoli from countless pillars, churches and gates to protect the volatile city from wars, plagues, earthquakes and the fires of Vesuvius.

However, the most powerful protection comes from the saint's blood. At least twice a year – including the anniversary of the saint's beheading – it performs a miracle on cue in front of thousands of witnesses. The dark, dried 'blood' in two glass ampoules miraculously turns to liquid, as it supposedly has done for six centuries.

The rest of the year, the blood is locked away in the Treasury Chapel of San Gennaro, an explosion of Neapolitan baroque in the otherwise surprisingly subdued Duomo. Superimposed on the site of a Graeco-Roman temple, the Neo-Gothic cathedral's interior features some over-the-top touches – like the golden light bursting out of a white-marble Virgin Mary above the altar – but the frippery is kept to a minimum.

There is, however, a ghostly caterwauling coming from beneath the altar. In fact, the wails from the crypt are so spooky I'd give it a miss if I didn't know what was down there. For nine days before the Miracle of the Blood, a group of women known as the Aunts of San Gennaro keep a vigil over the saint's bones, singing songs and prayers coded in Neapolitan dialect. The cultish echo reverberates as you walk down into the crypt, which is actually a small, underground chapel covered floor to ceiling in carved white marble with columns wrapped in red-and-gold cloth. A glass case under the altar displays a large, chipped terracotta urn containing most of Gennaro's remains, the knobbly ends of the long bones jutting out like stirring sticks. In the aisle at the back, the statue of the dignitary who brought the holy bones to Napoli is kneeling in supposed piety, while at the front, the wailing women are sitting on a row of plastic white chairs. There are only six of the old girls, but the noise they're making is loud enough to wake the dead. Or at least stir his blood.

Gennaro's sanguinary remains are stored far away in his Treasury Chapel near the entrance of the cathedral, along with the iconic bust said to contain bones from his decapitated head. Given that the Church claims to have skull fragments, a few long bones and a couple vials of his blood, you would think there would have been scope to create a life-sized, full-bodied articulated relic: a Six-Million-Ducati Saint ('*Signori*, we can rebuild him'). But they had enough trouble just building the chapel in his honour. The glass vials of San Gennaro's blood used to be stored in a rickety part of the cathedral until a plague in 1527 inspired the city fathers to promise St Januarius a new home if he would have a word with God about the pestilence. Once the danger passed, though, the ingrates dragged their heels for nearly eighty years. When work on the chapel finally started, it took another four decades to complete, mainly because a mafia of Neapolitan painters and sculptors, a kind of artistic Camorra, kept trying to beat up or bump off the foreigners hired to decorate the landmark chapel of their patron saint. The Bolognese artist Domenichino did most of the frescoes, but he became so convinced that the Neapolitans were trying to poison him he started switching dishes at random during mealtimes. Even so, he died in mysterious circumstances before completing his work, leaving another outsider to execute his vision of Paradise.

Faced with such a stunning result, you would never imagine that so much lethal strife lay behind the chapel's creation. What's most striking about San Gennaro's Treasury is the amount of love and money that's been lavished on this one large room compared to the sparse decoration of the rest of the cathedral. Two wrath-of-God statues of Peter and Paul guard the bronze gate to the chapel, with a bust of Gennaro overhead and a Latin inscription proclaiming him the 'the saviour of our homeland, Naples, from famine, war, the plague and the flames of Vesuvius through his prodigious, concentrated blood'. The room itself isn't that big, but it squeezes in seven altars, forty-two columns and nineteen bronze statues, without counting the dozens of paintings and masterpieces of carving and metalwork using virtually every medium available. As with most baroque artworks, the whole place could do with a good dusting – Dust Funds must be the Organ Appeals of Mediterranean churches – but the chapel is filled with so much overwhelming beauty, the only way to appreciate it is to break it down into bits that the mind can comprehend, like the three-dimensional allegory that forms the base of the main altar. Wrought entirely of silver, the scene depicts the transfer of Gennaro's bones to Naples, with Vesuvius erupting in the background and hosts of angels and people escorting the Archbishop of Naples as he carries the bones on horseback. Along the way, the stallion's hoofs trample Heresy, symbolised by (gulp) a man with books.

On the walls and ceiling, Domenichino's frescoes depict scenes from Gennaro's life. In reality, next to nothing is known about him, except that he was probably the bishop of nearby Benevento and martyred around AD 405, during the Roman Empire's last attempts to purge Christianity before the era of Constantine. The paintings show Gennaro and his friends being condemned to death-by-wild-beast in an amphitheatre, but the animals miraculously refuse to eat the Christians, so the governor orders them to be beheaded. Afterwards, a wetnurse collects the blood of the slain saint in two vials.

Within decades of his execution, the story of San Gennaro had already become intertwined with the city's fate, and by the eighth century AD his fame had spread as far as the British Isles, earning him mentions in Northumberland's *Lindisfarne Gospels* and the histories of the Venerable Bede. Curiously, though, there's no known record of the Miracle of the Blood until 1389 – nearly a thousand years after Gennaro's death.

So many relics materialised during the Middle Ages that sceptics tend to doubt the authenticity of all of them. Unless it's an outright hoax, though, the Miracle of the Blood is unique in that something unusual definitely takes place inside the reliquary – but no one knows why. The small glass balsamaries containing the 'blood' have different shapes: one is fat and round, about four inches high and a little over half full; the other is cylindrical and roughly half as big. According to the official Church-sponsored guide, the irregular shape of the vessels' necks indicates that they may date from the same era as Gennaro's execution. After 1631, the vessels were encased in a silver reliquary with a 12-centimetre, round glass 'window' in the centre and vertical handles that allow it to be turned upside down for examination during the Miracle. For most of the year, the 'blood' appears to be a reddish-brown solid, but when it liquefies it turns a lighter tint and froths and bubbles, supposedly even increasing in volume and weight.

The Church has never recognised the phenomenon as an official miracle; at the same time, though, it (understandably) refuses to let scientists open the reliquaries and take samples of the mysterious substance within. (Like any dangerous weapon, it takes two keys to open the compartment where the blood is stored: one kept by the chapel and the other by the Archbishop of Naples.) Boffins analysed one of the containers with prism spectroscopes in both 1902 and 1989 and detected traces of what could be haemoglobin, although they admitted that it might just as easily have been a type of red dye.

If the dark mass is blood, what's particularly mystifying for scientists is not the fact that it liquefies, but that it goes from solid to liquid and back again. Over the past two centuries, many explanations have been proposed, ranging from ideas as unprovable as divine intervention itself (such as psychokinesis by the masses or 'magnetic' forces from Vesuvius) to answers that are plausible but incomplete. The most obvious one is that the Miracle is simply an old-fashioned, hey-presto magic trick, though keeping it a secret for more than six centuries would have required a degree of discretion that would make the Mafia look like loose-lipped amateurs. Other theories are that the stuff in the vials is light-sensitive or has a low melting point and responds to the heat from the candles and crowds; however, sceptics have had a hard time coming up with such a magical material.

To date, the best scientific explanation comes from a group led by Luigi Garlaschelli, an organic chemist who attributes the Miracle to a natural phenomenon called thixotropy, which causes some gel-like substances to turn to liquid when they're shaken but revert to their solid state when left alone. He cites ketchup, mayonnaise and certain paints and toothpastes (not the most convincing examples, I know, but hear him out). His report in *Chemistry in Britain* in 1994 even gives a recipe for homemade San Gennaro's 'blood': a reddish-brown iron hydroxide solution.

'This gel is the right shade of brown without the addition of any dye; it becomes perfectly liquid when shaken, and, just like the relic, can even produce bubbles on its shiny surface,' he claims. The one hitch is that the process involves a form of dialysis that wasn't recorded until the early 1600s. However, Garlaschelli argues that medieval artisans may have stumbled onto the procedure. What's more, all the ingredients would have been readily available to a Neapolitan alchemist in the fourteenth century. In fact, at the time, the only known source of one of the compounds – ferric chloride – was unique to areas with volcanoes.

Then again, the Miracle of San Gennaro could be the real thing, proof of Napoli's special place among the saints and the importance that Neapolitans place on blood. To this day, the symbolic colour of the city is red, and the only local saint to rival San Gennaro is Padre Pio, who happened to come from Januarius' old parish of Benevento and reputedly bore the stigmata – the bleeding wounds of Christ – on his hands and feet for fifty years until his death in 1968. In any event, the debunkers of the Miracle of San Gennaro tend to miss a crucial point: even if the relic is the product of an alchemist's work-shop, the fact that it's put in repeat performances for more than six centuries and continues to stump modern scientists is pretty miraculous in its own right.

Wandering around the Duomo, I get to talking with one of the attendants about the big day. Dino's dark shirt is open down to his sternum, revealing a gold crucifix and a medallion of the Madonna of Pompeii for good measure. He tells me that San Gennaro's blood has never failed to liquefy in living memory. It's put on display three times a year: for eight days beginning on the Saturday before the first Sunday of May, to mark the translation of the saint's bones to Naples; for another eight days after the anniversary of the saint's death on 19 September; and then as a one-off on 16 December, to honour the saint for saving Napoli from Vesuvius in 1631.

This Sunday is the red-letter date, 19 September, and Dino is in charge of opening the doors to the cathedral. The blood is paraded through the church around nine a.m. 'And then begins the crying for the miracle. Usually the liquefaction of the blood takes place around ten, but we don't know – it's a miracle. If by ten o'clock or so, the blood hasn't liquefied, you can see in the eyes of the people that they're really nervous. There's a lot of fear – and dread. If there's no liquefying of the blood, the people fear there will be war, plagues, famine or earthquakes.'

Prego . . . prego . . . prego . . . prego . . . prego . . . prego . . . prego . . . prego . . . prego . . . prego . . . prego . . . prego . . . prego—
The fervent undercurrent of prayer flows through the cathedral, joining forces with the applause rippling from San Gennaro's chapel, where the priests have just collected his head and blood, carrying them all the way up the aisle until the noisy surf, the wave of affection, engulfs the altar. But it's still not enough – a human APPLAUSE sign is waving his hands at us, urging us to clap-*clap-CLAP* for San Gennaro; not necessarily for the three TV news cameras swooping and craning around us, but that won't hurt, either. Another official, one with an eye for detail, adjusts the mitre on the saint's head; as with any type of hat, apparently there's a proper way to wear a mitre, and the saint's has been riding too low on his metal brow after the trip to the altar.

The gleaming statue in its scarlet robe and headgear sits on one side of the altar, and his blood on the other, both of them facing the congregation and surrounded by candles and exotic red flowers with long, white stamens.

'See the blood now? It's dark red. But when it turns to liquid, it will be bright red,' whispers the old Sicilian next to me. One of his Christian names is Gennaro, so today is his saint's day. He grins. 'I'm going to convert you to *cristianismo* yet.'

I met Gennaro while we were waiting for the doors to open at the ungodly hour of seven thirty a.m. Speaking Italianised Spanish, he told me he'd visited Napoli from his home in Messina at least thirty times, but this was the first time he'd had a chance to witness his namesake's miracle. 'When I was a boy, I always dreamt of coming here but never thought I would. And now, I am here . . . of course, I'm old now.'

Gennaro also told me he was a doctor affiliated with the International Medical Association of Lourdes, which verifies the miracles of Our Lady at the shrine in France. Apparently a friend of his is one of the sixty or so people whose miraculous recoveries have been medically confirmed. She'd been hospitalised for over a decade with tuberculosis and also had one leg that was shorter than the other; after immersing herself in the water at Lourdes, she was cured of both infirmities.

'Are you Catholic?' Gennaro asked me.

'UmmMethodist,' I hem-hawed. 'Kind of like an Anglican.'

I've been skittish about using the P-word in Catholic countries ever since I told a Spanish girlfriend I was Protestant, and she gasped, 'Don't you believe in *Jesu Cristo*?!?' What's more, Neapolitans used to believe that the Miracle of the Blood wouldn't take place if heretics were present.

But my Sicilian friend didn't seem to mind, cracking good-spirited jokes to pass the time until Dino and Co. opened the cathedral. Several dozen of us were glued to the doors, with nothing to do but contemplate an S&M poster across the street advertising a design institute with a photo of a man straining at the dog leash around his neck. Once the doors opened, assisted by some good-natured pushing from the outside, Gennaro and I made the long trot up the nave and managed to bag an altarside pew.

By now, though, so many latecomers have pushed into the mosh pit that we have to stand to see. Orange-vested security guards keep the throngs from blocking the aisle completely. The crush is only slightly more restrained in the cordoned-off VIP section in front of us: we may all be equal in the eyes of God, but in organised Christianity, as in communism, some are more equal than others.

The plump Archbishop in his skullcap and finery is reading a homily about San Gennaro and The Christian Life as the congregation settles into dozy acquiescence, fluttering fans, handkerchiefs and papers to circulate the muggy, incense-laced air. A teenager is napping on his mamma's shoulder, while a baby howls at the back.

Then comes time for the miracle. Without spoiling the outcome for you, it looked to me like the stuff in the vials was already glistening on the surface when the priests carried the reliquary in. But the mere suggestion brings angry denials from Gennaro.

After one last Hail Mary, the Archbishop takes the silver reliquary in both hands, the glass portal in the middle facing the audience, and gently turns it upside down. The scarlet liquid immediately flows to the other side of the container, and the priests nod in affirmation. A man in stiff black formalwear twirls a white handkerchief over his head, and the congregation applauds as fireworks explode outside to herald another successful show by Napoli's patron saint.

'*Viva San Gennaro!*'
'*Viva Jesu!*'
'*Grazie, San Gennaro!*'
'*Grazie, Jesu!*'

But the miracle has happened so quickly – less than an hour after the relic was brought out – that there hasn't been enough time for a build-up of tension. The applause is more polite than rapturous; loud but not thunderous. People are twirling their hankies and clapping their hands overhead, but the saint would get a much bigger reaction if he had helped Italy score a winning penalty in the World Cup; as it is, it's more like he's performed a particularly good parlour trick.

Then again, some of the faithful are absolutely euphoric, like the woman near me who's moaning and kissing a crucifix, rocking side to side and clutching her rosary. Immediately, a female attendant starts circulating a collection box, but the woman waves her away, as if to say, *I'm far too overcome at this moment to reach into my purse for a donation. Can't a gal have some religious ecstasy in peace?*

Onstage, the Archbishop and the priests look particularly moved, closing their eyes and saying prayers of thanksgiving. They're still in the job for another year.

Gennaro is busy phoning a cousin back in Sicily to relay the good news, holding his mobile up so she can hear the applause. 'The miracle has just happened! It liquefied very quickly – *subito!* That's a good sign! It's going to be a good year!'

Afterwards, Gennaro invites me to go for a coffee before he returns to Sicily in the afternoon. At the café, everyone we talk to asks us about the miracle, a question that sounds both nonchalant and anxious: *tutto bene*? When they hear the miracle was *subito*, they smile as if to say they never doubted it, though they're visibly relieved.

'So what did the Archbishop have to say during his sermon?' I ask Gennaro.

'Oh, a bunch of stuff. I don't remember.'

All through the service, Gennaro had been making odd remarks, boasting not only about the hardness of his biceps, but also his thighs – 'Feel them! They're like a marathon runner's' – and asking me whether I'd seen the erotic artworks at Pompeii. Between prayers, he also mentioned that we were a lot alike, that we had an *attracción bilateral*. Unsure of what he was getting at, I decided to ignore his fruitier remarks: *Don't be so paranoid; it's probably just his tinted eyewear.*

Before he leaves, Gennaro offers to give me a tour of the well-heeled suburb of Mergellina by the sea. I've already been chucked out of my 'hotel' this morning because it turns into a knocking shop on Sundays: apparently couples book it by the hour. I've got a whole day to kill before my late-night flight, so why not visit a Sunday antiques market? It would be nice to see a part of Napoli that doesn't look like an outdoor laundry.

First, though, Gennaro needs to pick up his luggage at the Jesuit monastery where he's been staying here in the old town. The interior reminds me of an empty hospice – grey, cool and dead – everything that the streets outside are not. After chatting with the young mother at the reception desk (her baby's in the room next door), we wait for the old-fashioned lift to wind its way down. At this point, Gennaro does what most men who've just met do. He reaches over and . . . tweaks my nipple.

Now, I really don't know how to react. Nothing in my upbringing has prepared me for the proper response to geriatric nipple-pinching. Punching him to the floor is tempting, but possibly an overreaction. Maybe it's a Sicilian thing. Maybe the Cosa Nostra are all menacing kisses and manly embraces for the cameras, but when the director calls *Cut!*, it's all wedgies and nipple pinching. If I leave now, I'll never know. And it's not like I'm in any physical danger. No matter how hard his thighs or biceps, he's twice my age and half my height.

Gennaro's room is bare but nicer than mine, with a jerrybuilt closet in the corner that serves as an ensuite bathroom, though its walls don't quite reach the ceiling. For some reason, he's very keen for me to use the facilities. I pass, so he goes in himself, leaving me to ponder the situation to the accompaniment of an orchestral bowel movement; a veritable symphony of farts. I'm tempted to make a run for it, but knowing me, I'd leave something behind and end up having to skulk back, mumbling apologies and excuses as to why I'd left so suddenly. As you'll have noticed, I often get into these predicaments, thanks to my dead-cat curiosity and an inability to believe what's in front of me until it's nearly too late. The guy's staying at a Jesuit monastery – *Jesuits*, for God's sake! – and he's just completed a pilgrimage to see his namesake saint. I can't believe a man his age would seriously think . . . How old did he say he was? Sixty-nine? (*69 – oh, God.*) Does he really think this is going to end with me sucking off a sexagenarian or vice versa? (It occurs to me that there's some neat symmetry here with Penis Cakes, but I'm really not in the mood to go into it.) He must be out of his mind!

But – and this is where the dead cat crawls in – if I don't stay to find out, I'll never know. People will think I just made it up: *You went to Italy, a land of machismo, to see the Miracle of San Gennaro and wound up being molested by a pervy pensioner named*

Gennaro? Yeah, right. And to be honest, I'd begin to doubt myself, too. Maybe it *is* my imagination. There's only one way to find out.

After a particularly noisome explosion, Gennaro emerges from the water closet with his trousers buttoned (*thank God*), but his belt undone (*uh-oh*). He calls a taxi and gets his luggage together, asking me to hold open his duffel bag while he stuffs some wrapped platters of pastries inside. After zipping it up, he suddenly throws his sweaty arms around me and grabs me in a headlock disguised as a hug: '*Un abbraccio!*'

Then, apparently aroused by the smell of his own excrement, he announces, '*Un bacio!*' Even now, with his face moist against my cheek, I'm thinking, *Well, Italian men do kiss each other – it's traditional.*

'Now you give me one! Now you give me one!' the fat old man's insisting, my head trapped in his slimy embrace.

I push him away and let it be known that I'm not keen on *baci* with boys.

'But you live in London! Lots of men kiss in London!'

That would be news to most of my friends, but that's beside the point. I remind him that I'm American, the implication being: *I'm a red-blooded male, goddamit.*

Even so, on our way down in the lift, he keeps telling me, 'I think you enjoyed that kiss. Really – you did. I can tell.' And while we're waiting in reception, he turns his back to the girl and asks, 'Is it true what they say about tall men, that they've got big . . . ? Look at my hand' – and he gives his index finger an erection by way of illustration.

For reasons I still can't quite fathom, I get into the taxi with him. But then he tells me I'm going to have *two* kisses waiting for me at the train station.

That's it – stop the cab. I've had enough of the Sicilian copro-phile trying to cop a feel. I hop on a double-decker sightseeing bus to clear my head. But my subconscious is clearly working overtime. It's only much later in the day that I realise I've bought my other half a souvenir box of chocolate *Baci*.

The evening air is humid, hovering on the cusp between balmy and cool, and the slanting rays of the sun burnish the city's yellow façades golden. Teens and twentysomethings meet to laugh and flirt amid the streetmarket stalls on the Via Duomo, while the police keep an eye out for thieves among the endless piles of sweets.

Inside the cathedral, hundreds of Neapolitans are clamouring around the altar while a priest as pale as his collar holds the blood of San Gennaro before them. He tilts the vials from side to side as proof of the miracle and holds it against their fore-heads and chests, allowing them to kiss the reliquary. At the same time, he scolds others for jostling to the front; there are no shortcuts to the miracle.

Dino is standing in a doorway on the side of the nave, but he can barely hear me for the clamour of bells overhead. 'Sorry,' he says and disappears inside. The chimes fall silent, and he returns with a shrug. 'Electronic.'

'Did you kiss the blood?' he asks.

I shake my head.

If only I could explain to him: 'Instead, Gennaro kissed me.'

CHAPTER EIGHT

LAND OF THE BELLICOSE BOVINE
COWFIGHTING IN SWITZERLAND

PART ONE:

COW-MAD COUNTRY

A lesser woman might be jealous or, more likely, worried. But Frédéric Boson claims his French girlfriend understands his passion, insofar as any foreigner can. For although it might seem peculiar to the rest of the world, it's as common as skiing, fondue and cowbells in this corner of the Swiss Alps.

'If you meet someone else from Valais, you ask them, "Do you prefer your girlfriend or your cows?"' he tells me.

'What's your answer?'

'My cows. We have a strange relationship. It's like *love* with your cows.'

Rather than a love that dare not moo its name, though,

Frédéric's bovine devotion transcends the bounds of merely physical or even platonic *amour*, hovering somewhere between spiritual kinship and outright worship. His prize-winning cows come as close as any species could to being members of his family, and like other farmers, he treats his favourite as nothing less than royalty, calling her the Queen of the herd. Whereas other people might lavish a similar level of adoration on their household pets, Valaisan cows are barnyard animals weighing 600 to 800 kilos – combative milk machines the size of water buffalos – that could impale their owners instantly if the temper took them. They may be called Pamela, Bella, Venus or Madonna, but don't let the feminine names fool you: these cows have horns. In fact, they look like big, black bulls with udders: the cow world's equivalent of she-males.

The ancient alpine breed of Herens cattle has fighting in its blood, with cows prone to lock horns to determine their leader during the difficult trek to pastures high in the mountains. Every spring and autumn, villages in this rural canton in south-west Switzerland hold head-butting battles of supremacy to see which cow merits the title of *La Reine des Reines*: the 'Queen of Queens'. One of the premiere *Combats des Reines* takes place in Martigny in October against the backdrop of the Alps and the town's ancient Roman amphitheatre. 'It's fantastic because you're in a Roman coliseum,' Frédéric enthuses. 'You feel like the gladiators.'

As any Spanish bullfight aficionado will tell you, bulls get their belligerence from their mamas. Unlike Spain's embattled tradition, though, there's no torture, death or matador involved in Swiss cowfighting. Locals still chuckle about the Austrian agitators who visited one year, intent on exposing lurid examples of bovine abuse. Once they witnessed the regal treatment of the cows, they left the Swiss to enjoy their 'Battle of the Queens'. Besotted farmers have been known to spoil their girls with wine and cake and lavish victory kisses on their drooling mouths. After all, a calf from a champion cow can sell for many times the normal price. For the Queen of Queens herself, though, the prize is somewhat humbler, but authentically Swiss: a shiny new cowbell.

Over the years, cowfighting has attracted a few of the usual vices, as well as some unusual ones, such as clandestine horn sharpening and the nobbling of cows. What you won't hear about is the kind of bestiality reported in some Swiss-German parts of the country: stories of perverts who rape and mutilate cows. Frédéric doesn't even like talking about them. 'If someone did that here, we would take up arms and go after them,' he says, comparing the temperament of French-speaking Valaisans to that of the obstreperous Basques and Corsicans. 'We are like cows. When we have problems, we fight' – he grins – 'but mainly with our mouths.'

As a proxy for battle, cowfighting provides a way of keeping the peace, not just between farmers, but also men and women. The fact that hidebound farmers should revere the female of the species may seem strange considering that Swiss women weren't able to vote in federal elections until the late date of 1971. Perhaps tellingly, though, it was a tiny commune in Valais that led the push for female suffrage, granting women the vote in 1957. An old cowfighting proverb may help explain why: 'The man governs in the stable, but the woman governs at home.'

Though a full-time obsession, cattle breeding is a part-time job for Frédéric. He's also trying to make a go of it in the hospitality industry by running a hotel near Martigny with his girlfriend, Marie, and their partner, Hadrien, who's originally from Versailles.

Hadrien has offered to pick me up in town this morning, but he's obviously unimpressed by my choice of accommodation: a hotel next to a petrol station with pea-green carpet on the walls and a Swiss-German manager who seems genuinely shocked that anybody would want to stay at his establishment. Goggle-eyed and blinking, he receives the odd visitor with a kind of Teutonic bewilderment, as if he's just stumbled out of the forest into a clearing and encountered an extraterrestrial. He can't work out whether it's hostile or not, but just in case, he'd better kill it.

'Why are you staying *here*?' Hadrien asks me as politely as possible, carefully avoiding contact with the upholstered walls. I have wondered that myself. My credibility takes a knock every time I tell people where I'm staying. Then again, I've been in much worse places – like the hotel in Belgium that stored the remote controls for the TVs at the front desk to prevent their clientele from stealing them.

'Hotels are not a good business in Switzerland,' Hadrien comments as we drive over to Frédéric's farm. The minimum wage is 3,000 Swiss francs (£1,300) a month, compared to just half that next door in France. Despite the economic difficulties, the three friends are hoping to run another hotel in the area once their current management contract runs out.

'Why don't you go somewhere else?'

'Because Fred can't go too far from his cows,' he laughs. 'But I don't mind.'

As big as a mountain and as soft as a young cheese, Hadrien is a rare find: a humble Frenchman. 'Although I think Paris is the most beautiful city in the world,' he says – acknowledging a fact as incontestable as the earth being round – 'I couldn't live there.' It's too fast-paced, expensive and crowded. Having met Frédéric while studying hotel management in Lausanne, Hadrien has adapted well to the Swiss-French way of life. 'To come here, I think you have to be a little bit . . .' – he pauses to chew it over – 'humble. The people are difficult to get to know, but once you work your way into their hearts, you have a friend for life.'

And then there's the location. Martigny and Valais as a whole are two of the real 'finds' during this journey, offering the best of many worlds with scenery so consistently stunning it could spoil you for life. Wedged into the Rhône Valley near France and Italy, Martigny is an hour and a half from Geneva, with a de rigueur castle, pavement cafés and enough old architecture to offset the modern stuff's lack of character. Thanks to a local philanthropist, Martigny also punches above its weight on the cultural scene, with sculptures adorning most roundabouts and a mix of world-class and boutique attractions. The Gianadda Foundation regularly manages to convince major touring exhibits to add a little-known *ville* in Switzerland to their itineraries, complementing the town's permanent exhibits: Gallic-Roman archaeology, obscure classic European cars, a museum that brings the scientific sketches of Da Vinci to life and the foundation's endearingly bonkers array of modern art on its grounds, not least of which is a gigantic breast amid the landscaping. Just up the road is the ski resort of Verbier and just over the border, to the south-west, is the French town of Chamonix, site of the first official Winter Olympics and the highest peak in the Alps, Mont Blanc. To the east of Martigny, in the German-speaking part of Valais, stands the equally famous resort of Zermatt and the archetypal, picture-postcard, Toblerone-box alp: the Matterhorn. And less than an hour south of Martigny, on the Italian border, is the Great St Bernard mountain pass, the ancient shortcut between northern and southern Europe, with its hospice for stranded travellers and some namesake dogs on hand for the tourists. During winter, when the pass is blocked by snow, the St Bernards actually live down in Martigny. 'Everyone knows about St Bernard dogs, but very few people know they come from here!' a local told me. Hence, the latest brainwave: not only are they planning to build a St Bernard museum, they're also talking about letting the furry lifesavers roam the streets (presumably without their legendary casks of brandy).

Unlike manmade monuments, the Alps never look smaller in real life than you imagined them. Returning to Switzerland from a flat land – and most countries are topographically challenged by comparison – you suddenly remember what a mountain's supposed to look like. You can't help but have the same reaction as the early travel writers, those Pursuers of the Picturesque who hyped the romance of rocks simply because the scenery was unlike anything they'd ever seen before. The gap around Martigny is broad enough to let in lots of light but narrow enough for you never to forget that you're in an alpine valley. On one side – the bit that stays shaded until noon at this time of year – the mountain wall bristles with conifers; on the opposing, sunsoaked side, terraced vineyards pattern the slopes like solar panels tilted at steep angles to absorb every last bit of light, with nary a centimetre wasted. 'Sometimes the stone wall is actually bigger than the land it supports,' Hadrien points out. 'The land will be only two metres wide, and the wall three metres high.'

Frédéric's farm lies between these extremes, in the valley where the land flattens into a plain that looks barely two miles wide, full of meticulously cultivated crops that seem even tinier against their granite backdrops: tidy fields of corn turning gold in the autumn sun, bonsai pear and apricot orchards, and origami apple trees twisted into daisy chains consisting of more branch than trunk. 'Valais is a big garden,' Hadrien declares, explaining that the Swiss grow everything from asparagus to strawberries in the vale. The warm wind from the south that dumps rain on Lausanne and Geneva also blesses Martigny with a microclimate comparable to the south of France. In fact, the Rhône that flows through the valley is the same river that re-emerges on the other side of Lake Geneva and runs through south-eastern France to the Mediterranean. 'So the wines here could be called "Côte du Rhône".'

When we arrive, Frédéric is trying to chase some calves into a trailer, darting back and forth across the pasture like a bucolic Benny Hill. I offer to help, but he says the young bulls would try to gore me, so Hadrien and I watch from the relative safety of the barn door. This seems as good a time as any to ask him about the differences between the 'Swiss-French' and the 'French French'. As an honorary member of the Order of the Priceless Sardine, it strikes me that this part of Switzerland is paradise for anyone who admires the idea of the French life-style but not necessarily the reality.

'But nobody likes the Swiss!' scoffs more than one friend of mine. And I have to admit, before coming here, I wouldn't have disagreed. My past dealings with certain bureaucrats convinced me that the Swiss had combined Germanic officiousness with French inefficiency to create a truly infuriating national character. However, I now realise that this gross generalisation

THE 'CORPSE' WORE SHADES: A penitent plays dead during Galicia's Rigor Mortis Procession.

LUBING UP:
A Turkish wrestler
makes sure every last bit
is drenched in olive oil.

HE'S A KILLER, I TELL YA!
I still have nightmares about
the oil wrestler who whipped
me (the, uh, one on the left).

I DON'T KNOW WHAT THE
GAY FANS SEE IN IT
Turkish oil wrestlers grapple
with their sport's unique
hands-down-the-pants hold

OUR PATRON OF PILES AND PENISES:
Portugal's St. Gonçalo is upstaged by a priapic pastry during the annual 'Phallus Festival'.

ANOTHER BLOODY MIRACLE:
The Archbishop of Naples checks that
the dried 'blood' of the city's patron saint
has liquefied on cue – as it's supposedly
done for more than six centuries.

COWFIGHTING IN THE COLISEUM: Swiss 'queens' lock horns in a Roman arena in the Alps – after being subjected to wearing some ridiculous crowns.

A TOUGH CUSTOMER:
Ireland's last matchmaker does
his best to help a desperate case
from America – and a friendly
woman from closer to home.

TOO PC OR NOT PC? A St. Nicolaas and his 'Black Pete' uphold Dutch tradition...

...while two coloured Petes pretend to bundle a black schoolteacher off to Spain in a sack.

probably doesn't apply to the fifth of the population that is Swiss-French. Valais is like France with a Germanic sense of hygiene. 'France is kind of a big brother, but the Swiss-French want to keep their distance,' Hadrien says. 'And also, because people here are honest and hardworking, they see the French as being lazy, dirty and prone to showing off.'

He uses the term *civique* to contrast Swiss francophones with the French. Valaisans still have a sense of civic solidarity, of doing things for the common good rather than purely for their own benefit, he says. 'In France, people are always trying to find a way around the law, but here, they don't do that. Plus, there's a lot of crime in France. Here I think nothing of leaving my car keys in the ignition. If an outsider locks his doors when he leaves his car, they feel insulted. And in a way, they're right to.

'Sometimes it's a little freaky,' he adds, gazing at the fields and the massive alp above us. 'Things are almost too clean. But you feel very safe.'

A few minutes later, as if to prove the point, Frédéric's uncle comes up to us, all firm handshakes and flapping arms. He works on the farm, and he's angry with Hadrien. 'If I would've known you had someone coming from England, I would have cleaned the barn! It gives a bad image! It's not worthy of Switzerland! *C'est catastrophe!*'

Now, as barns go, you have to understand that this Swiss cowhouse is absolutely state of the art. It's only two years old – so new that the wood still smells freshly cut. The interior is all exposed beams, light-brown timber and pale-grey metal, with sunlight streaming in through the windows in the peaked roof. Gigantic Swiss rolls of hay have been stacked neatly on the floor, and clean straw has been strewn on the ground like a token attempt at casualness: the agricultural counterpart of scatter cushions. The central corridor between the docks where the cattle feed is wide enough to drive a mini-tractor through, and there are grids in the floor to siphon the excrement away from the living area into a big green septic tank outside. It may be unworthy of Switzerland, but I reckon in Britain, if you took out the cows and made some minor adjustments, you could find people who'd be happy to move in straight away.

Taking a break from cow chasing, Frédéric greets me with a manly handshake. At first glance, he could be a Frenchman in all but nationality, with his bags of Gallic charm, a goatee that's filling in his cheeks and a winning tendency to pronounce 'cow' as 'koh'. He also has longish, tussled footballer's hair, though his rectangular glasses reflect an intelligence lacking in many grown men who head balls for a living.

As he ushers me into the barn to see his prized Queen, I ask what's the most important part of preparing for the cow-fighting this weekend.

'Silence.'

I can't tell whether that's an answer or an order. The dark, horned Queen stands tethered to a feeding dock inside, all alone except for a lesser cow two stations away.

'The physiological aspect is important, but also the psychological,' Frédéric says in a hush, tapping his temple. 'If they do a lot of fighting beforehand, it's not good.'

While she was up in the Alps this summer, Fercle injured her leg in a confrontation with a cow that was menstruating. According to Fred, the fight should have never happened; the cowherd should have kept them apart. 'When a cow is menstruating, it's like doping.' She feels no pain and will fight to the end. Fercle got barged against a water tank. As a result, she won't be able to compete this weekend. 'I don't want her to go just to see what happens. That would be disrespecting the animal.' Just as importantly, if she got hurt, she might not want to fight again.

Besides, the Bosons already have a much-envied track record: they've raised fifteen queenly fighting machines in as many years and also run a highly successful produce business. 'We are like the Mafia. We do everything as a family,' Frédéric jokes.

Herens breeders treat their cows like family partly because their herds are so small. Even the relatively wealthy Bosons have only five. So it's fair to say they know their cows about as intimately as any decent human could. On the wall next to Fercle, a chart in protective plastic lists her lineage going back eight generations to 1963 – a decade before Fred himself was born. 'I knew her mother, her grandmother before her, and her sister.' In fact, Frédéric named Fercle after his own grandmother's cow.

'Just like some people name their daughter after their grandmother,' I suggest.

He laughs but doesn't disagree. As Fercle snuffles some dried white bread from his hand, he caresses her massive head and drapes his arm around her neck, struggling to explain a very special kind of love.

'When it comes to breeding the cows, it's exactly like horses. You know the psychology of the mother, and you try to find a bull with a similar psychology. Everyone has in mind the bull that would be the first love of the cow. But,' he adds quickly, puffing his chest and pointing to his heart, '*I* am her first love.'

Earlier, Hadrien had told me that the Bosons had to put down one of their beloved cows, Gitane, and sell her for beef. As the chef at their hotel, Frédéric prides himself on using only Herens beef on his menu, but he would never think of eating Gitane. 'He'll eat from other cows, but not his own.' For Fred and his cows, it's not that meat is murder; it's borderline cannibalism.

He leads Hadrien and me through a sliding door to the next room where four young bulls are penned together. Their horns and bodies are much smaller, but Frédéric assures me they're much more aggressive.

'Then why don't you use the bulls for fighting?'

'It would be too dangerous.'

In other words, the only things the males are good for are their meat and their sperm (female readers: insert your own joke *here*). It's like Frédéric's father says: 'We use the bulls in the winter for breeding, and then we eat them.' In a final affront to their masculinity, a cow gets its pedigree from its mother rather than its father. 'As far as I know,' Frédéric explains, 'it is the only breed where the female is queen.'

Come to think of it, I've never fully understood why 'cow' is one of the worst things you can call a woman in Britain. It's not a common term of abuse where I come from. But then Fred mentions that cows have periods every twenty-one days and pregnancies that last nine months.

'You can imagine this leads to men making comparisons,' Hadrien deadpans.

'But cows are more quiet.'

What makes Herens cattle unique is that they establish strict hierarchies instinctively: if they're in a group of five, they'll lock horns and duel to determine a queen; if that group then goes into a pasture with another ten cows, they'll all duke it out to decide the ruler of the fifteen, and so forth. 'You don't decide who's queen. The cows decide,' Frédéric says. Traditionally, it was each queen's job to lead the rest of her herd up through the steep, rocky terrain to the cooler pastures in the mountains during the *inalpe* at the start of summer. Once there, the cattle would face off in impromptu confrontations in their never-ending search for the fresh grass further up the slopes. In early autumn, before the first snows, the cows then make the return trip down the mountains in a custom known as the *desalpe*.

Frédéric spent all last summer up in the mountains with his cows, roughly a hundred days in a cabin without running water or electricity.

'It was . . . paradise,' he sighs wistfully. 'There was nobody up there. Only my *kohs*.' And occasionally Marie.

'I couldn't do it,' Hadrien chuckles. 'I need to have people around me.'

After a summer of mountain climbing, the cattle are in peak condition for cowfighting at the Battle of the Queens in Martigny.

'It's like football,' Frédéric says. 'You go on the Alps for a hundred days, and then you come down for the cowfights. The event on Sunday is like the World Cup.'

Fred does this a lot – comparing cowfighting and football – and it takes me a while to figure out why. It turns out he used to play professionally, as goalie for first-division Genève-Servette. And suddenly it all makes sense: 'To be goalkeeper, you have to be a little bit crazy because you're all on your own. Mentally, you have to be very strong – not for when things are going well, but when they're going badly.' He smiles. 'You walk into a café and people may not say anything, but you can tell from their eyes that they're disappointed in you.'

By his own account, though, Frédéric was good at his game: at one point, he was loaned out to a second-division team to try to boost its performance, but some of the players resented him. 'It's just like in cowfighting,' he says, reversing his metaphors. After he'd saved a goal during a match, one of the opposing team members purposely kicked him in the knee when he was already down. 'But we didn't have any other goalkeeper, so I had to keep playing like this –' Fred hops on one leg to demonstrate. 'And in the remaining seventy minutes, I *never* conceded a goal!'

After the match, a doctor X-rayed his knee but couldn't see any serious injuries, so Frédéric played on his bad leg until he was in too much agony to continue. Another physician examined him and realised that he had been playing with a fractured kneecap *for six weeks*. The injury effectively ended his career, and he was determined not to follow the route of so many Swiss footballers when they're put out to pasture. There's no shortage of life-insurance companies in Switzerland, and it's not unusual for former footballers to parlay their popularity into careers as local life-insurance salesmen: 'Hello, my name is so-and-so, and I used to play for such-and-such,' Fred mimics. Instead, he returned to his first loves.

We drive to a pasture to check on some of his other cows in a narrow, rectangular plot tucked between a pear orchard and a cornfield: fruit, meat, milk and veg all lined up in a row. For people like me, who couldn't tell the difference between a Jersey or a Jamaica Brahman, the Valaisan view of the cow world is refreshingly simplistic: white cows are for food; dark ones are mainly for fighting. Or as Frédéric puts it: 'Milk cows are stupid. Really, really stupid. But Herens cows are very intelligent.' The modern breed usually has a black coat with reddish highlights that enable owners to tell their cows apart. 'It's amazing,' Hadrien tells me. 'He can recognise his cows from four hundred metres away. And when he goes into the stable, they stand up to greet him.'

Sure enough, the three cows stand to attention as Frédéric passes on the basic principles of their psy-*koh*-logy. 'If you are sweet with the *kohs*, they are also sweet with you. You see some farmers, and they don't have a relationship with their *kohs*. At a fight, if a *koh* fights well, she'll search you out because she's happy.'

He does a puff-chested strut by way of demonstration and introduces me to his herd's second-in-command.

'Look at that face!' he gushes, in a tone that makes me think I'm meant to be looking at a paragon of beauty, not a 600-kilo bruiser with bulging eyes, a battered nose and two wonky horns – one bent up, the other down.

'She has a face like a boxer,' he enthuses. 'With some cows, you can still see some femininity. But she doesn't have much femininity.'

You can say that again. If it weren't for the udders, I'd think Dimitri was a bull. She's even got a war wound. One of her horns snapped off during a fight, so they've used dental tape – the same kind used on human teeth – to bond it to the stump. According to Frédéric, horns are like fingernails: warm to the touch, with living flesh inside but a dead exterior. The farmers start shaping the cows' horns when they're very young in hopes of producing the perfect fighting weapons. 'On Sunday morning, they have someone who blunts the horns because the day before, everyone will be filing and sharpening them. You could slice meat on them. And the farmers will say, "Oh, I didn't do anything! I don't know how it happened!"'

He wraps his arm lovingly around Dimitri's neck and informs me that the tips of her horns carry ten tonnes of pressure per square centimetre. 'She could kill me in one second,' he says dotingly. 'But she never would.'

'Do cows ever get seriously injured during the fights?'

'It's like boxing. It's shocking and bloody, but it's just bruises and scrapes. The farmers have their prizefighters treated at a special animal hospital in Bern. I think it's possibly better than an English hospital for people.'

However, not all injuries are fight-related. The Bosons decided to build their own barn for their cows after an incident with Dimitri at another stable: whether by accident or intent, someone stuck a pitchfork in her eye, Fred claims. 'We called the best eye doctors – for *humans* – but the cornea was damaged.'

'Is cow-nobbling very common?'

'It's like life. If you have one hundred people, ninety will be normal, but you get ten who are psychopaths. The ones who hurt cows are psychopaths.'

'People may fight over their cows – and they do – but to hurt the animal is showing disrespect,' Hadrien adds.

'You've lost your right way of thinking when you own a cow,' Fred says, tapping his head. 'It's like a football fan in England.'

'A hooligan?'

'Yes! Exactly! Like a hooligan!'

Or mooligan.

No one knows this better than Fred's long-suffering girl-friend, a down-to-earth girl from Bordeaux who joins us later.

'So did you know what you were getting into with the cows?' I ask Marie.

Frédéric answers for her. 'She fell in love.'

'With him or the cows?'

'You have to do both,' he laughs.

She smiles happily. 'That was an obligation.'

*

Cuckoos aside, the cow comes as close as any animal to being Switzerland's national mascot. In fact, moo juice is the key ingredient in one of the country's eternal contributions to humankind: milk chocolate. (Swiss cows also wind the nation's clocks and guard its numbered bank accounts, but I'm not supposed to tell you that.) Depending on your political views, Switzerland's hallowed neutrality might appear to reflect stereotypically cowlike behaviour. 'Bovine' is usually a synonym for 'dull', 'docile' or even 'stupid'; similarly, Swiss neutrality is often confused with pacifism. However, just as the native Herens breed is actually a race of natural-born fighters, Swiss society is much more militaristic than you might think.

My first trip to Switzerland was as a journalist covering the World Economic Forum in the Swiss-German ski resort of Davos, an annual pow-wow of the great and the good and the despicably awful. A fax came through that a group of peaceful protesters was planning a ski-in at the event, and sure enough, about thirty or so students and adults turned up at the train station disguised not altogether convincingly as holidaymakers – the giveaway was the token contingent of Third-Worlders shivering in saffron robes.

Anyway, in a true democracy – particularly the world's oldest – you'd think that the authorities would have allowed these no-harmniks to shout their slogans and wave their banners in the freezing cold and then scuttle back to the cities, content that although they hadn't changed anything, they'd stuck it to *der Mann*. What's more, the foreign dignitaries weren't going to be in any danger; they were safely locked away in the forum, in a bunker made ugly by the gods of concrete. As it turned out, the poor do-gooders didn't get anywhere near it. The minute they emerged from the station, a squadron of jackbooted police in riot gear surrounded them like Robocops with weird wicker shields. They were backed up by dark vehicles with wire-mesh panels to corral the protesters and keep them from marching down the main street. In a cruelly ironic touch, the furthest the anti-globalisers got before giving up was the local McDonald's. Never has Ronald McDonald looked so pleased with himself.

I've always wondered if that was a one-off. But as I'm strolling through Martigny on Saturday morning before the *Combat*, I pass a parade of the usual floats and adorable children – followed by marching soldiers, armoured cars and a couple of tanks. Granted, this year's cowfighting fair has an army theme – *'Mobilisation Générale!'* – but the only other time I can remember seeing tanks in the streets was during a military coup in Peru. And before coming here, it hadn't been apparent to me why such a stable democracy – home of the Geneva Convention – would even need an army. After all, the threat of an attack by the Swiss Army wouldn't necessarily strike fear into your heart. The US military, for instance, is fearsome if only because of the ever-present danger of an oxymoronic death administered via 'friendly' fire or a 'smart' bomb. Rather than shock and awe, though, the Swiss Army would more likely inspire an aw-shucks reaction amongst its enemies: 'Run away, the Swiss are going to whittle us with their blunt knives or – the horror! – poke us with that fiddly bit that no other nationality knows what to do with!' As wrong as this may be, the poster for this year's fair does little to disabuse you of the notion: it shows a comely Swiss miss frolicking in an army helmet.

But the real eye-opener – and reminder for the West today – is just how heavily Switzerland has relied on the military to keep it *out* of war, especially during those times when the Alps just weren't enough. The Swiss have long had a muscular democracy, and their centuries-old neutrality didn't just happen by accident. For years, they kept the peace at home by exporting their warmongers for profit. More than a million Swiss mercenaries fought for foreign armies between the late 1400s and the early 1800s, mainly on the Continent, though some also served in the British Army and a few hundred fought for the North during the American Civil War (to this day, Swiss Guards protect the Pope at the Vatican). In *One Million Mercenaries*, historian John McCormack quotes sources as diverse as Shakespeare and Machiavelli as paying homage, often begrudgingly, to the 'Switzers', who would 'fight for any God and man' and 'were notorious for their ferocity and brutality'. The English took a particularly dim view of the prostitution of war, probably because they often found themselves having to fight against Swiss soldiers, described by the Prince of Orange as 'the main nerve' (not to say only nerve) of the French Army. Predictably, the French took a more favourable view of their hired allies. 'The Swiss sell the liberty of their bodies to retain the liberty of their country,' observed a French commander during the Thirty Years War. Napoleon also regarded them highly, declaring: 'The Swiss are good soldiers and will not let you down.'

That's because they came from Switzerland's mountainous *hirtenland*: cowherding country. 'Nature and necessity have framed them to war, for a mountainous region . . . breeds a rude people, patient of hardness, and of warlike dispositions, so as they seem to be born soldiers,' observed a British traveller in 1617. Likewise, Thomas More would have happily rejected any Swiss applications to his *Utopia*: 'They set little store by nice houses or clothing and are only really interested in breeding and raising cattle. They live mainly from hunting and stealing. They seek eagerly for every opportunity to pursue the warfare for which they are born.'

Switzerland formally outlawed mercenary service in 1859, but the military still plays a complex role in keeping the country neutral – and unified. The Swiss Army was mobilised during both world wars to resist any invasions, and the country maintained one of the biggest land-based armies in Europe during the Cold War. Whereas even such a relatively 'new' democracy as Spain has abolished military service, Switzerland still requires its men to do time in the national militia. For more than a few males, these breaks are an opportunity to network with the old boys' club: many officers are also doctors, lawyers and company directors. On a broader level, though, military service forces Switzerland's two main competing linguistic groups (not to mention Italian and Romansch speakers) to work together in the name of national unity.

At least, that's the theory. 'Here we have more in common with the Italian and French parts of the Alps than with Bern and Zurich,' Frédéric informed me. 'We are part of the mountains.' These alpine territories also used to be part of the Duchy of Savoy – Valais didn't formally join the Swiss Confederation until 1815 – and to this day, farmers on the French side of the border hold up traffic during the seasonal *desalpes* of their cattle. Later this month, Martigny's Italian counterpart, the town of Aosta on the other side of the Great St Bernard Pass, will host its very own cowfight competition, known to French-speaking Italians as the *Batailles des Reines* or *La Battaglia delle Regine*.

Within Switzerland, the world of cowfighting highlights the rivalries between German and French speakers. In contrast to their national standing, where they're outnumbered three to one, francophones actually constitute the majority in Valais: 60 per cent versus the roughly 40 per cent who call cowfighting *Kuhkampfe* and speak a peculiar dialect of *Deutsch*. 'But it's a German unlike anything you'll learn in school,' Hadrien told me, shaking his head. 'It's not even *Schwitzerdütsch* – Swiss-German. We went to a cowfight in that area, and I couldn't even understand the numbers of the cows as they were being called out.' Historically, the two cultural groups have had very different ways of viewing the world. Given their minority status, though, there's not a lot the Swiss-French can do about it. 'They feel they've been invaded by Germans, and in a way they have,' Hadrien said.

My interpreter, Patricia, gave me a case in point over a dinner of fondue and Fendant at the Café du Valais. She and her husband mentioned a recent referendum on whether the children of immigrants should automatically be granted Swiss citizenship. As with votes on strengthening Switzerland's ties to the EU, the Swiss-French were mostly in favour, but the Germanic majority blocked it. The far-right Swiss People's Party, dominated by Swiss-German billionaire Christoph Blocher, campaigned against the proposal with ads depicting a Swiss passport bearing a photo of Osama bin Laden. During national elections, Blocher's group also scored an upset victory, winning 28 per cent of the vote, making it the largest party in parliament.

'It is giving a bad image for Switzerland,' Patricia argued. 'If people think that we are a country that doesn't like *étrangères*, what will happen to tourism?'

I didn't want to say it, but it seems to me that your average tourist to Switzerland knows more about cannibalism in Papua New Guinea than the workings of Swiss democracy, and for many visitors, especially those who stash money in Swiss bank accounts, their only interest in news from Switzerland is the latest snow report. The country could fall to fascism, and they wouldn't care, so long as they could ski.

What makes the Swiss-French so likeable, though, is that they bother to be concerned about the impression they give their neighbours. They're a kind of Ultimate Bourgeoisie, forever worried about what *les Joneses* and *die Schmidts* will think, even though their own standard of living is generally much higher. The only time people here allow themselves some smugness is when I tell them I live in Britain.

'You live in London? You poor thing! What terrible weather!'

For the most part, though, everyone I've met speaks very highly of the British, which is remarkable considering what some of the English have said about them. In *Miss Jemima's Swiss Journal*, the Victorian author recounts the adventures of her Junior Alpine Club in 1863 on one of the first package-holiday tours to Switzerland, conducted by Mr Thomas Cook himself. Having left Martigny, Miss Jemima and her companions continue trekking through the Rhône Valley in their hoop skirts and starched collars. 'Luxuriant as is the vegetation and exquisite the views, yet here we saw many poor miserable cretins and goitres,' she writes. 'Indeed, this splendid district has the character of being the most miserable and melancholic in Northern Europe. Superstition, ignorance, poverty and the dirty habits of the people, combined with the unhealthiness of a close low valley, are said to be the causes of this visible wretchedness.'

Her jibe about 'superstition' was a dig at Catholicism (Miss Jemima got very excited upon visiting Geneva, the 'Protestant Rome'), and Valais is still a deeply Catholic canton: in many places, priests still bless the first cheeses of the year. Thanks to the likes of Miss Jemima and Mr Cook, though, Valais' economy has been transformed.

'It's because of the English that people started coming here for the mountain air and the climate,' Frédéric told me. 'In Valais, we are going directly from agriculture to tourism. Fifty, maybe even only thirty years ago, if you had a cow, you were rich. Because the poor only had sheep. And if you had the *Reine*, you were *really* rich.'

Cowfights have taken place on the Alps for centuries, but the locals didn't start organising official *Combats des Reines* until the 1920s. In the past few years, one of Switzerland's main TV companies has started broadcasting the cantonal finals live. Last year, an overwhelming majority of viewers watched the final three hours. Why? 'Because everybody wants to go back to the authentic culture,' Frédéric explained.

Like so many events I've been to, cowfighting mirrors a resurgence of regional, if not national, pride. During the Seventies and Eighties, many farmers gave up on Herens cattle because they produce about half as much milk as other breeds. However, the Herens population numbers around 15,000 now, most of them bred for fighting. 'There are only three reasons for keeping cattle: milk, meat and fighting. Without the cowfights, this breed would have been wiped out. It's only the passion of a few that keeps them alive. Other breeds produce more milk, but this race is only for the Alps.

'If you lose a fight, you really feel as if you've lost everything. And you have. Here if you have the *Reine*, you are someone. You can have a Mercedes, a Porsche, a big house, but that's nothing,' Frédéric continued, echoing More's critiques of cow-coveters five centuries ago. 'It's easier to have those things than to have the *Reine*.'

'Money isn't enough,' Hadrien agreed.

Frédéric recently turned down an offer to sell Fercle for 40,000 Swiss francs. That's over £17,000 and about twenty times the market rate. Prices have been driven up by wealthy Valaisans who've made their money in Geneva.

'Everyone wants to have a cow in Valais now. It's like a fashion. I suppose when you're in Geneva taking your cocktail, it's very nice to be able to say, "I have a cow in Valais." But I tell you something,' he smiled, wagging his finger for emphasis, 'a man can have a lot of money, but he will never have a winner.'

PART TWO:
GRUELLING DUELS OF DROOL

At first, the cowbells sound enchanting, rounding out your typical Swiss Alpine Experience. Early on the morning of the *Combat*, the pyramidal peak above Frédéric's village is wreathed in cloud, while here in Martigny, the sun has yet to put in a personal appearance. Its rays are already warming the vineyards on the far side of the valley, but on this side, next to the vertical forest obstructing the dawn, the sunlight seeps over the brim of the mountain and filters down through the peaks in bands of blue, grey and violet mist. On the edge of town, farmers in workcoats and overalls are fretting in a patch of field smeared with excrement. Cattle the size of baby elephants are wandering across the grass, each one packing up to 800 kilos of bovine momentum that's potentially dangerous at both ends. Ever-mindful of Frédéric's warning – *ten tonnes of pressure per square centimetre* – I do my best to navigate round their horns, but I'm also wary of their backsides. Though I grew up on a ranch, I can't remember whether cows can kick. One thing's for sure: they're masters at projectile defecation. And the noise they make isn't so much a moo (or *meu*) as a sonorous growl from the days when dinosaurs walked the earth. Each and every one of the beasts is wearing a bell that's almost as big as its udder, strapped onto a leather collar at least eight inches wide and tuned to a slightly different pitch to distinguish it from the rest of the herd. Together, the melodic buckets crowd out any Sunday morning church bells – and practically every other sound in the valley – as if a deranged group of bellringers had been set loose in an industrial kitchen and started improvising with pots and pans. After a few hours of this, you're tempted to scream: *Will somebody just knock off that racket?!*

Frédéric has been here since six a.m. helping to weigh the cows by wrestling them into a narrow green trailer that's actually a scale. The queens then proceed to the relative privacy of a white tent where a female veterinarian with an ultrasound machine – just like the ones used on pregnant women – makes sure they've given birth during the past year, as the regulations require. From there, the cows go to have their horns checked. If they're too sharp, the officials use sandpaper or files to blunt them, the rule of thumb being that you should be able to balance dice on their tips.

For a time, the cows were also subjected to blood tests, but those were stopped because no evidence of doping was ever found. 'If someone was doing wrong, we could see. Everybody would know,' Frédéric reckons. And anyway, the farmers have plenty of natural tricks up their sleeves. Some owners mix the cows' food with wine and even blood to give them a taste for battle. 'But the farmers do these things mainly for themselves and their own minds,' Fred says. 'If a cow is six hundred kilos, I don't think one litre of wine is going to do much. It would probably take more like fifty litres, and even then the cow would probably be so drunk it would pass out.'

We agree to meet up later in the amphitheatre – provided that I can find it. I'm so disoriented by the barging beef machines and the noise of the bells, bells, bells, bells – and so preoccupied with dodging the squirts and cowslicks from the brutes' backsides – and of course, the two-pronged weapons on their frontsides – that I have to ask an old-timer where the arena is.

'Right there!'

I've (stupidly) managed to walk right past it. In my defence, from out here on the street, the 2,000-year-old coliseum looks like an old stone wall, and an unimpressive one at that: it's barely eight feet high. Once you go inside, though, you realise that it's a 5,000-seat arena sunk into the ground. Modern wooden stands have been built on top of the ancient concentric circles, and the inner stone wall – the barrier between the audience and the cow ring – is at least ten feet high in its own right. The knobbly grey walls are decorated with the banners of cowfighting's quintessentially Swiss sponsors: a bank, an insurance firm and a mineral water company.

The farmers lead their queens into the stadium via the entrance that would've once been used by gladiators and wild beasts. 'Watch the owners,' an aficionado advised me. 'They're funnier than the cows!' Many farmers use secret gestures to beckon their cows to the sidelines and keep them from fighting too much at the beginning of the competition. They may flick their fingers or stick their hands in their pockets – or they may have treats like bread or salt stashed in their trousers. When the judges tell them off, the old boys feign innocence, puffing out their cheeks and miming Gallic shrugs, as if to say: *What do you expect? She loves me!* To counter this interference, five *rabatteurs*, or 'pushers', have the unenviable job of prodding the horned behemoths into battle.

Cowfighting is often portrayed as the bovine answer to boxing, but it reminds me more of Turkish Oil Wrestling (sadly, I may be the only person in the world qualified to make that comparison). The preliminary rounds consist of a dozen or so combatants pairing off against each other simultaneously, and, like the finals in Oil Wrestling, sometimes there's not a lot of action on the field. A few curmudgeons have even gone so far as to imply that cowfighting is boring. In its defence, I'd argue that it's no duller than your average spectator sport: the crucial ingredient is drink. Many aficionados start drinking early and often, downing white Fendant or red Gamay from plastic glasses or guzzling it directly from the bottle. For fans – and there are entire families here – this is a big day out, a chance to see their heritage played out in a Roman amphitheatre, surrounded by the Alps, with litres of drink to tide over the *longueurs.*

Frédéric, for one, is riveted. 'This is a microcosm,' he tells me as I join him in the stands. 'Everybody knows everybody. Everybody goes to the same pubs and the same fairs.' Whereas all I see are a bunch of dark cows with white numbers painted on their sides, he knows their lineage and owners' names. The mother of Number 62, for instance, was a Queen of Queens with the unflattering name of Moustache.

A typical cowfight begins inauspiciously, with the two animals burrowing into the turf and rubbing their mastodon jaws in the dust.

'They're women. They have to put on their make-up,' cracks a man next to me, teaching his son the finer points of cowfighting and chauvinism.

Then the cows drool some more and squirt some excrement, paw the ground without looking at each other and shove their faces in the dirt again. But as soon as their horns make contact, clanking and clattering against each other, the fight is quickly engaged. They headbutt each other, their skulls colliding with an almighty crack that's muffled only by the bells (always the bells). A cow loses if it walks away from a fight or gets knocked back three times. Occasionally one queen will bellybust another through the rope and out of the ring, snapping the fence poles like matchsticks.

Then a five-year-old bull – I mean cow (it's hard not to mistake them for males) – struts into the ring, her head dipped slightly but horns erect. Fred informs me that Number 122 is the daughter of one of his family's bulls. 'For me, she's the favourite. The owner's from my village. I think in fifty years, the man has never had a cow like it.'

As the potential queen starts duking it out with her horns, though, she suddenly rears back her head. 'Ooh! That's either in the cheek or the nose, but you can see by the way she twisted her head that she was hurt.'

She makes a break for the exit, but her elderly owner gives her some dry bread to boost her morale. 'Had it been my cow, I wouldn't have brought her here, because she's too young,' Frédéric observes. 'But the owner's in his seventies – he might not be here next year!'

Another combatant gets fishhooked in the nostril, flinging a glistening stream of blood on the ground. 'That is like a boxer. It looks bad, but it is just a superficial wound.'

'Do the cows ever try to gore each other?'

'Yes, but it's not good. A cow that does that cannot be Queen. It is not gentlemanly.' He laughs. 'We have a gentleman's code of honour.' If a rogue cow tries to horn in on a duel, for instance, the *rabbateurs* will ward it off. 'It's the same with people. Ninety per cent of people respect a fight between two men. But there's always ten per cent who want to stick their horns in. And it's incredible: that ten per cent of cows corresponds to the same ten per cent of owners! The nastier the owner, the nastier the cow.'

Most of the finer specimens of the Herens breed range in colour from glossy black to tawny red, but the next round features a rare relative, an Evolener cow distinguished by a splotchy red coat and a white stripe down its spine. 'A hundred years ago, all cows in Valais were like her,' Frédéric explains.

Number 128, aka Benarès, shoves a black-coated opponent across the turf and pushes away another, bigger cow before seeing off a third challenger. With each victory, she bays to the crowd like a champion. By the time she qualifies for the group final, the spectators' cheers are running full throttle. 'They want her to win because she is a reminder of the way the cows used to be. Normally, you wouldn't expect her to win because the older types aren't as strong as the black ones.'

There's a break for lunch around noon, and suddenly, all

around us, the most delicious-looking picnics appear from out of nowhere: dried hams to be carved with Swiss Army knives; baguettes and rounds of crusty bread, cheese wheels, grapes, apples, pears and plenty of wine. Not having packed anything, I join Frédéric and his family for a quick lunch of Raclette and Fendant in one of the food tents outside the arena and then go for a walk around *Le Comptoire*. It's like a Swiss version of the state fairs I grew up with in America, an expo selling everything from kitchen sinks, furniture, safes, skis, TVs, tractors, toilets, taxidermy and hygienic paper dispensers to mini-lathes and miraculous buff-and-go gadgets that keep your shoes gleaming just long enough to separate you from your cash. There's a Canadian pavilion hosted by a big-bearded lumberjack (which may explain the worrying number of plaid shirts on sale), plus fairground rides, waffle stands and a big Swiss Army outpost, complete with watchtower, in keeping with this year's theme. And dotted throughout are a multitude of eat-and-drinkeries, many of the latter specialising in wines, beers, spirits and liqueuers, so that you could easily have a four-course liquid lunch – topped off, of course, by a visit to the milk bar.

For the finals, I sit ringside with Frédéric's father, a man with businessman's hair but a farmer's features. His skin is so red it looks painful to the touch, though the steady flow of Fendant from his friends and fellow VIPs must act as an anaesthetic.

As head of the group that organised this year's *Combat*, Mr Boson is entitled to the best seats in the house. In contrast to a Spanish bullfight, that means we're on the sunny side of the amphitheatre; the standing section is left in the shade. The emcee is making increasingly ridiculous pleas for people on the far side to stand up so they can pack more people into the stadium. 'Standing is good for the legs!' he declares to jeers and whistles. The scorn continues as a pink-faced man with a politician's smile starts droning a speech expressing his gratitude to all the dignitaries and their mothers. His voice gets sucked into a whirlwind of derision.

'People here are very anarchic,' a guy next to me chuckles.

The grass in the ring has long since been worn away, and the arena has turned into a dustbowl, the cattle kicking up particle clouds that choke the spectators. The emcee announces that the local fire brigade is going to spray the field with water. After a lengthy pause, a lone fireman steps into the ring carrying a puny hose that stretches only halfway across the field.

The heckles come hailing down; even the emcee's at it: 'The fire department of Martigny doesn't do things halfway!'

Meantime, a local tells me that the cows fight only two or three times a year. 'Because after this, they have a big pain in the head. But I don't know what people in England will think if you print that.'

My interpreter explains: 'The British are famous for loving animals. I remember we once met an English couple in Crete. They were quite something,' she says, allowing herself a chuckle. 'They wanted to save all the cats in Crete. And of course you know how fast cats breed. But they were rounding up all the cats and sterilising them. But they couldn't sterilise them fast enough. And the locals, they didn't know what to think!'

Maybe it's sympathy pains, but between the dust, wine and bells, my head's starting to hurt, too. The sad-sack fireman finally manages to dampen at least half the field, and the competition gets underway. Benarès, the red-and-white cow from this morning, enters the arena to applause from the crowd; she takes a salutary crap in response. Alone in a field of fourteen dark finalists, she quickly locks horns with Number 22, pushing and shoving in a grudge match.

Benarès falters, and 22 – aka Pommette – breaks the stalemate. The old-fashioned, red-and-white cow places fourth in her category, with a gash in her cheek and blood staining the cuticle around her horn. The queen of her group is a cow called Yoko, who's awarded with only polite applause. After all, she and her owner hail from St Nicklaus in Upper Valais; they're Swiss-German.

The finals grind on through the afternoon as the shadows lengthen across the field, with many of the cows exhausted but driven by instinct to fight. One of the most impressive matches is between the biggest cow in the competition and a much smaller queen. Iris weighs 677 kilos – a mere strapling compared to hippo-sized Banko, who's no less than 838 kilos. As the clear undercow, Iris is the crowd's favourite, but she's breathing so hard by the end it looks like a dwarf is trampolining inside her belly. Banko uses her sheer bulk to force her back but gets gored in the process. Blood seeps through the chestnut fur on her forehead. However, she quickly cows Iris. Then she paws the dirt, takes a ruminative crap, and goes on to bully another cow.

Fickle as ever, the crowd shouts its approval. 'It's very rare for the big ones to fight so much,' Mr Boson explains. 'Normally it's the small ones. People want to breed big cows, but there's usually nothing in their heads. They're stupid.'

It's just like with people, I can hear Fred say . . .

Putting that theory to the test, Banko faces off against Tina, a former cantonal champion who weighs 'only' 705 kilos.

Banko immediately engages her, but Tina twists her head and bulldozes her back.

'*Fantastique! Fantastique!*' an aficionado shouts.

But the encounter soon settles into a deadlock, with the two heavyweights circling around in the dust. Banko suddenly makes a break and nails Tina in the neck, shoving her back twenty feet.

'*Incroyable! Incroyable!*' Mr Boson hollers.

By now the smaller cow has a bloody horn, but she manages to duck under Banko and hammer her head into her larynx, ejecting a thick stream of drool from her bigger rival. Banko finally gives up as the crowd cheers the performance of both cows in the best fight of the day so far.

The sun has long since disappeared behind the mountains by the time Tina fights in the final match of the competition, dispatching a cow named Esméralda to become Martigny's Queen of Queens.

'*Exceptionnel! Exceptionnel!*'

The spectators hurry out of the stadium to get in a solid hour of drinking at the fair before it closes. 'Normally, the *Combat* ends earlier so there is plenty of time for drinking and talking about the cows, but there won't be much time tonight!' an aficionado tells me on our way out. 'The quality of the cows was excellent. You're lucky to have seen such a good match.'

I'd hate to have seen a bad one.

In the congratulatory tumult outside the amphitheatre, Tina is standing under a tree on the field where it all began this morning, patiently waiting for a lift home. Her owner, a young farmer named David Moulin, is swigging wine straight from the bottle and exhaling firewater fumes. He says Tina has won four times at Martigny, but this was the first time as a fully grown adult in the heavyweight category. 'I feel superb. I've won other awards, but this is the peak.'

'So what clinched it for you this time?'

His answer is as pure as it is simple, one that any Valaisan cowlover would understand: *'Passion.'*

CHAPTER NINE

PADDYWHACKED
MATCHMAKING IN IRELAND

PART ONE:

ALL THE WOMEN LOVE WILLIE

Welcome to Lisdoonvarna!

That's what the expat from Boston thinks as she wedges herself into the pub. A corporate jet-setter based in Ireland, she doesn't have much time to meet men, and given that she's on the far side of thirty, time may be running out. Not that she's looking, of course. She's just here for a good time – the *craic*, as the Irish call it. Then again, you never know – it could be like that Hollywood movie, the one where a wisecracking Yank falls for an Irish charmer: dark, handsome and presumably hung like a donkey (never mind what they say about the Irish Curse). Sure enough, the moment our

Bostonian sets foot in The Matchmaker, she's hit with her first chat-up line of the evening:

'Yer boobs – are they real?'

Welcome to Lisdoonvarna! A Lourdes of Love for romantics; for others, a Guinness-fuelled den of iniquity, a 'culchie' Sodom and Gomorrah, a country-and-western rutfest stuck way out in the far west of Ireland – the very edge of Europe – just a few miles from the Cliffs of Moher, where Hibernia plunges into the sea, resurfacing again to form the Aran Islands. Like Connemara to the north, County Clare is about as Irish as modern Ireland gets, one of the last vestiges of 'real Ireland' (whatever that is), where a former spa town continues a custom once widespread throughout the country and the Continent: matchmaking.

At the centre of Lisdoonvarna's annual lovefest – 'Europe's Biggest Singles Festival' – is Willie Daly, 'Ireland's last matchmaker', a horse trader by day and Love Doctor by night. Willie's father was a matchmaker, as was his father before him, dating the Daly love-doctoring dynasty back to the late 1800s. Over the past four decades, Willie's vocation has grown from an intensely local practice to an international affair. His father and grandfather used to conduct their business in discreet consultations in pubs and homes, but Willie's work is now very much out in the open. Country fairs, weddings and even funerals used to be the only places for singletons to meet people outside their villages; in recent years, though, Willie has made matchmaking missions to Irish bars in Dublin, London and New York, and every day he gets hundreds of letters from would-be brides and grooms all over the world. Whereas phones were still rare in rural Ireland when he started out, nowadays his clients keep in touch via mobiles and emails, and Willie's reputation has been parlayed into an Internet dating site for the Diaspora. For the past four years, he's had an 'office' at the front of The Matchmaker pub, with a window facing onto the high street, where potential clients can fill out a form to add their name to Willie's hopelessly tattered Book of Love.

'I just keep it for looks,' he grins through his beard, caressing the four-inch sheaf passed down from his grandfather. The layers of paper demark different generations, the strata of love and desperation, bound with eroded cardboard and held together by a shoestring and scraggly Scotch tape that has long since turned grey and curly.

Every weekend from late August until early October, for the duration of Lisdoonvarna's Matchmaking Festival, Willie mans his office from around nine o'clock until necessary, inter-viewing prospective grooms and would-be brides who become bolder the more they drink. 'I'm happier with this system now,' he tells me. 'It's more public. People used to be shy, but they're losin' that shyness. It'll be quiet at the beginning, but as the night goes on, they're anything but shy, if you know what I mean.'

Earlier this evening, I helped Willie tape up the signs around his office, a small, rectangular room painted cream with pink highlights and a black-and-white chequered floor. Like the rest of the pub, Willie's office is bright and modern. In fact, The Matchmaker is barely distinguishable from the Oirish theme pubs you'll find anywhere in the world; it's a pub chain waiting to happen. There's even a Vietnamese guy pouring the Guinness. But there's only one flesh-and-blood Matchmaker. Willie receives his visitors behind a dark, wood table positioned so that his clients can sit with their backs to the open doorway. The three signs in the window provide some added protection from gossips and gawkers on the street, though people can still peer in if they want to – and this being a small town, they do want to. Above Willie's head, the sign stuck to a mirror is handwritten in black marker on a white background:

MATCHMAKING
ON NOW
COME IN

The admonishment outside the door is even more insistent:

WHAT ARE YOU WAITING FOR?

After all, Willie's clients may not have much time left. Ireland has one of the youngest populations in Europe, but the demographic at Lisdoonvarna tends towards the liver-spot end of the age spectrum. Some singletons are so far gone they've started saying things like 'I'm sixty-four years *young*'. What's more, the men and women who pack out the pubs and hotels this weekend are so old, they actually – brace yourself – know how to *dance*. Not pogo mindlessly into each other or waggle their limbs in chemical-induced ecstasy, but really dance, coordinating their steps and movements with their partners. They'll be two-stepping, foxtrotting and jiving around the dancefloor to Irish country-and-western, which one woman describes as 'American country music taken one step back'.

Whether this is an improvement, I can't tell.

Despite the best efforts of the band, it's still too early for the crowds on this Thursday night. However, Willie has a steady following in his own right. For many women of a certain age, the main attraction of the Matchmaking Festival is the Matchmaker himself. All the women love Willie: soft-spoken with light eyes, he has longish white hair combed back high off his forehead and a peppery white beard. To country-loving women, he represents an irresistible mix of clean-living ruggedness. He's a gentle man – a gentleman in the literal sense – compared to the rough farmers who have dirt under their nails and no idea of how to treat a lady. Willie's wearing a dapper blue shirt that highlights his eyes, and he has a checked blazer folded underneath his bench, for when he goes around town introducing people. He keeps a blue comb in his pocket and regularly touches up his lip balm. And what woman could resist Willie's smile? The gaps in his grin do the winking for him. Women do doubletakes outside the window, and he smiles at them, kissing his first two fingers and waving so that the other half of his hand flutters in an odd *toodaloo*-type gesture.

Willie reckons he's around sixty years old, but he doesn't know for certain. The priest at the time – 'a lovely man' – was fond of a drink, and instead of noting infants' names in the parish register, he'd write them on bits of paper that were stuffed in his pocket for a moment of sobriety that never arrived.

As he's telling me his stories, women keep interrupting, teased, permed and perfumed for their big night out. One asks if she can have her photo taken with the world-famous Matchmaker of Lisdoonvarna.

Willie sweet-talks her. 'It's not often I get to have my picture taken with a beautiful woman.' She giggles like a sexagenarian schoolgirl.

Another one who doesn't look a day under sixty bustles in amid a cloud of cream chiffon, her unnaturally red hair hovering in a coiffed V over her head.

'I must get your photo in there!' Willie says, pointing to his book. 'I like the hair.'

She happily fills out one of Willie's application forms. Under the space to describe what she's looking for in a man, she scrawls 'smart, tall' – and a third qualifier that looks to me like 'mick'.

In deepest Ireland, surely that's a given.

'*Rich,*' she says. 'And no crutches – I want a man to take me out, not keep me in!'

The moment she leaves through the invisible revolving door, in totters a fiftysomething babe with a platinum-blonde bouffant, white miniskirt and enough make-up to compensate for her sidekick's plain-Jane appearance. The two women are sipping a milky yellow substance that smells like liquorice.

'Pernod and lemonade,' the blonde tells me. 'You know what they call it?'

I have no idea.

Feigning embarrassment, she whispers in my ear: 'The Open Legs Drink.'

While she cackles, her friend grimaces at the lack of action on the dancefloor. 'They're not dancing!'

'No, foreigners don't dance,' Willie explains. 'They just like to listen to the music.'

'I feel sorry for the fella who's playing more than anything,' she grumbles into her drink, the liquorice taste making her frown even more.

Willie does the gentlemanly thing and offers her blonde friend a dance. After a few twirls on the dancefloor, he returns to see whether he should shut up shop for the evening and spend the rest of the night introducing couples in the pubs.

'There isn't much prospects tonight,' he sighs after an hour or so, returning from the doorway at the sparsely peopled bar.

As if to prove the point, in stomps a short, intense man on a coach tour from Cork. Joe has big ears, a big nose and big, tinted glasses. The bald island atop his head is fringed by ridiculously black hair wisping across his forehead. An over-sized cross dangles between the buttons on his shiny short-sleeved shirt. This man could single-handedly drive a stake through the stereotype of the charming Irishman.

'Mr Daly, fix me up with a nice girl now,' he says, with the urgency of someone who is double-parked and has just popped into the shops to pick himself up a woman. He plonks down across from the Matchmaker. 'I don't want a girl who will rip me off. Not like the last one I found. She was from Galway.'

'No, they're all nice women in here.'

'So go on, what have you got?' He twists the book round and starts flipping through the pages. 'I can't see too well. What sort of woman would you find for me?'

Willie eyes him reluctantly. 'Well . . . she'd be a little taller than you . . . blonde . . . works in an office – so a nice professional type . . .'

He's winging it as he goes.

Joe nods eagerly with each detail.

'. . . not good-lookin'—'

'She's not good-lookin'?' Joe's not completely put off, though. After all, she might have other ways of making up for her lack of looks.

'She's what they call *attractive*. She's the kind of woman who could make herself look good with make-up.'

'But if you woke up to her in the morning, you wouldn't be frightened.'

'She's not good-lookin', but you can make her up to *be* good-lookin'.'

'Is her picture in here?'

'I don't think it is, no.'

'Can you bring 'er here now?' Joe asks, tapping the table.

'Well, I'll have to see if she's about, I haven't seen her here tonight.'

'But you could find her for me.'

'I know where she lives and I could see if she's interested.'

Willie stands up to survey the bar while Joe flips through the pages of his directory *d'amour*, pausing at the Asian Celtic Connection section. 'I don't want no Asian women,' he tells me, now that Willie has turned his back on him. 'I'll tell you the truth. Now this is the God's truth. You can have the most beautiful, lovely Thai woman in Thailand, but once you take her out of her culture and she comes here' – he flips his hands as if rotating a jar – 'she turns *old*.'

It strikes me that this might have something to do with a lack of sunshine and fresh vegetables or possibly the effects of year-round potato consumption on the complexion, but instead I try to suggest a logical alternative.

'Maybe you should take an ugly old Irishwoman to Thailand.'

He stares at me blankly. He's not interested in anything Thai. He wants a take-away woman right now.

'And I don't want a woman with ties, either,' he tells Willie. 'I'm going travelling on the Continent for the next couple of months. I've got a motorhome, and I won't be back till Christmas. Will that girl be prepared to travel?'

'Well, you'll have to ask her,' Willie sighs.

'So if I come back tomorrow night at nine o'clock, you'll have her here for me?'

'I'll see what I can do.'

'And how old is she?'

'Forty-two.'

That seems to fit the bill.

'And no ties!' Joe shouts on his way out.

Next morning, I set off for Willie's farm several miles outside Lisdoonvarna. In the bar of my hotel, the 'First-Chance Dance' has already begun. Three couples are waltzing away – all of them women – while two men of a similarly certain age shyly sip their pints and look on in frustration. There's a lingering scent of neglected bachelorhood: mothballed suits, farmyard pheromones and lashings of the worst cologne of all: desperation. Ireland's ban on smoking in pubs seems to have stuck, but judging from the odours wafting across the dancefloor last night, the legislators overlooked the importance of tobacco as a masking agent for all manner of smells. 'The air used to be full of smoke,' a woman told me. 'Now it's just Guinness farts.'

As a foreigner, I'm obliged to describe the west coast of Ireland as romantically 'wild' and 'rugged' – the Irish Tourist Board makes you sign a contract at the airport – but the clear-eyed truth is that County Clare isn't as spectacular as other parts of the country. For mountains, Clare has hills, and its tumbledown stone walls are overgrown with briars. Any emerald greens are shot through with bogrushes and bracken. It's the kind of landscape you'd expect to peter out self-pityingly into the ocean: *Don't mind me, I'm just going to go drown myself.* But that's when Clare comes into its own: the waves battering the rocks at Doolin, the moulded moonscape known as the Burren (best photographed in close-up) and the 600-foot drop at the Cliffs of Moher, with an Irish busker included in the ticket price. Fortunately, though, if you like your nature soundtrack-free – *was there Muzak in the Garden of Eden?* – the Celticness® is optional, thanks to the wind. So Clare does have its moments. On the whole, though, the county suffers from comparison with its neighbours. If Connemara just across Galway Bay is the craggy, stoic face of Samuel Beckett, then Clare is the bushy physog of a farmer.

In fact, Clare and neighbouring County Kerry are the historical heartland of the 'culchies', the good, honest country folk derided as 'muck savages' by the citified Irish. Unable to beat the stereotype, local yokels have joined in making fun of themselves by setting up their very own National Culchie Festival and banning Dubliners from the competition. Although everybody may laugh about it now, the east–west divide runs much deeper than the tedious city–country conflicts you find everywhere in the world. The Most Evilest Englishman in History famously banished Irish Catholics 'to hell or Connaught' – the region west of the Shannon River – and some locals can still recite, with a little catch in their throats, the famous assessment by Cromwell's surveyor that the area was 'a savage land, yielding neither water enough to drown a man, nor a tree to hang him nor soil enough to bury him . . .' Curiously, what they fail to recall is the last bit of the phrase: '. . . yet their cattle are very fat.' It just doesn't fit the myth.

Now, I have to confess that before meeting Willie, I suspected he was a bit of a blarneymeister milking the fat cow of Oirishness. Depending on what you read, he's variously described as a matchmaker, a horse trader and even a horse whisperer. If it didn't stretch the bounds of credulity, you wonder if he wouldn't add Leprechaun Tracker to his CV. Besides the variable fee he charges for his services, he also owns a bar – Daly's over in Ennistymon – and he offers 'Love Trail' pony-trekking trips for singletons.

Horseplay may seem unlikely training for a career in match-making; then again, consider how many horsy euphemisms we have for love and otherwise. A virile man is a 'stud' or 'stallion', his female counterpart 'a young filly'. If the couple like each other, they may 'get their oats', 'knock boots', 'get their legs over' or even 'ride bareback'.

The equine link with human coupling comes from the days when most people travelled on foot and horse traders were the bucolic bon vivants, the country connoisseurs who knew of every eligible boy and girl in the county. Horse trading at fairs and markets brought them into contact with farmers who were well off enough to pay to keep their own bloodlines going. So matchmaking was a natural – and socially necessary – sideline. In 1934, a professor from Harvard spent a few months living on a farm near Lisdoonvarna to write an 'anthropological study' on *The Irish Countryman*. Conrad Arensberg noted that although matchmaking was common throughout Europe, 'in Ireland its importance is such as to make it the crucial point of rural social organisation'. Even in those days, the Irish got married later than their foreign counterparts, and for different reasons. Arensberg reported that 62 per cent of Irish men and 42 per cent of women between the ages of thirty and thirty-five were unmarried, compared to an average of about 25 per cent for both sexes in the US and England. 'Other countries usually delay marriage longest in the urban professional classes. But in Ireland, it is the country people who marry latest,' he wrote. This was partly due to poverty – many farmers couldn't afford the dowries to marry off their daughters, and few owned enough land to sustain large families. But it also had to do with the absolute power that many mothers had (and still have) over their sons. The traditional Irish mammy ruled her household with semi-divine authority, and it was her ironhanded benevolence that kept her family – and Irish society – together at times when external forces were doing their best to tear them apart. The downside came during the transition of power, when mammy had to abdicate to her daughter-in-law. 'What's the old saying?' Willie mentioned last night. 'More than one woman in the kitchen is a recipe for disaster.'

The mammies fought their corner particularly hard because in the unwritten rule of the countryside (not unlike the jungle), it was the old who were driven out of the family home if they didn't play happy families. As a result, to this day many 'mammy's boys' don't marry until their mothers die. If they did find a bride, the new woman of the house was under intense pressure to prove her worth by producing offspring. 'No matter how much money you have, no matter how good-looking you are, if you don't have children, you are no good,' a childless woman told Arensberg. 'But if you are ugly as the worst and have children, you are all right. The man wants children just as much as the woman. He is afraid others will tell him he is no good if he hasn't any.' Then she added a phrase that's as profound as it is heartbreaking: 'Children are the curse of this country, especially if you haven't any.'

Around the time Arensberg was anthropologising the Irish, Willie's father would have been making matches in County Clare. Meanwhile, in North Kerry, the man hailed as 'Ireland's last great matchmaker' was just beginning his career. By all accounts Dan Paddy Andy O'Sullivan – 'the Man of the Triple Name' – was much better at matchmaking than horse trading. Despite his poor eyesight, he was responsible for 400 marriages, increasing Ireland's population by some 2,000 children in the process. In thirty years, only one of his matches was a failure, he claimed: the wife was so religious as to be frightened of sex. She eventually returned to her father's home, and her husband lived out his days with a 'housekeeper' who gave birth to a son and a daughter: somewhat ironically, they wound up becoming a priest and a nun.

That's one of the many surprising – and often poignant – stories in *Dan Paddy Andy*, a fascinating book by John B. Keane (best known for his play *The Field*, which was also a film starring Richard Harris). When Dan Paddy Andy was just starting out, priests still prowled the countryside at night with sticks and terriers to hound amorous couples out of the hedgerows. From their pulpits, they denounced O'Sullivan for opening the first dancehall in the area (with the tin-eared name of the Pallodium), way before the age of rock 'n' roll: at the time, the 'Devil's music' was usually played on an accordion. Nevertheless, Dan was convinced he was fighting the good fight by finding wives for men like Dinny Doodawn, who had his bits burnt as a child and had to go to London to repair his 'undercarriage'. O'Sullivan convinced another young suitor to let a doctor photograph him in the nude so that he could prove to his prospective father-in-law that he had all his 'faculties'. Then there was his tried and tested advice to a couple that was having trouble conceiving: 'Don't leave the bed until you haven't the strength to lace your shoes.' And if that didn't work, he knew of at least two couples who were so desperate for children, they decided that the wife should go on her own to a festival such as Lisdoonvarna, in a place where she wouldn't be recognised, to be impregnated by a 'young, vigorous and lusty rustic', to use Keane's words.

O'Sullivan reckoned that he had three fraudulent enquiries for every sincere one, and he was always on the lookout for conmen trying to trick women out of their inheritances. "Twas the hair oil and the tie pin that put me onto that buck in the first place,' he said of one rogue. On another occasion, a couple of brothers told him that they wanted to find a single woman to serve both of them; they couldn't afford two wives. When the time came to baptise their children, they planned to toss a coin to decide which one was the father. Dan responded by banging their heads together and literally kicking them out of town. Unbelievably, though, the brothers did end up finding a woman who acted as wife to them both. And this all took place in rural Ireland in 1946.

As you might expect, Dan Paddy Andy was full of old-fashioned wisdom, though it wasn't entirely predictable: 'Better for a man to fall in line with a woman than be expecting her to fall in line with him. 'Tis a deal easier for a man to skip into step. Give her the handling of the money as well and you'll never want, no matter how hard the times.' He empathised with the men who sought out his services – 'They does be dribbling from the mouth in desperation' – and detested those who mocked the less fortunate. One incident in particular sums up his life's work. A well-to-do man was making fun of a poor, would-be suitor in a pub. O'Sullivan grabbed the eejit by the collar and shouted, 'Every man is entitled to a woman, you begrudging thief, you!' It's worth keeping that in mind when considering matchmaking at Lisdoonvarna.

Dan Paddy Andy met his Maker in 1966, and the media soon conferred the title of Ireland's Last Matchmaker onto Willie – not counting the 'Cupid Curate' who founded the Knock Marriage Bureau in County Mayo in 1968.

Arriving at Willie's farm, I find him out feeding some of his calves. He's sporting khaki cords, wellies and a pastel-yellow buttondown: a dapper man even while doing the chores. We chat as he mixes the powdered milk substitute with hot water from his tea kettle. For some reason or other, he mentions my age.

'You look younger than thirty-four.'

'Aw, I think you flatter everybody you meet.'

He grins. 'Well, with a lot of the women, you want to make them feel special, even if they aren't that good-lookin'. Did you see that one last night with the bun in her hair and the miniskirt? Any other night and she would've got plenty of takers. She would've been treated like a *queen*.'

Like many homes in the area, Willie's farmhouse is similar to any bungalow you'd find in a middling suburb, only this is plopped in the middle of the countryside. Inside, the lino-floored kitchen has an old-fashioned cooker with a grill for toasting bread on top, a clapped-out dishwasher held together with black tape, and a picture of Christ on the wall, with a panel of insect killer hanging from the empty socket meant to illuminate the Messiah. Another patch of bug poison adorns one of the wooden cabinets, and in the kitchen window, a pair of shorts has been draped to dry over the head of the Virgin Mary: possibly the closest she ever got to getting into a man's pants. For a few years now Willie's been separated from the mother of his seven children (he has eight in total), but his daughters drop by regularly to beat back the onslaught of male untidiness. Today it falls to Grainne, Marie and Sarah, who can't help but try to bring some order to the place whenever they visit. 'This is a bachelor's flat,' says Sarah, as she bravely attempts to do the washing up. 'I mean, just look at it.'

Over tea and shortbread, Willie tells me that his success rate was nearly a 100 per cent in his first couple of years making matches. 'But very quickly that changed.' He tends to blame this on modern women being overly 'fussy' or 'picky', a reminder that matchmaking has always been a very male-oriented business. Giving him the benefit of the doubt, though, the truth is that women have moved on, and men have been left behind. Eligible females continue to leave the countryside, a phenomenon that seems to be widespread in Europe – at the Rooster Run in Spain, for instance, the men were complaining about a lack of women. In Irish families, the eldest sons inherited the land, so unmarried daughters had no choice but to leave, usually moving to cities in Ireland, England or America; and once they adjusted to city life, they rarely returned to the country. West of the Shannon River, the ratio of men to women is easily ten to one. Willie says about 70 per cent of the people who seek his services are men and the other 30 per cent women. 'And a lot of the women probably aren't as young as they need to be.' Most of his clients are in the forty-four to seventy-five age bracket.

Given that he's reluctant to divulge his success rate, Willie's incredibly precise about his clients' nationalities: humouring me, he tells me that most are Irish, but 7 per cent come from America (mainly women); 1 per cent are German; 2.5 per cent hail from the Philippines, with a bunch of enquiries from Thailand, too; and 5–7 per cent visit from England. English women often find the festival overwhelming, he reckons. 'They don't know how to socialise like Irish people. They're too well-behaved and they miss out on a lot of fun.' He obviously hasn't seen an English hen party rampaging through Temple Bar in Dublin.

The good news is that his hit rate has rebounded in recent years. 'At the moment there's a lot of interest in the Irish male.

He's wealthy now, and he's got a lovely house. The EU has been very good to him.' Earlier, he pointed out a couple of boxy, two-bedroom houses along the lane that used to be home to families of seventeen and eighteen children. 'But there's no kids on the road now. Give it eight or nine years, though, and this area will be repopulated. Ireland is boomin' right now. That's the only word for it – boomin'. But in some ways we've become too well off in Ireland. You become too well off, and you lose your traditions too fast. And it makes people greedy.'

'So what's the most important factor in matching couples?'

There's a moment of pensive biscuit-munching before he replies. 'Within reason, physical attraction. But personality is also important, too.'

'Was Joe from last night a typical client?'

He seems relieved to say no. 'I don't think that man's looking for a wife. I think he just wants a girlfriend for a couple of months or so.' He'll end up putting Joe off with the Irish version of *mañana*.

Willie goes into the next room to show me some of the hundreds of letters he keeps stuffed in a chest of drawers, next to a couple of mounted English saddles. In one, a Yorkshireman has included a photo of himself, potbellied and posing in the messiest corner of his house, with his leg cocked at a carefree yet composed angle, as if he regularly gets the urge to vogue in his own home.

'He might want to slim down a bit if he wants to find a woman,' Willie chuckles. 'He wouldn't get many takers like that.'

But the majority of Willie's cases are local men who are desperate to find wives. It's not uncommon for them to show up at the dances with their bank details and the deeds to their houses to help speed up the courting. For many farmers, though, it's the dancing itself – the mere opportunity to get close to female warmth – that represents a huge part of the festival's appeal. 'They want to be where they can grab *hold* of a woman,' Willie says, clenching his fist.

Back in the Seventies, the matchmaking coincided with a music festival immortalised in 'Lisdoonvarna', the song by Christy Moore. However, general rowdiness put a stop to the event after complaints from locals and Dubliners with holiday homes in the area. 'Even the first year it was so funny, it reminded me of the Battle of the Boyne,' Willie laughs, describing how scores of men were lined up on either side of the river in Lisdoonvarna throwing bottles at each other.

'I remember it was a Friday night and I was on the radio being interviewed, and I think my wife was in the hospital havin' the baby—'

'Me,' Sarah interjects, while washing the dishes. She's smiling, but not laughing. 'I was bein' born and you were on the radio, ya old fecker.'

'It was on Friday evening' – he's still chuckling – 'and, Jesus, by Sunday evening, I couldn't believe it. There must've been at *least* twenty fellas piled on each other pure drunk. They were thrown in together in a big lump.'

Christy Moore and the other musicians managed to revive the Lisdoonvarna festival briefly, but they had to relocate it to Dublin after being rebuffed by Clare's county council. Again, 'middle-class Dubs' were blamed for blocking the proposal to hold the concerts in their original venue. Young musicians were particularly disappointed. 'It sounded so romantic,' lamented the lead singer of folk-rock group The Frames. 'It's the kind of Ireland I have only ever seen in American films.'

The mind reels . . . Nowadays, many locals complain that the Matchmaking Festival is nothing but a tourist gimmick that rakes it in during the fair's three-month run. That may well be the case, but Willie seems to see very little of the money.

A couple of his relatives have stopped by on their way back to Dublin, so he pops out to say hello, leaving me to speak with Sarah. Dark-haired and pretty, she's just the type of woman that the local men would like to see more of. But she's a student in London, and she's not sure whether she'll come back to Ireland. Although her dad would like nothing better than for one of his kids to follow in his footsteps, she admits that she couldn't handle the emotional strain of the work. Willie acts as a friend and counsellor, providing year-round support to many farmers in the area. She tells me about the hard cases, the men who probably will never find partners, and the phone calls in the middle of the night from the farmers driven to the brink by loneliness. 'I *really* don't like matchmaking,' she says. 'I call it a vocation, actually, rather than a job, I don't think there's any profit from it at all, to be honest.'

By the evening, the late-breaking sunshine has turned into a real Irish rain: all the centuries of suffering condensed in heaven and then poured out, drenching you to the soul – and if the rain doesn't get you (thanks to the miracle of modern fabrics), the mist will. On the field outside my hotel, boys no more than ten are playing football in the downpour. A few inches more, and they'll have to switch to water polo.

Before visiting Willie at The Matchmaker, I head over to the Roadside Tavern to indulge in my newfound favourite meal for the second night in a row. I'd never appreciated the potential of boiled bacon and cabbage with potatoes, assuming it was one of those dishes you have to be brought up with to appreciate. Boiling three already flavourless ingredients to hell and back has never sounded very appetising. However, I've now seen the error of my ways. The bacon is thick with flavour, chewing to the same consistency as the potatoes, which turn to mash in your mouth while the bacon fat acts as butter. The cabbage is there to soak up all the creamy white parsley sauce, plus the English mustard that I add to give it a kick. And it's all heaped on a plate so hot the table's still warm after it's been cleared away. The Polish waitress may not speak English very well, but she more than makes up for it with her mental telepathy. She brings me a Guinness the moment I sit down.

Apart from that, though, it's destined to be a night full of misunderstandings.

By the time I make it over to The Matchmaker, a group of friends and acquaintances are already huddled around Willie in his office. I take a seat next to an overweight, ponytailed guy with glasses and a chain of red volcanic welts running up and down his neck: he's popped his pimples especially for the occasion. We get to talking, two guys hunkered down on a bench, and he tells me he's been drinking since eight thirty.

'Thats not too bad,' I offer.

'Eight thirty . . . *in the morning.*'

That explains why his head keeps wanting to roll off his shoulders.

'So what's your type, then?' I ask, gesturing towards Willie's book on the table.

He rears back, glaring at me with drunken umbrage. 'Not male. *Not* male!'

'What? No, I meant what type of woman . . .'

I go over to the other corner of the room – as far away as I can get – to lick my wounds. 'All I said was, "What's your type?"' I moan to the guy next to me.

'That was your first mistake,' he chuckles. 'Y'see, here that can mean "Do you like men or women?"'

That should make me feel better, though somehow it doesn't. My new longhaired neighbour is a free spirit who has come to Willie to find out where he can tie up his donkey for the night. You see, Declan scrapes a living by offering donkey rides to people. 'I'm through payin' rent,' he says with a grin. Instead, he roams the country tethered to a beast of burden. Truly, one man's freedom is another man's—

'When are the Koreans coming?' he asks Willie.

'They said they'd be here tonight, but they may leave it until tomorrow.'

A Korean TV crew has been in touch about filming a feature on Lisdoonvarna, and Declan, demonstrating an innate flair for paddywhackery, has donned an Irish football shirt from the Korean World Cup in their honour.

'Shall I bring my donkey tomorrow, then?'

'Yeah.' Willie nods enthusiastically. 'Walk up and down the streets offering rides to people. Then tie it up on the corner. They'll love that!'

But it's not just his ass that women love about Declan. He's got the kind of cheeky, carnivorous grin and thick bohemian hair that certain women – especially professional types – find irresistible, in an opposites-attract, high-flyer/low-life kind of way. Declan confesses that his main concern tonight is finding a woman with a dry bed for the evening; he doesn't want to sleep in the rain with his donkey.

While Willie inspects the dancefloor, an American woman working the room peeks into his office, spots Declan and me, and within seconds has pulled up a chair for a conversation-cum-interview. Charlotte is a big-boned, big-haired woman from San Diego who's wearing a dress with strings that crisscross her cleavage. I notice this only because it's impossible not to notice: she's leaning forward in her seat, scrunching her arms together to focus the full impact of her frontage on Declan.

'So! Where are you from?' she says in that very American way of hers, smiling brightly and clasping her hands as if to say, *Let's get to know a little bit about each other: namely, your salary; marital status; and sperm count (before I jump your bones).*

Declan tells her he's Birmingham Irish, which understandably means nothing to her: 'Huh! That's interesting!' She puts a coy, enquiring finger to her lips. 'Didn't I see you earlier walking up the street? I'm sure I remember your hair. You had a donkey . . . and you were wearing these . . . cut-off . . . *jeans* . . .'

She can barely keep from drooling.

Declan gives a modest, aw-shucks chuckle. 'Yeah, that probably was me.'

'So have you guys registered?'

In other words: *Are you single?*

I explain that I'm attached – I'm just here writing a book.

'What about you?' she asks Declan, hopefully.

'Nah. I'm a bit short of funds, y'see.'

Her eyes dim. 'Oh. What do you do?'

'I have a donkey. I go around the country giving donkey rides.'

And . . . *whoosh!* The light in her eyes goes out.

'Oh! That's . . . interesting.' She turns to me – *attached or not, at least this guy has a job.* 'So who's publishing your book?'

I tell her, and ask whether she's of Irish extraction.

'No, but I've dated a lot of Irish men . . .'

'So you decided to come to the source.'

She seems offended – strange, that – and makes her excuses.

'I don't think she liked either one of us,' I tell Declan after she leaves.

'That's a shame. She had nice boobs.'

We decide to take a look at the dancefloor, wading through the crowd and the amplified heehaw of country music. We're stopped halfway by a couple of women who were talking to Willie earlier, both thirtysomethings who've come all the way over from Waterford, a town more than three hours away. The dominant one – Emma, I think – is a divorcee with dyed-black hair the texture of fried seaweed. She's sipping her wine with exaggerated sophistication, a cocktail-party pose consisting of one arm cocked on her hip and the other hand holding her wine in a woman-of-the-world manner: *I am one classy broad.* Her friend Claire, also wearing a blowsy blouse, is a pretty redhead, all soft and feathery, who recently broke off her engagement. She clutches her drink shyly, uncomfortable with the cattle-market reality of matchmaking. 'I don't like it. You know how when someone puts pressure on you to fix you up? That's what it feels like. It feels like everyone in here is trying to fix you up.'

It turns out that Willie had indeed tried to fix Claire up with Declan, much to the amusement of her fry-dyed friend. 'He said you had a *donkey* . . . and a *cart* . . . and we were like, *eenh!*' She imitates a buzzer and slices a finger across her throat. 'I'm sorry, I'm sure you're very nice, Declan, but – *eenh!*'

This seems unnecessarily rude to me, but Emma swears it's the only way. 'With Irish, Scottish and Welsh guys, you have to be very direct. Otherwise they just don't get it.'

True to type, Declan shrugs off the ridicule and focuses on her better-looking friend, leaving me to shoot the breeze.

Emma's a painter-slash-writer who's here to do something on Lisdoonvarna, having already braved the International Bachelor Festival that takes place every summer in Ballybunion, not far away in North Kerry. That event was originally called the Gay Bachelor Festival, but it changed its name in the Seventies: the last thing they needed were more men. 'It's like fifty weddings with no brides,' jibes my crispy-fried companion. As for the men at Lisdoonvarna, well, 'they're on the hunt in a way that you never see in Ireland'.

Having established that she's not just any old quarry, she informs me that fewer Americans are coming to Ireland these days, partly due to lingering fears of flying after 9/11 but also because they've realised their greenbacks don't go very far in the Emerald Isle: Ireland offers such poor value for money, only high-end tourists can still afford to visit. She also reckons that the Celtic Tiger's roaring economy is distorted by its status as a tax haven, with much of Ireland's GDP coming from tech firms owned by US parents. 'The money that the American multinationals are making is on our books, but it's not staying here. We're being used as a place to pass money through.'

Somewhere along the way, amid such weighty topics, she mentions that she and her friend have camped in a tent, despite the rain.

'You don't look like you got dressed in a tent,' I say, attempting a compliment.

But she doesn't take it that way.

'What?! I beg your pardon? Did you say I look like I got dressed in a tent?'

'What? No, no, no . . .'

This just isn't my night. I beat a retreat to Willie's office. Within minutes, though, the serenity is interrupted by a trio of twentysomethings searching in vain for the Matchmaker. Instead, they settle for me. The ringleader, Elaine, is a short, busty blonde: a chatty maneater who will end up marrying a thin man, if only to pick her teeth with his bones after devouring him. Like other women under fifty, Elaine and her gang are lamenting the lack of young men on the menu.

'But Willie says these men have twenty years of lovin' stored up.'

'*Ohhh*, God!' she cackles. 'Imagine the ex*plo*sion!'

For lack of any other prey, Elaine seems to take a shine to me. I should stress, however, that it's nothing personal; if anything, it's Pavlovian. Practically any male under fifty would be a surefire ladykiller at Lisdoonvarna. It's as if the women can scent that you're still capable of producing fresh testosterone. One whiff, and they're in heat. It's like stumbling into an Asylum for the Criminally Nymphomaniac.

Elaine's especially keen after I mention that I'm staying at one of the most expensive hotels in town – through no fault of my own, you understand; I booked there on Willie's recommendation. The Hydro Hotel occupies the high ground above Lisdoonvarna's old spa buildings. It's so big it's almost a living creature in its own right, requiring constant care and attention, even though it's shut four months of the year. It reminds me of the stately hotel in *The Shining*, only with rain instead of snow.

'Ooh . . . I'll bet you have a bathtub – and a double bed.'

I do indeed. (There has to be some reason for paying Hydro prices.)

'I just have a single bed and a shower in our B & B. And I *really* want a bathtub and a nice, fluffy double bed.'

Elaine won't take no for an answer, and she won't leave until I promise to meet up with her later at the disco in the Hydro.

I could've also told her that my room has an impressive amount of German porn, but that would've only encouraged her. My TV seems to have more German channels than English ones, and they all turn to porn commercials at night, dead-eyed enticements to dial phone numbers with the prefix of 888, so you get a bunch of Teutonic Robovixens barking *Acht! Acht! Acht!* into the camera. It's about as erotic as sticking your privates in a vacuum cleaner. Then again, some people like that sort of thing. My guest information folder is written first in *Deutsch*, then in English, reflecting Ireland's enduring popularity among German tourists. It's tempting to make a connection with the fact that Ireland was officially neutral during the Second World War (while some IRA factions actually backed the Germans), but apparently that has nothing to do with it. Earlier I met a trio of Germans who had hopped on a flight from Frankfurt to Ireland at the last minute to come to Lisdoonvarna. 'German people like Ireland because it is very traditional,' one of them told me. 'We have lost most of our traditions because of the last war, so it is nice to come here where people are more relaxed.' I should point out that he didn't look at all relaxed at the time, stiffly gripping his pint of stout.

For the moment, I continue to hide out in Willie's office. An American spots me and decides to keep me company. Sarah's a manager from Boston who works for one of those American multinationals I'd been told about, flying around Europe and spending barely sixty nights a year in her home in Cork. 'It's pretty stressful,' she admits. 'So what do I do? I come to Lisdoonvarna to get a good buzz!'

While most of us take after our parents to some degree, I'd guess that Sarah looks more like her father than her mother.

This may explain the greeting she'd received as she entered The Matchmaker.

'Yer boobs,' a man grunted, leering into her leathery cleavage, 'are they real?'

Sarah just laughs off all this as part of the Lisdoonvarna experience. After all, she's a return customer. She and her friend, Alice, came here last year as well. While the band in the room next door cranks out 'Heartache Tonight' by the Eagles – surely an odd choice – she tells me what to expect at the Hydro this weekend. 'We stayed there last year. I had gone out on the town that night but came back stone-cold sober. I walked through the door, and it was like a battle zone. There were people splayed all over the floor and crawling over each other to get up the stairs.' The men who could stand tried to block her going up the stairs, while those who couldn't tried to grab at her legs. 'And I was like, "Get off. It's quarter to four. It's not like any of us is going to be any good at this hour of the night anyway. It ain't gonna happen for ya!"'

For fun, Sarah and Alice had also registered with Willie. 'I put down a fake number, but my friend put down her *real* number. And she was, like, *inundated* with phone calls from farmers who hadn't been on a date in years!'

She tells me Alice wound up going on quite a few dates but, as a businesswoman, she found conversation with farmers a chore. 'It was always the same story – about their farms: "I get up . . . I milk the cows . . . and then I have some free time during the day . . . and then I feed the cows . . . and then I put them in the barn . . ."'

While we're talking, Alice pops her head around the doorframe. A portly woman with a flatline face that tells you she still doesn't – and frankly may never – see the funny side of it, she explains that she got phone calls from at least sixty farmers. 'And some of the guys are, like, sixty-five years old,' she says with a frown. 'Did you sign up with him?'

'No, I'm safe.'

'He's not that good.'

In fairness to Willie, though, his job title is Matchmaker, not Miracleworker.

'Don't bother with Willie,' Alice advises me. 'Just go out here and find a girl you like and pick her up.'

'But I'm—'

'Yeah, yeah. Whatever.'

As she leaves, Sarah confesses that she also tried her luck with some farmers after Lisdoonvarna. 'But it's painful. It's downright painful. I went out to dinner with one. He hadn't been out on many dates, and he still lived with his mother. He was a very nice man, but we didn't have anything in common.

'But you know what?' she continues. 'Because of the price of land, a lot of property developers have paid these farmers big money, so they're millionaires. But they have zero social skills. A lot of them will come up to you and say, "Hi, I'm lookin' for a woman," and you're just like, "Oh man, if I put my marketing hat on, I could really do somethin' with this. I have some friends who would love to meet you."'

'You really think American women would like them?'

'Do I think women would like men who own their own home, have plenty of money, and are just waiting to shower it on women who they want to love and cherish for the rest of their lives? Yeah, I think they would.'

However, she concedes that her potential clients might need some coaching. 'Some of the men I met here last year, they had tags on the back of their dress slacks because they had gone out and bought a new pair of trousers – special – for the festival but like, they forgot to take the *tag* off the back. They're real farmers: it's like, "I'm drivin' my tractor, I'm puttin' on my dress slacks, and I'm goin' to town." It's an incredible innocence.'

'But you like it?'

'I *love* it. It's so . . . refreshing.'

'Even though you don't find it attractive.'

'No. It's nice to know that it still exists. Because I live in a very cynical world. So to see something like this' – she smiles wistfully – 'it's really refreshing.'

Returning to the Hydro around midnight, I'm bracing myself for debauched scenes straight out of Sodom and Gomorrah: shagging in the corridors, barnyard noises from the bedrooms and an Irish orgy in the lobby (for some reason, though, I imagine everyone fully clothed in an Irish orgy). Alas, Sarah must have exaggerated last year's shenanigans; either that, or people just haven't drunk enough yet.

The dancing is segregated into a disco for the teens and twentysomethings at the back of the hotel and a country hoedown for the oldies in the main bar. I spend most of my time wandering disconcertedly between the two, wondering where I fit in. In the disco, kids with gelled bedheads are wheeling and whirling to all the old Irish favourites – 'Like a Prayer', 'The Cheeky Song', that sort of thing – while in the tightly packed bar, oldies-but-goodies are two-stepping and foxtrotting, turning the dancefloor into a musical clockwork that looks fun . . . if you know the steps. The atmosphere is warm and well lit – the better to show off their moves – with dark wood and upholstered seats on the sidelines, whereas the disco is designed to imitate big-city clubs, with strobe lights and squirts of dry ice breaking up the darkness, plus a couple of poles for the dancers and a couple of Poles swinging around on them – waitresses at the hotel enjoying a rare night out.

As I dither between the rooms, I'm collared by Elaine, the Man-Eating Colleen.

'JR, the disco!'

So the oldies' bar it is. As I find a hiding place on one of the settees, easing into the pheromone fug, one of the Polish girls wanders in, taking a break from the disco. Given that we're the only under-fifties within a fifty-foot radius, we soon get to talking. Actually, Alina, as I'll call her, is only twenty. She's been working here for two months, and already she's reconsidering her choice of career after her first Irish love festival.

'You wouldn't believe how many men come up to me and say after a few minutes of conversation, "Come up with me to my room. This is my room number." In Poland, you have to go out, have a date, some conversation, maybe go out again, and then do something. Here, sometimes security has to physically separate a couple in the disco because they're trying to have sex!'

As she says this, a couple of fiftysomethings are gnawing each other's necks on the next sofa over.

'And the men – they're so old! One came up to me and said, "I am rich, I have ten cows. Marry me." And I thought, "My grandfather has cows. That is not rich to me."'

Now if he'd said tractors . . .

She points to a short man with thick glasses who's feeling up a woman across the table from us. I saw him this morning strutting through the breakfast room with a jumper knotted around his neck, greeting all the *laydeez* he'd met last night.

Alina says he also tries to kiss all the waitresses good-morning.

'They tell me each year less and less people is coming to the Matchmaking Festival. Next year, maybe it will be empty – only this kissing man will come.'

We keep chatting like this until three o'clock, when the shutters slam across the bar, security men block the passage-way to the disco and the music in the oldies' bar comes to a toe-tapping, two-stepping halt.

I say goodnight to Alina and head up to my room. Turning the corner in the foyer, I notice a familiar face among a group on an overstuffed sofa: it's Declan the Donkey Man. He's cosying up to Claire, the blowsy redhead, while her fry-dyed friend who'd been so rude to him is fielding interest from a couple of one-night suitors.

'JR, come over here!' she barks at me.

It's too late to act like I haven't seen her, so I do as I'm told.

'Quick, sit down here and pretend you're with me,' she whispers.

At this point, my Southern upbringing kicks in, though I hope I'm not going to end up fighting with some farmboys over a woman I'd happily offload.

She manages to convince them otherwise, and they take their copulative intentions elsewhere. I ask Claire how she's wound up with Declan.

'That Matchmaker knew too much about me,' she smiles tipsily.

'How's that?'

Fry-Dyed explains: 'While we were sitting in his office, he told her, "What do you think about that fella there?"'

'Trust me to pick a man with a donkey and a cart!' Claire gushes.

There's a phrase you don't hear every day.

'It's because I have no willpower.' She glances fondly at Declan, who's not even listening to her; he's too busy talking to a guy on the sofa.

'I know what you mean,' purrs Crispy-Fried, nodding at me. 'This one's rather cute, too.' She turns to blast me with her bedroom eyes, the skin around them creased like sheets. 'You *are* rather cute,' she slurs as coquettishly as she can. 'Stay here.'

Apparently the women have ditched their tent for a B & B. While they go outside for a cigarette, I congratulate Declan on having found a bed for the evening.

'I know!' he says, raising his pint. 'I haven't bought a drink all night! And I'm not tryin' ta be flash or anything! I'm just bein' myself!'

Hang on – if he's going to be sharing Claire's bed at the B & B, where does her friend think she's going to be staying? *She doesn't seriously think* . . . I try to make an escape, but she catches me in the act.

'Goodnight,' I mumble hastily.

'You *are* rather cute.'

She's the second woman I've met tonight who's on the pull to upgrade accommodation. Is it me or my double bed?

I'll never know.

PART TWO:
'A STRANGE SIDE OF IRELAND'

After due consideration (a whole second's worth), I've decided I can't face another night of the Lisdoonvarna Lovefest. I've had enough desperation for one weekend. Instead, I'm planning to skedaddle out of town after dinner and make a pilgrimage to Doolin – apparently the Mecca of Irish music – and round off the evening at Willie's bar over in Ennistymon.

But first I pay a quick visit to the Love Doctor himself. The Matchmaker is just starting to get a good Saturday night buzz going, and Willie's in his consultation room, toodalooing at the curiosity-seekers in the window. A gaggle of certain-aged women come in, weekenders from Dublin who are looking for 'Drink, Dance & SEX', according to one of their info sheets.

Chances are, then, that they wouldn't be interested in the teacher from Galway who comes in shortly afterwards, braving the gauntlet of oiks who are clutching their pints and heckling any man who dares cross Willie's threshold. A gentle soul in a sensible jumper, this teacher will do anything to find love.

'Good sense of humour,' he lists as the qualities he's looking for in a woman. 'Not motivated purely by money. Family values.' As for his own interests, he writes: 'GAA' – the ultra-wholesome Gaelic Athletic Association – 'horseriding and reading.' In short, he's a nice guy: the kind that many women say they're looking for but can never quite bring themselves to go for.

Ever optimistic, Willie reckons he knows of a suitable match. 'I think he's a good-lookin' fella, don't you?' he asks me. 'He looks a bit like that . . . like that bloke off the telly. What's his name?'

I don't know who he's talking about, but it's obvious the man deserves someone who will appreciate him.

I can't take any more of this.

Before heading over to Doolin for the evening, I take a stroll down the high street to see the other pubs, stopping at a place with an ultra-Oirish name and a sign advertising Thai bar food. Two nurses from Galway are sitting in the window seat, one redheaded, the other brunette. This is the third time I've bumped into Orla and Michelle this weekend. They were in the Roadside Tavern earlier this evening, and they were in The Matchmaker last night registering with Willie.

'We're only here for the *craic*,' Orla had told me.

'So is that a decoy?' I'd asked, noting the silver band on her finger.

'No, that's . . . that's nothing to worry about,' she averred, twisting it nervously while waiting to pay her fee.

Tonight, though, she and Michelle are regretting having signed up; even more so when they find out that Willie didn't charge everyone a registration fee. As likeable as she is, Orla is clearly a control freak who's suddenly found herself out of control. Her first thought this morning was: *I've gotta get my sheet back.*

'Especially after what you wrote as special interests!' Michelle giggles.

'We just came up for the fun, and everyone we met was sixty-plus. And then, the first young guy I met when I came up here was a guy from home, and he doesn't want to see me, and I don't want to see him. But as I say, we're only here for the *craic*.'

You hear that so often in Lisdoonvarna, Willie ought to put it on a T-shirt – I'M ONLY HERE FOR THE CRAIC – alongside the others he sells: ON THE PROWL.

Over a drink in another pub, the girls give me their take on the event. They reckon it appeals to the older generation that missed out on the sexual revolution that took place in virtually every other Western country except Ireland; divorce, for instance, wasn't legalised until 1997. Although younger women are more independent these days, old-fashioned attitudes still prevail.

'Have you been to the Lovely Girl Competition?' they ask me.

'What's that?'

'The Rose of Tralee.' The annual beauty contest that's held every year in County Kerry and beamed round the world to the Diaspora.

'They always describe the winners as' – they smile in unison – '"lovely girls".'

Considering the alternative, Orla and Michelle are more than happy to take me up on my offer to skip the lovefest and go bar hopping. We drive over to O'Connelly's, a pub in Doolin that's famed for being the epicentre of Irish music, which of course means that the Irish are actually few and far between. 'We were in Doolin last night and we were the only two speakin' English,' a man from County Kerry had told me at dinner.

Well, this *is* the Gaeltacht, but the others weren't speaking Irish: they were conversing in Dutch, Italian, Spanish, French and, of course, German. Not for nothing is it called Little Doolinburg.

The interior of O'Connelly's feels like it's been put together to squeeze in as many people as possible. Tonight, though, there's not much of a crowd, and the musicians are packing up their instruments early, leaving us to shoot the breeze among the backpackers and the combined funk of wet socks, farmyard pheromones and underwear worn more times than its two sides should allow.

Fortunately, the scene over at Daly's is altogether livelier and more intimate. The bar is a rectangular nook in Ennistymon's main street, a room barely ten feet wide with flagstones on the floor and farm implements on the walls. It's run by Marie, one of Willie's dark-haired daughters. 'Oh, you'd like her. She's single, very pretty, very nice,' he'd told me not long after I'd met him.

'*But I'm—*'

The Matchmaker just can't help himself. A mother of one, Marie is Willie's best hope for carrying on the other family business, but she's reluctant to take on the mantle of Matchmaker. Though she empathises with the lonely farmers who frequent her bar, she also seems well aware of the disappointment that men can cause.

A dozen or so people are gathered around the fireplace, sitting on all manner of irregular chairs and stools, swapping songs and stories. We take a seat at the back of the room, among the framed news clippings of Willie and past world events.

A woman named Theresa is singing a cappella in a voice so pure and compelling it leaves the rest of us spellbound. At least until the next singer, that is. He warbles a bog-standard Irish misery tune about a poor man wrongly accused of a crime and how 'they' – and we all know who *they* were – took a rope and they strung him up and then they took his knife and cut him down and so on and so forth.

'*Cheez*us,' Michelle giggles. 'Why don't we just slit our wrists now?'

But Orla's more appreciative. 'Y'know, I'd never come to this sort of thing normally – and I live in Galway, where there's plenty of pubs that offer traditional music.'

Some time around two in the morning, Marie sweeps us out onto the street, and the three of us stop to admire the building across the way. The murals on its façade have turned a smoky sepia in the half-darkness.

'That looks like a lovely old pub,' Michelle sighs.

'It does, doesn't it?'

We stand in silence, each of us imagining different histories for the place. How many generations must have passed through its doors? How many romances must have been kindled inside? If its walls could talk—

'What's it say there?' Michelle asks, straining to decipher the stylised Celtic lettering above the windows.

Orla has better eyesight: '*Est . . . ablished . . . 19 . . . 93.*'

We've just been paddywhacked.

Back in Lisdoonvarna, we arrive at the Hydro in time for last orders. In the oldies' bar, the emcee is announcing the final act of the evening.

'Here's Dennis O'Shea with his new album, *Back to Tennessee!*'

A man in rust-coloured trousers and a swirly shirt opened down to the top of his paunch takes the stage. His hair is a carefully moulded *mélange* that adds a good few inches to his height – *Look, laydeez, I got hair to spare!* But all that's irrelevant, as is any idle musing about whether he's set foot in Nashville once, let alone twice. The fact is, he's so happy to be here, possessed by the pure joy of singing, that you can't help but take your ten-gallon off to him. The room kicks into country-and-western overdrive, and for an instant, I picture the farmers dancing with cows: a bovine barndance.

Must be the Guinness.

Out in the lobby, the scene is like a nursing home after the women in white have been round with the meds. People are passed out in the alcoves, snoring into the upholstery of the high-backed chairs, oblivious to the noise from the widescreen TVs in front of them. Those still standing are doing their best to remain upright, their pints providing crucial ballast to keep them from falling over.

One of the few sober people in the vicinity is the woman with fried seaweed for hair. She's looking even more frazzled than last night, but she's recovered her dignity and accompanying sense of superiority, holding her wineglass in that pretentious cocktail-party pose – *I am a classy piece of ass* – while her friend Claire is being hit on by yet another man. This one has a ponytail and quirky headwear.

'What happened to Declan the Donkey Man?' I ask Emma.

'I don't know. I think he took his donkey and left.' She shrugs. 'Claire and he got together last night, and they got together again today, but that was when she realised it just wasn't going to work out – what with the donkey and everything.'

I bite my tongue, but I can't resist. 'Did she at least get to . . . get to—'

'Ride his donkey? No. And I'm sure of that – I slept in the same room as them.'

'So who's this guy?'

'This is Sean. He builds things. We met him building outside in the garden of our B & B. But you'll never guess what he builds: *full-scale* stone circles.'

I'm not even sure what that means, at least in the confines of a B & B's backyard.

One thing's for certain, though. Whatever cuteness I had last night has disappeared, along with her beer goggles. Whether it's because she's sober or sick of Claire getting all the attention, her personality has defaulted to self-righteousness with more than a hint of disdain. 'Last night I had a drink and a dance and enjoyed it. But tonight the nature of the event was very different – it was very un-Irish. Almost animalistic. There were gangs of men who made it clear that they just wanted one thing. And they were very . . . very *forceful*. I had to shout at six of them and physically punch about four of them. And the funny thing was, once I put them in their place, they sort of snapped out of it and became very Irish again. Very respectful.'

She frowns. 'Men used to be very respectful. All the respect that they had for their mammies was transferred to their wives. But not here. Not this weekend. You've seen a strange side of Ireland – not one that many people see.'

Next morning as I prepare to leave, it's raining so hard even the Irish are impressed. Guests are standing in the doorway of the Hydro, stupefied by the cascade.

'Oh, God!'

'*Cheez*us.'

Inside, though, hope springs eternal. Willie has set out his Book of Love in the lobby, right in the hotspot between the reception desk, the grand stairway, the sandwich and drinks buffet, and the entrances to the bar and the restaurant. The First-Chance Dance is already in full swing, and those who aren't dancing are watching the All-Ireland hurling final on two widescreen TVs. Willie's standing at the centre of the action, wearing a dark-blue blazer that matches his eyes, his smile winking away as he talks to Mary, who's probably in her forties but has the figure of a thirty-year-old. She's been coming to Lisdoonvarna from County Waterford for nigh on twenty years.

'This is one of the girls I've admired for a long time, but it's never quite come to pass.' Willie smiles, giving her a good ol' hug.

She laughs him off. 'Maybe when we're in our wheelchairs.'

As they catch up, she mentions that she's just bought her family's ancestral home by buying out her siblings' shares – all eleven of them. The slate-roofed cottage has been home to at least four generations, and she's planning to keep it as a country getaway.

Willie's so impressed, he shakes her hand – a chance to re-establish contact. 'Congratulations, Mary,' he says. 'The Irish are the worst for tearin' down old houses and puttin' up godawful mansions.'

'It's the money,' she agrees. 'Money is the root of all evil. You get too much money, you lose yer values, yer sense of history.'

'And traditions.' He nods and pauses to touch up his lip balm.

'Oh, look! Willie's been kissing last night!'

'No, no,' he chuckles embarrassedly.

But it's too late. Mary leaves to meet some friends, giving me a chance to ask Willie if he has many female admirers.

'No, no. When I was younger, but not so many as there used to be.'

I ask him about a Finnish woman I met last night, her white hair dyed a brittle blonde. She'd dropped by his office for the second night running and seemed more than a little miffed when Willie left her with me while he did the rounds.

'We were *friendly*.'

'It looked to me like she wanted to rekindle your friendship.'

'You have to be careful in matchmaking—'

He breaks off to catch a busboy trundling past. Ruddy and redheaded, the guy must be the only Irishman working at the Hydro.

'I had a nice girl for you just now,' Willie tells him.

'No, I don't want a girlfriend now. I want a she-male, a transvestite. Great big boobs and' – he cups his hands for girth – 'a huge *dick*.'

Willie recoils with laughter as the man hurries on his way. 'I like that boy, but he's got a vile tongue. I introduced him to some German girls, and he said some *vile* things to them. But it didn't matter because I don't think they understood a word he said!

'But you have to be careful in matchmaking,' he continues, back on message. 'Occasionally you'll meet someone, but it doesn't happen often. People come to you looking for a partner, and you can't be seen to abuse yer position, because it would come back at ya pretty quickly. Besides, we get so many Americans in here, they'd fuckin' sue ya!'

In the past, Willie has blamed the breakdown of his marriage on the demands of matchmaking. 'People say it's funny you bein' a matchmaker and separated,' he tells me. 'I say, *Cheezus*. I was married twenty-five years. That's more than most.' He's been separated for about three years. 'I have a girlfriend now,' he adds, repeating it in case I missed it. 'I have a girlfriend now.'

This is the first I've heard of her. Funny he should mention this at the *end* of the weekend. I ask if she's a young beauty like his mother, who was twenty-three when she married Willie's sixty-year-old father.

'No, no, my girlfriend's in her early forties.'

'Was she here?'

'No, she stays away most weekends. Which isn't a bad thing.'

There's that winking grin again.

I thank him for his time and venture out into the rain. Before leaving Lisdoon, I reckon I've worked up just enough of an appetite for one last trip to the Roadside Tavern. I order a pint of stout, vegetable soup with soda bread and Irish butter, and, of course, boiled bacon and cabbage – nothing too heavy, you understand; I just had breakfast. While I'm waiting, I thank my *Crusty Rucksack* travel guide for directing me to this place, which seems as traditional as Lisdoonvarna gets. The part of the dining area where I'm sitting is light and refurbished, but the heart of the pub, the bar, is dark and atmospheric. The different ambiences are united by the wallpaper, which is nothing more than old newspapers overlaid with postcards from every corner of the world, from Dallas to Saudi Arabia, Italy to India and even the Burren just up the road, their once-bright colours muted to the same tone by a yellowish-brown lacquer of nicotine.

Come to think of it, now that smoking's been banned, how will pub chains recreate the tobacco patina of traditional boozers? Maybe they can import the wallpaper from their smoke-heavy branches in Bangkok and Bangalore. I foresee a huge import–export market in nicotine-stained furnishings. Nicotined wallpaper: it'll be big.

A middle-aged German couple enters wearing matching white anoraks. They take a seat next to an old man ploughing his way through his Sunday lunch.

'What is that?' the woman asks the white-haired eating machine, practically probing his plate with her finger. You'd think she was inspecting a curious deposit left on the shelf in her toilet bowl.

'Boiled bacon and cabbage,' the old man announces.

She checks the menu, tilting her head to adjust for the bifocals. 'Ah yes: "Traditional Boiled Bacon and Boiled Cabbage with Potatoes."'

'What would you like?' the waitress asks them.

The Germans don't understand the Polish girl's English, so the Irishman has to translate: 'Boiled bacon and cabbage.'

'Yes,' the woman says. 'Traditional Boiled—'

'They want boiled bacon and cabbage.'

On my way out, I could swear I hear someone call my name.

It's Declan, nursing a pint and looking more dishevelled than ever. He greets me with a transatlantic fellas-in-da-hood handshake.

'What happened to you? I saw Claire in the Hydro last night with another guy.'

Declan shakes his head and rubs his face. 'Ahh . . . ya can't trust 'em, can ya?' He laughs. 'Still, it's just a bit of fun, isn't it? No harm done.'

CHAPTER TEN

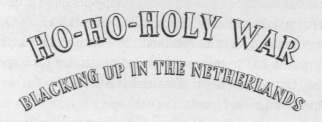

PART ONE:

A BLACK CHRISTMAS

Tell someone you're taking your family to Amsterdam at Christmastime, and you're likely to get the reaction I did when I mentioned it to a fellow parent in London.

'What – with the *kids*?' she gasped, unsure whether to report me immediately to Social Services or to Immigration to have us stopped at the airport.

After all, Amsterdam isn't your typical family-holiday hotspot. When it comes to social issues, the rest of the world tends to view the Dutch as either brave trailblazers or, less charitably, laughable liberals. For decades, self-styled progressives in Europe and America have advocated 'Dutch solutions' to drugs, homosexuality, prostitution, euthanasia and economic issues, whereas conservatives often depict the Netherlands as a latter-day Sodom and Gomorrah: to hear them talk, when the Dutch aren't puffing away on pot or rumpy-pumping prostitutes in a red-light district, they're bicycling off to a gay wedding or offing grandma at a while-you-wait, lethal-injection kiosk.

In truth, there's something to shock just about everyone in Amsterdam – and plenty of things you'd rather not have to explain to your four-year-old: the 'Canna-biscuits' on sale in convenience shops (very convenient, indeed) . . . the hempy pong emanating from the threshold of the Cheech & Chong Café . . . the Santa doll with his yule log standing to attention in the window of an adult toyshop . . . and the lovely old church ringed by immigrant hookers in glass closets, leering at passers-by.

As a pre-Christmas destination, though, Amsterdam is certainly unique. While Scandinavian countries tout for tourism and bicker about which is the 'true' home of a mythical character, the Dutch maintain a modest silence, confident in the knowledge that they have the real thing: the original Santa Claus. However, their *Sinterklaas* – his name was Americanised in New Amsterdam – dresses like St Nicholas, a bishop, instead of a 'jolly old elf' in the corporate colours of Coca-Cola. Likewise, his belly tends to be of European proportions rather than an American-sized bowl of jelly, and when it comes to delivering gifts, the '*Sint*' prefers a white horse to a reindeer-powered sleigh. Far from suffering the frigid temperatures of the North Pole, he spends most of the year basking in sunny Spain. Come November, he fires up his steamboat to travel to the Low Countries, arriving three weeks before 5 December, the eve of his feast day. For children throughout the Netherlands – and parts of Belgium and Luxembourg – the arrival of Sint

Nicolaas is a thrilling event celebrated with songs, sweets and processions. For adults, though, the sight of Sinterklaas and his entourage can be more disconcerting and, in its own way, *shocking* than the hash on demand, oversexed Santas and vending-machine hookers that you expect to see in Amsterdam anyway.

What you *don't* expect to see is hundreds of white Hollanders blacked up like Sinterklaas' Moorish servants, parading in daylight through the world capital of laissez-faire liberalism, where at least one in four residents is a dark-skinned foreigner. These light-eyed Black Petes, or *Zwarte Pieten*, wear curly wigs, their lips made thick with make-up and their faces painted so dark it looks like they've dipped their heads in tar. Joking, capering and sometimes even mimicking black accents, they gambol along the streets and canals like human golliwogs in sixteenth-century attire. Everywhere you look, from corner shops to major department stores, holiday displays are festooned with dolls and cartoons of the *Sint* and his grinning sambo of a helper, shinning up ropes and chimneys. Just a few decades ago, children's books even depicted Black Pete with a broken chain around his ankle. Back then, he was still the *Sint*'s devilish sidekick, armed with a switch and a bag to whip naughty children and bundle them off to Spain, similar to his counterparts throughout the Continent. Nowadays, though, he's had a postmodern makeover as the kiddies' friend, the deliverer of gifts and goodies.

Even so, Christmastime in the Netherlands remains somewhat . . . *controversial.* Many black immigrants (and white liberals) object to *Zwarte Piet* on the grounds that he's an offensive caricature. Muslims aren't that fond of the tradition, either, though not because Black Pete was originally a follower of Mohammed. The guy they don't like is the *Sint* himself, a Catholic saint who strolls through mixed neighbourhoods wearing bishop's robes and a hat with a big, golden cross on it. In this respect, Muslims are strangely allied to Christian fundamentalists. 'Black-stocking' Calvinists in the Dutch Bible Belt – yes, there is such a thing – also object to the *Sint*'s papist appearance. In response, most white Hollanders swear blind that Black Pete has absolutely no racial overtones. What's more, they claim, the *Sint* has nothing – *nussing!* – to do with religion (never mind his name, clothes and the big cross on his hat). Aside from the slurs on the saint and his sidekick, what these defenders of tradition detest is the *Sint*'s capitalistic offspring, 'the fat man from America' who poses such a threat to their original custom that some towns and department stores have started banning Santa until after the *Sint* is safely out of Holland on 6 December.

Got that? So far, the quintessentially Dutch characters of Sinterklaas and Black Pete have managed to survive these annual onslaughts. But they may yet fall victim to escalating tensions in Dutch society. A black coalition has petitioned Parliament to ban *Zwarte Piet*, and *Sinterklaases* have been physically attacked in public by Muslim youths. Even more worryingly, at least one *Sint* has received death threats, reflecting the increasing violence in recent years that has the Dutch despairing that their tolerant, carefully constructed society is on the verge of collapse. The gory murder of a Muslim-baiting filmmaker named Van Gogh – a relative of Vincent himself – triggered revenge attacks on mosques and Islamic schools and came two years after the killing of a gay right-wing politician who had also stirred up anti-immigrant sentiment. Meanwhile, some crackpot imams have continued to advocate the beating of women and execution of homosexuals, and the media continue to fuel fears of 'terrorists in our midst' (two of the 9/11 hijackers, including ringleader Mohammed Atta, supposedly visited a radical mosque in the Netherlands while living in Europe). The birthrate among immigrants continues to outpace that of so-called native Hollanders, with the number of Muslims having grown from virtually zero to one million, or 6 per cent of the population, in barely thirty years. Some forecasters predict that Amsterdam and other cities will soon have Muslim majorities. Consequently, it shouldn't have been that surprising when the Dutch followed the French in rejecting the draft EU Constitution in 2005, partly due to fears about extending membership to Turkey. Throw in a floundering economy and the Netherlands' pioneering role in the slave trade, and the quaint old tradition of *Sinterklaas* turns into a powderkeg of the recurring themes in modern Europe, including the most combustive issues facing Western societies today: race, religion, immigration and the decline of 'native' European culture in the face of American commercialisation. 'This is a very good moment to ask white people to look in the mirror because of all the problems we have with the Muslims and ethnic groups and terrorism,' says a politician campaigning to ban Black Pete. 'Because if they don't change their minds, the whole situation will explode. It will *really* explode.'

And if the Dutch can't find a solution, what hope is there for the rest of us?

As the founder of Holland's biggest rent-a-*Sint* agency, Henk van der Kroon oversees at least thirty *Sinterklaases* and 120 Petes, dispatching them in teams to visit homes, offices, shopping centres and even football clubs from early November right up until the eve of St Nicholas' Day. 'I am what you might call the senior *Sinterklaas*,' he declares, puffing on a cigar.

Bald on top, with clipped white hair on the sides and a big Christmas ball of a belly, you might also say that Henk is the stereotype of a blunt Dutchman. However, his eyebrows hint at a softer side to his gruff exterior. Set at a sympathetic angle to the rest of his features, they make him perfect *Sinterklaas* material. The *Sint*-in-Chief is sitting at a pocked Formica desk in his apartment-cum-office in a townhouse just outside Amsterdam's centre. This is the headquarters of *Sinterklaas Centrale*, up several flights of narrow stairs from a Turkish café and convenience shop. Given that the historical St Nick hailed from what's now Turkey, this seems fitting. But Henk corrects me. 'When people say Sint Nicolaas was a Turk, that is not right.' He wags his head, arguing that Asia Minor was under Graeco-Roman rule at the time. Henk was especially fond of Greece in his youth, and he still speaks the language – in addition to English, French, German and a little Italian, all of which come in handy when he plays the *Sint* for embassies and tour groups.

If only he spoke Arabic or one of the Berber dialects.

Once upon a time, you see, Henk was out on assignment with three or four Black Petes in a racially and religiously mixed part of Amsterdam South. Resplendent in his long white beard, rich scarlet robes and gold-crossed mitre, Henk had been hired for a special promotion. This being Holland, he wasn't promoting anything so crass as a new car or chocolate bar or other aspect of Christmas Inc., but something high-minded and infinitely worthy: recycling. The local authorities had installed new recycling bins in the neighbourhood, and the *Sint* and his Petes were meant to stand in front of one, rewarding good citizen-recyclers with marzipan candies moulded in the shape of – you guessed it – little recycling bins.

What the organisers failed to tell Henk, though, was that his special appearance coincided with clocking-off time at a primary school just up the street. *Sinterklaas* and his Petes were suddenly mobbed by hungry schoolkids. And that's when the sweets distribution turned sour. '*Hundreds* of children came,' Henk recalls. 'They saw Black Pete and thought, *Fantastic*! But there were also Muslims' – he lowers his voice, adding a catchall term for non-white immigrants – '*Allochtoonen*.'

While most of the younger kids and their parents launched into typical *Sinterklaas* songs, gleefully waiting for the Petes to dole out the sweets, a group of older boys, Turks and Moroccans, muscled to the front, grabbing as much candy as they could. Armed with his crook, Henk tried to impose some saintly order, but the ruffians responded by shouting abuse and knocking the boxes out of the Petes' hands, littering the ground with candy recycling bins. It was a recycling riot! A marzipan mêlée! Before Henk knew it, the boys were attacking him, knocking his mitre off with their shoes, as children as young as four began to cry: *Mummy, they're trying to kill Sinterklaas!*

Hopelessly outnumbered and unable to fight back – even when provoked, it's not the done thing for *Sinterklaas* to deck children – Henk and his Petes beat a retreat to their car while some quick-thinking mothers provided cover, forming a dam of adults against the juvenile tide. 'And the *Allochtoonen* – the Moroccan and Turkish boys – they were jumping against the car.' The *Sint* and his men roared off uninjured, though their car was damaged. 'It was a disaster!' Henk shakes his head.

'And all the Dutch mothers and children were *crying*. Shock – *trauma!* It was all very traumatic. And that is something that you can never do in my country. This is something that is a . . . a *big crime* in a certain way, to demolish over a hundred years of tradition.

'Dutch children have respect. Sint Nicolaas is a holy man, you have respect. But those people have no respect,' he growls, still appalled by *those people*. 'And they must have as much as possible. Even when they have one treat, they want more, more, more, more. Dutch children don't *run* to steal – never. Never. And that is the opposite of the Muslims. They *run* to take it. That's the difference. The Muslims have not had this tradition. The only thing they know is surviving – take as much as you want. And even if your friend is also Muslim, you can knock him down because you must have it.'

He takes a puff on his cigar and leans forward. 'So the consequence of that is that we have lost a lot of good Sint Nicolaases. They don't want to play *Sinterklaas* any more. Even *now* we have a shortage of Sint Nicolaases because of these incidents. They happen every year. *Minor* things, but the Sint Nicolaases feel threatened.'

The attack on Henk made the front page of the Netherlands' top-selling broadsheet, right below *De Telegraaf*'s banner, next to a photo of him in his robes with an uncannily prescient title, given current fears of terrorism: *Streetfighters Terrorise the Sint*. 'It was a very hot item in Holland,' he chuckles. The date was 29 November 1996. 'And that was the first confrontation. Before, there had been small things, but that was the start. After that, we take measures.'

With its ominous understatement, the word 'measures' immediately conjures up images of a *Sinterklaas* kitted out with

007-style accoutrements. I imagine bullet-proof robes, crosiers that turn into electrified cattle prods, beards that expand into nets to nab evildoers and mitres that hide mini-cannons firing tear gas and rubber bullets. He could even have his own TV series – and they could call it *The Sint*.

But the Chief *Sinterklaas* doesn't look like he'd appreciate my idle reverie (and I *would* like to get some presents this year). Like most people I've met on this trip to the Netherlands, he's not in much of a jovial mood. It's been only a few days since a Dutch–Moroccan slaughtered director Theo Van Gogh on the streets of Amsterdam in broad daylight in retaliation for a TV film he made. Van Gogh's ten-minute movie featured four Muslim women in see-through chadors recounting how they had been beaten, raped and forced into marriage, while the camera revealed Koranic verses that apparently justified wife beating; the text was inscribed on their half-naked bodies. By all accounts, Van Gogh lacked the artistic genius of his great-great-granduncle, but he definitely had a knack for creating controversy, usually through the cheapest trick in the book: causing offence. Via TV, newspapers, books and the Internet, he would deride Muslims as 'goatfuckers' (and much, much worse) and hypothesise whether diabetic Jews smelt like caramel when they were cremated – a particularly tasteless jibe in a country where 80 per cent of the Jewish population died in the Holocaust.

Van Gogh's next project was going to be a film about his fellow controversialist, Pim Fortuyn, the gay right-wing politician who had urged his countrymen to be out and proud about their prejudices. When challenged about his own anti-immigrant remarks, Fortuyn's stock response was: 'How can I be against Moroccans? I have slept with so many of them.' To liberals' dismay, Fortuyn was on the verge of a landslide victory when an animal rights activist (of all people) shot him dead. 'With Fortuyn, everybody feared that the killer would turn out to be a Muslim,' a Dutch friend told me when I arrived. 'And this time, it was.' Following Van Gogh's murder, he said, the country is in a state of shock. 'It would be very hard to overplay it. We feel that we used to live in a tolerant society, and we now have this inkling that it's all ended.'

The new intolerance has had a knock-on effect on *Sinterklaas*. 'This year we were threatened on the telephone that they would kill Sint Nicolaas in an al-Qaeda way,' Henk says, slicing a meaty finger across his neck. 'It could be a joke of Muslims,' he adds quickly. 'So I haven't informed the press. Of course, I've informed the police. But that is a very serious matter.' Henk says he would not send a *Sint* to a predominantly Muslim neighbourhood without an overwhelming security presence. However, attacks could take place anywhere. 'When we have an appearance on the streets in Amsterdam, I always warn the police in advance, and the police always provide protection. Sometimes they're in plain clothes – you don't see them – but we don't want incidents.' He's also started hiring four or five Moroccans to act as Black Petes in mixed neighbourhoods. 'When I go to an area and I am afraid, then he can shout in a very loud voice in his own language: "Shut up or I'll kick you down!" and then they run away, because most of them are thirteen, fourteen, fifteen years old.'

'But I have to say' – he's nothing if not fair-minded – 'the majority of Muslim kids, they have respect for Sint Nicolaas. It is always the small minority who are really extremists. Maybe fundamentalists is a better word.' He points in the direction of what is possibly the most infamous 'jihad' mosque in the

Netherlands, just a few minutes' walk from his home. At El-Tawheed Mosque, radical imams have preached that Christians and Jews are mere 'kindling for the fires of hell', peddling a book that advocates wife beating and throwing gays off tall buildings, preferably headfirst – if they survive the fall, they should be stoned to death. 'And they refuse to stop this mosque,' Henk says incredulously. 'I cannot understand this. *I cannot understand this*. This is *impossible* in my country. We are an open and a liberal society.' He's not ranting or even raising his voice; he's more frustrated than anything, bemused at how the Dutch dream has gone so wrong. In the Netherlands, he says, you can be whatever you want – a Hindu or a homosexual. 'And you can say everything – *everything* is allowed here. You are allowed to make an insult, but it's at your own risk because the other party can take you to court. And they [the Muslims] cannot understand that!'

Sinterklaas highlights this clash of cultures. 'At our schools, all the Muslim kids learn the Dutch *Sinterklaas* songs and sing them very well, and of course they hear from their friends that Sint Nicolaas is coming this evening, so we can put our shoes out in front of the hearth, and so they come home to their old father, a Muslim man, and ask if Sint Nicolaas is coming to their house. And *then* you get a confrontation because he is absolutely *against* it, and Sinterklaas *doesn't exist*. Or they ask their father if they can put their shoes before the hearth, and that is the start of the conflict.

'We are confronted with a multicultural society and the Muslims see Sint Nicolaas as a symbol of Christianity. Well, it isn't. Of course, with the mitre and the staff he looks like a bishop, but this is a fairy tale. It has *nothing*, absolutely *nussing'* – he flaps his hands over his coffee – 'to do with any kind of religion at all.' As proof, he says, he gets many requests to visit Jewish families.

Somehow, though, I doubt that would be a selling point for their Islamic cousins.

He frowns when I ask him about *Sinterklaas*' other long-running controversy, the debate over Black Pete. 'That was another attack on our tradition that came from – how can I say? – *idiot* Surinamese people who want to depict Black Pete as a symbol of slavery and how bad we were as white men.'

This doesn't seem so unreasonable to me, given that most of the blacks in the Netherlands come from former Dutch colonies such as Suriname.

However, Henk says Black Pete's roots have nothing to do with South America. Instead, he's a by-product of Spain, which ruled the Netherlands for a spell in the 1500s.

'It's so simple,' he says, flapping his hands in exasperation. The story goes like this: Spanish aristocrats and clerics liked to show off their wealth by having everyone in their households, including their servants, dressed in fine livery. 'So they had some *nice* black boys from Africa' – Henk smiles – 'because it was something exotic to have a black boy or black man with beautiful clothes. And the more pages you had, the more important you were.' Like most of the tradition's defenders, Henk prefers to call Pete a 'servant' rather than a 'slave'. 'A slave is somebody who doesn't own his body. As you know, there were no slaves in Holland.'

Well, not many anyway.

'That was the business we did overseas, on the other continents.'

So that makes it all right, then.

But he's way ahead of me. 'The Dutch, we were very bad.

Actually, we invented slavery, I think. That is a black page in our history. But it has nothing to do with Sint Nicolaas. It had nothing to do with racism at all in the past or now.'

Back when the Black Pete controversy was really hot, Henk says one family did request a couple of White Petes – men without face paint – but their appearance was a flop; even the family decided it had been a mistake. Likewise, some *Sinterklaas* processions have experimented with multicoloured Petes. 'But that was more shocking. There were too many protests, also from blacks who said, "That is not our tradition. Our tradition is Black Pete!"' He laughs. 'Even more funny is that we have Negroes playing Black Pete, and they want to have their faces painted darker.'

For Henk, the Black Pete debate is a slippery slope. 'Because if you have Green Petes one day, the day after you're going to get people asking why women cannot be Sint Nicolaas. No, no, no.' He shakes his head. 'This is a self-correcting matter. Nobody accepts a female Sint Nicolaas or Green Petes or whatever.'

And *Sinterklaas* has enough troubles as it is. Henk's bookings have fallen more than 20 per cent over the past few years, from 501 at this time in 2001 to just 393 as of late November. This is mainly due to the current economic slump, but it also has to do with changing demographics. 'Muslim families never invite *Sinterklaas* into their homes. And they're having more children,' Henk says. 'So that could be a reason why slowly the *Sinterklaas* tradition will go backwards.'

However, a recent survey gave him some comfort. Dutch people were asked what they feared most: terrorism ranked number one, and the loss of *Sinterklaas* number three. Henk can't remember what the percentages were, and he realises the poll may have been spurious, but it seems to confirm his view. 'Dutch people absolutely do not want to lose the Sint Nicolaas tradition, but the – how can I say it? – the composition of Dutch society has changed. That is the problem.' He winces. 'That is the problem.'

'Do you see a solution?'

'No, I don't see one.'

I try to be upbeat, pointing out that the Netherlands has always managed to absorb immigrants in the past.

'My country is the biggest example of integration,' he agrees, proudly recounting all the groups that have contributed to Dutch society since the fifteenth century: Portuguese Jews, French Huguenots, East European Jews, Indonesians, Antilleans, Ghanaians and the Surinamese. 'We have always had open doors. All the integration ran smoothly and fantastic. But – *but* – then came the biggest mistake in Europe: the Muslims. And that is a completely different story. They can't understand tolerance, freedom of speech, freedom of religion – they don't know this. They come out of this *primitive* environment, and they don't accept the Constitution. The law of the Koran is more important and stands above the Constitution.' He shakes his head. 'I am very pessimistic. Very pessimistic.'

The phone rings, and he answers it in his blustery Dutch.

'That's a student who wants to play Black Pete,' he tells me. 'If you want, you could also come and write down your experiences. I have no problems with that.'

'As Black Pete?'

'Yes.'

'Oh . . .' My voice quavers, struggling to avoid commitment. I picture myself blacked up like a tar baby, beaten by shoe-wielding thugs and trying to make a getaway in the Sintmobile. And that would be nothing compared to the hiding I'd get from political-correctionists in Britain if I dared to write about it. *As tempting as it may be, Henk . . .*

'You could even earn some money,' he says on my way out. 'We always pay some sort of compensation, because you cannot find volunteers to do it.'

It's the need for compensation that worries me.

It may sound like an oxymoron – or possibly a kinky accessory – but the Dutch Bible Belt is a real, honest-to-God location, though by now it's so thin it's more of a Bible G-string. Stretched diagonally from the south-west to the north-east, it represents the Netherlands' Calvinist core, bypassing the capital and dividing the historically Catholic region in the south from the liberal Protestant areas of the north. Right in the middle of Calvinist country – less than an hour from Amsterdam – lies the town of Barneveld, where Christians in their dourest Sunday best have a host of 'black-stocking' churches to choose from. Mainstream Protestants and Catholics also have a presence in the area, as is inevitable in one of Europe's most crowded countries, but the dominant religious inclination tends to be of the hardcore-Calvinist variety.

Within the Netherlands, Barneveld is best known, if at all, for its poultry – and the fact that several years ago, when it had a devout Calvinist mayor, the man snubbed *Sinterklaas* by refusing to shake his hand. As with strict Christians and Santa Claus in Britain and the US, Dutch Calvinists view the *Sint* as a Catholic distraction from the true 'reason for the season'. That's why I was so surprised to learn that a museum in Barneveld is hosting an exhibition on *Sinterklaas*.

'The current mayor is a Catholic, so it's okay,' says Priscilla van Leeuwen, curator of the Museum Nairac and possessor of a wicked sense of humour.

When I first called her, I explained that I was keen to get out of the capital and see the diversity of the Netherlands, 'to show that it's not just one, uh, one—'

'Blob?' she joked. 'Not one pot-smoking blob – wearing clogs.'

Contrary to my expectations – I imagined gables galore, women in lace caps, even the odd horsedrawn carriage – Barneveld is a disappointingly modern market town with a bright new shopping district and discreet loudspeakers playing *Sint* songs to get you in the spending spirit. The Museum Nairac is one of the few old structures left in the centre, its big inverted 'V' of a roof weighing down on a redbrick ground floor. Yet in a single exhibition room, Patricia has managed to pull together a collection of rare books, icons, photos and artefacts tracing the saint's transformation from *Sinterklaas* to Santa Claus, as well as the evolution of Black Pete. 'Sint Nicolaas is not typically Dutch,' Henk had told me. 'You have him in many other countries. Only Black Pete is typically Dutch.'

But first the skinny on St Nick. As the bishop of Myra (now part of Turkey) in the fourth century AD, Nicholas became famous for destroying pagan temples, casting out demons and performing miracles that eventually made him the favoured saint for children, as well as a slew of less innocent and often mutually dependent occupations, namely sailors, pawnbrokers and prostitutes (it's not for nothing that St Nicholas Church in Amsterdam lies between the port and the red-light district). St Nick's all-around-good-guy image made him one of the most popular saints in Europe in the Middle Ages, with many countries and cities adopting him as their patron. In the Netherlands, the first known record of a celebration for children on St Nicholas' Day comes from near Rotterdam in 1360. Medieval 'boy bishops' would also play the role of the saint, with a cortège of subjugated devils. Similarly, a fourteenth-century icon from Russia shows Nicholas casting out a demon . . . depicted as a little black devil.

With the Reformation, Protestants throughout Northern Europe tried to purge their countries of Catholic saints and festivals, unwittingly helping transform Christmastime into the semi-secular holiday we know today (in a double irony, it's their spiritual descendants who are leading the fightback to 'reclaim' Christmas as a holy season). Protestants emphasised Christ's 'birthday' – 25 December – rather than St Nicholas' Day on 6 December, and *Sinterklaas* markets were banned.

Given that public parties were forbidden, the *Sinterklaas* celebrations moved indoors, with children leaving their shoes in front of the chimney overnight to receive goodies. The saint's physical presence was limited to a gloved hand that reached around the door, throwing sweets to the children, while a booming voice enquired whether they had been naughty or nice. Even then, the long arm of the law tried to quash 'papist idolatry' in the privacy of people's own homes. Incredibly, some of these statutes are still on the books. A local TV station reported this week that officials in Tiel, less than an hour from Barneveld, had found a seventeenth-century law still in force forbidding children from putting their shoes out for St Nick.

In the backlash, however, St Nicholas came out of hiding to parade throughout Europe and America in various incarnations. In England, the festive spirit was personified – apparently for the first time – by Ben Jonson and other playwrights as a character called Sir, Lord and eventually Father Christmas. Across the North Sea, the earliest known record of a *Sint*-type figure riding through the Low Countries comes from 1783 in an area that now straddles the Dutch and Belgian borders. Around the same time, the first references to 'St A. Claus' and the like began to appear in American newspapers, particularly in New York, the city formerly known as 'New Amsterdam'.

Back in the Old Country, St Nicholas travelled around with devilish sidekicks who did his dirty work for him, beating children and threatening to kidnap them. To the horror of social workers, many of these scare figures survive to this day, making Christmas as diverse as carnival on the Continent: the Germans have *Knecht Ruprecht*, a rod-wielding servant smeared with soot who operates under countless aliases (including Beelzebub); the Austrians have *Krampus*, a chained demon with fur, horns and a long red tongue similar to the Yuletide devil feared by Czechs and Slovaks, and the Swiss have *Schmutzli*, a soot-faced figure in a brown robe who used to threaten to gobble up children. For sheer nastiness, however, the French top the league with *Père Fouettard*, whose faintly comical name – roughly translated as 'Father Whipper' – belies his gruesome origins as a child-killing butcher in one of the St Nicholas legends.

Compared to chained devils and child-killers, the Dutch contribution might seem relatively tame. However, Black Pete has proved to be much more controversial than any other Continental bogeyman. An Amsterdam schoolteacher named Jan Schenkman invented the character in *St Nicholas and His Servant,* published around 1848, the cover depicting an angry black man chasing after naughty children. Schenkman's work popularised the idea of *Sinterklaas* arriving in Holland by steamboat, and he also crystallised the *Sint*'s Spanish connection, a link that may hark back to Spain's occupation of the Netherlands in the 1500s or the simple fact that it was the land of marzipan, oranges and other exotic treats. His anonymous servant soon turned into a Moor dressed in sixteenth-century clothes. Given that he made his debut fifteen years before the Dutch abolished slavery in 1863 – the first record of Pete having a name dates from the same year – it's no wonder that blacks have found him objectionable. Over the years images of him have ranged from a lightly tanned page to a googly eyed sambo with a broken chain on his foot.

The debate over Black Pete began in the late Seventies and early Eighties, amid growing immigration from Suriname, the Dutch Antilles and Ghana. However, most of the experiments in changing Pete's skin colour proved short lived. Instead, his personality changed, along with his relationship to the *Sint*. He became a quick-witted prankster rather than a thick-skulled enforcer, and he began to speak Dutch without a 'black' accent. His bag turned into a sweets dispenser, making him the firm favourite among kiddies, who identified more with his rebellious mischiefmaking than the *Sint*'s reverent demeanour. For native Hollanders, these changes were the solution to the Black Pete controversy. 'That was in the PC years,' Priscilla says offhandedly. 'Of course, political correctness changes over time. There is a slight hint of slavery, of course, but nowadays the Black Petes are not his slaves. And sometimes they even patronise him because he's an old man. He tends to forget things.'

So the custom's not racist; it's ageist. While many Dutch feel they've gone far enough in adapting their beloved Pete, the image of a kindly white man and his clownish sidekick still rankles with some blacks. In Amsterdam, I met a local councillor who is petitioning Parliament to abolish Black Pete or, at the very least, make him a different colour. A Surinamese immigrant, Iwan Leeuwin is also chair of the Dutch branch of the Global Afrikan Congress, formed in Barbados in 2002 (nice work if you can get it). To help me understand the issue, he actually drew me a picture in the town hall where we met. 'This is the *superior*,' he said, pointing to the *Sint* on horseback he'd drawn on the board in green ink. 'And the Black Petes are the inferiors. The solution is that we should cut this out radically,' he said, making crosses through a posse of stick Petes.

'This is not just happening on the fifth of December; it is happening *all the time. All the time* white people in Holland are feeling they're superior to black people. If all people are equal, then you have to stop these things. Because you are showing the world, you are showing the kids, this is the superior, that's me, I'm white. And blacks – down there. And it happens at school, when you're looking for work. And this whole problem with the Muslims right now: it's just because they don't get respect. If they got respect, they wouldn't get violent.'

What's struck me in talking about the culture clash in the Netherlands is how often the term 'respect' comes up in conversation. In fact, future generations may look back and see it as one of the buzzwords of our times, from Aretha Franklin to the black American concept of 'dissing', or 'disrespecting someone', that has crept into English on both sides of the Atlantic (even politicians as diametrically opposed as George Galloway and Gordon Brown have jumped on the 'respect' bandwagon). Whereas white majorities in Northern Europe and the US seem to have long since forgotten the meaning of the word – the

Protestant God made us all equals – other cultures still take face, and the loss of it, deadly seriously. Like Fortuyn and Van Gogh, Iwan said he believed that people should be free to talk about their concerns; the difference is that they should talk *respectfully*.

Instead of Black Pete, then, maybe they should adopt 'Straw Pete'. One of the most fascinating displays in Barneveld shows a Dutch version of *Struwwelpeter*, the macabre German nursery rhymes that date from the same period as Black Pete. With their scary illustrations of children having their thumbs snipped off for sucking them or burning to ashes for playing with matches, they exemplified what was actually called 'black pedagogy': scaring kids straight. Nowadays, the politically correct tend to view them as examples of Victorian-era child rearing at its worst. But in their day, adults and children loved the cautionary tales for their extreme sense of humour. In the story that Priscilla has featured, St Nicholas punishes three boys for taunting a 'woolly headed' black man on account of his skin colour. 'Foaming with rage', the saint dunks them in a giant inkstand 'because they set up such a roar / and teas'd the harmless black-a-moor'.

To think we like to imagine we invented racial tolerance.

Meanwhile, *Sinterklaas* and his European counterparts have been fighting the Fat Man from America. Ironically, though, European immigrants made Santa what he is today (and towns such as Holland, Michigan, even hold Dutch-style *Sinterklaas* processions). Thomas Nast, a German-born caricaturist, drew Santa as a rotund, bearded man in 1863, and another German native copied the English Christmas card and introduced it to America, depicting a red-suited Santa on the cover in 1885. And it was a son of Swedish immigrants who turned Santa into a global superstar clad in a red suit with white trim. Starting in 1931, Haddon Sundblom painted Santa as the pitchman for Coca-Cola's Christmas campaigns – even modelling him on a retired salesman.

I ask Priscilla why the Dutch haven't capitalised on their links to Santa, considering the way Scandinavian countries cash in on the North Pole. She thinks a lot of people don't even realise there is a connection. The Dutch name for Santa is the *Kerstman*, or 'Christmas Man'. 'He's such a different chap. We don't recognise *Sinterklaas* in him at all. There's nothing in common except the presents.'

Despite the inclusion of Santa in the exhibit, the museum has received support from the National Sint Nicolaas Committee, formed in 1993 to keep *Sinterklaas* from dying out in the Netherlands. 'People were afraid that Santa Claus would take over the market,' Priscilla says. This is partly because 5 December is slightly more complicated than Christmas. Rather than just buying something and swaddling it in wrapping paper, Dutch families traditionally disguise their gifts as a clever 'surprise' and write a poem poking fun at the recipient. The percentage of Dutch households celebrating *Sinterklaas* dropped from 77 per cent in 1983 to a nadir of 16 per cent in the early 1990s, according to some surveys. And that's when the crusade against Santa began. The northern town of Assen led the fightback, banning Santa until the *Sint* has left on 6 December. Department stores posted No Entry boards for reindeer and Christmas trees, and the local Sinterklaas Committee urged police to lock up any trespassing Santas. The Dutch rallied around their tradition, which now survives in at least 60 per cent of households.

'*Sinterklaas* is alive and well. He was beginning to look a little anaemic, but he received a blood transfusion just in time,' Priscilla says. Although the Dutch have tended to be international in their outlook, and proudly European, they've also realised that they need to preserve their culture. 'On the one hand, you have to think big, but on the other hand, people are starting to realise that the old customs and the place where you come from are very important and that it's important to keep your own identity. You can be European, and you can also be your own nationality.'

What hits you first is the howling: *Peeeeeeeeeeeeeeeeeeee-eeeeeeeeeeete!!!!!!* Hundreds – no, *thousands* – of kids are wailing and screaming, jostling each other ahead of *Sinterklaas'* dramatic arrival in Amsterdam. Some are dressed as the *Sint*, sporting cut-out mitres on their heads, but many more are kitted out like their idol, Black Pete, in feathered caps and brightly coloured breeches. They even have dark make-up smeared on their faces. They're crowding the locks and bike paths along the river belting out *Sint* songs and waving little orange flags stamped with caricatures of the grinning duo as they fidget in the cold for a first glimpse of *Sinterklaas'* steamboat.

I've cycled into the city with my friends, an Anglo-Dutch couple who live in Amstelveen, just south of the capital. The leisurely half-hour ride – more of a two-wheeled stroll, really – has reminded me how immensely liveable this city of less than a million souls is. Last time I was here, for a preliminary trip with my family, the sky was grey and drizzly, but this year the sun is beaming, providing a reprieve from the gloom in the national psyche. With Hans and Abi in the lead, and their four-year-old riding shotgun, we've pedalled through autumnal fenlands, past a statue of Rembrandt beside a windmill, along-side reflective canals and the wide Amstel River. We've travelled through the often outlandish architecture of the outskirts to the timeless grace of the waterside houses in the centre, their gables and windowpanes like the wigs and faces on characters out of an eighteenth-century play.

'We'll have to make a short cut if we want to catch *Sinterklaas*!' Hans exclaims over his shoulder. We pick up the pace, trundling across tram lines and bridges. Only in Amsterdam would you find yourself bicycling to chase a boat: Follow that Saint!

As any tyke will tell you, the *Sint* steamed into Holland yesterday, arriving fresh from Spain in a televised event covered by 'serious' news presenters. For several days, the *Sinterklaas Journaal* has been giving kids urgent updates on the *Sint*'s progress in a ten-minute slot before the Dutch version of *Sesame Street* (in which Bert and Ernie are openly gay*). Each year the bulletin focuses on a different theme, such as a mini-drama over a delay in the *Sint*'s departure – will he make it to Holland on time? – or the dimwitted antics of Black Pete. Last year children were informed that a *Zwarte Piet* had gone slightly bonkers after eating too many sweets. The cutaways showed him crashing into a girl on his bike and taking the wrong turn at a junction: the arrow pointed right, but he turned left and ploughed into a lake. *Silly Pete!*

Towns take it in turns to receive this free gift of publicity, and last November it was bestowed on Zwolle, east of Amsterdam. Amid all the excitement, however, what the *Sinterklaas Journaal* failed to report was the frantic dredging

* Only joking.

that took place in the run-up to the *Sint*'s arrival. The leaders of Zwolle were terrified the *Sint*'s steamboat would churn up the water, bringing the swollen corpse of a recent drowning victim to the surface, live on national TV.

From the moment the *Sint* makes landfall, he miraculously multiplies so that every town and village in the country hosts its very own *Sinterklaas* parade. In Amsterdam, the *Sint*'s arrival is heralded by hundreds of male and female Petes cavorting in orange vessels that chug up the river and into the canals. The blue signs on the sterns reveal their provenance: 'Madrid', 'Valencia', 'Alicante' and any other vaguely familiar Spanish location. They're singing and dancing onboard, doing the Mexican wave, accompanied by bands of other Black Petes playing oompah music and *Sinterklaas* jingles on brass instruments. Puttering alongside them are boatloads of lucky children whose parents have decided to go for a Sunday cruise in the family dinghy.

A big white policeboat cruises into the canal, dwarfing the other vessels. A sound like a shrill foghorn echoes across the water. It's the *Sint*'s steamboat, decked out in balloons and streamers. Its stovepipe chimney blasts great clouds of white noise into the air, sending the Petes running for cover as the brass bands merrily toot and bang on their horns and drums. The *Sint* stands at the prow, next to the sign marked SPAIN, waving regally as he floats under the series of raised bridges leading to the harbour. The throngs of two-headed giants – parents with kids on their shoulders – wave back, fluttering their *Sint* flags in the air and following him as he makes his way up the canal. Hordes of parents are pushing their bikes along the paths. It's a bicycle traffic jam!

'You'll notice there aren't many black faces in the crowd,' Hans remarks.

Or brown ones, for that matter. The *Sint*'s arrival coincides this year with Eid ul-Fitr, the celebration marking the end of Ramadan, the month of fasting. Eid has its own name in Dutch, a legacy of the country's colonial past in Indonesia. In neighbourhoods throughout the Netherlands, Moroccans, Turks and Muslim Indonesians usually celebrate *Suikerfeest,* the 'sugar feast', with banquets, new clothes and special prayers at the mosque. After the recent arson attacks on mosques and schools, though, this year's celebrations are much more subdued. 'The feelings and emotions are gloomy,' a Moroccan man told me. 'All the discussion is about extremism, the attacks and the current situation of Muslims in the Netherlands.'

While Muslim immigrants focus on the *Suikerfeest,* native Hollanders will spend the next few weeks counting down to the *Sinterklaasfeest* on 5 December. Every night for the next three weeks – or as often as their parents can manage – Dutch children will kneel before whatever passes for fireplaces in their homes and leave their shoes or clogs out for the *Sint*, plus a carrot and straw for his horse. When they awake each morning, they'll find a gift that's small enough to ensure their parents don't go bankrupt by the end of the holidays: gold coins or alphabet letters made from chocolate, marzipan animal figures or baked goods dosed with ginger, nutmeg, cloves and aniseed – often all in the same cake or cookie (having circled the globe to find them, the Dutch still can't get enough of their spices).

The *Sint*'s waterborne cavalcade glides into the wide old harbour in front of the Scheepvaart Museum, an elegant monument to the country's maritime past, with a clipper ship on one side and what used to be the dockyards of the East India Company on the other. Two men are watching the spectacle, balancing infants on their shoulders like bags of articulated jelly.

'New fathers,' one of their partners smiles. Leigh is originally from the States – even when you're not looking for them, you bump into Americans in Amsterdam – and she makes a point of telling me she runs an espresso café, not a coffee shop. In her dangly earrings and pashmina, she's got that typical Kashmir-by-way-of-Starbucks look. 'When I first came here, I didn't know what to make of Black Pete. But it doesn't seem to bother our best friends.' She shrugs. 'They're black. *And* gay.'

If only they were disabled.

'Originally Black Pete was Moorish, you know,' her partner, Melle, informs us. 'For a while they tried to make him politically correct. You had Rainbow Pete—'

'I thought he was gay.'

'*And* Wheelchair Pete – people thought, "Why should all Petes be able to walk?"'

'What next?' Leigh laughs. 'Terrorist Pete?'

Ho-ho – uh, *no*. The cannons firing every few minutes keep me jittery, though no one else seems to fear any attempted Sintocide. After docking at the Maritime Museum, *Sinterklaas* will stop for some light refreshment with city officials and then mount his white stallion to begin the on-land parade. He'll make a circuit around the centre, riding through Dam Square, where he will tactfully overlook the flowers and manifestoes wreathing the base of the National Memorial:

TOLERANCE! FREEDOM!
FREE SPEECH!
WHERE?
NOT IN HOLLAND ANY MORE!

Likewise, the *Sint* carefully avoids the red-light district, as well as the Catholic church that bears his name (even though he is Amsterdam's patron saint). 'If he did go into the church,' Hans explains, 'that would make it a religious event.'

Instead, the parade stays secular to a fault, with commercial endorsements in the form of amoebic corporate mascots, cars pitching New York Pizza and a gigantic plastic bag advertising *pepernoten*, ubiquitous little gingernuts with a liquorice kick. There are floats and big papier-mâché effigies, baton twirlers and medieval damsels on horseback, a kilted pipe and drum band, a forest of men on stilts, revellers wearing hobbyhorse heads and Jules Verne diving suits and even the odd wino stumbling through the proceedings, draining a bottle dry as he soaks up the attention.

But the crowd's favourite is Pete, in all of his multitudinous incarnations: hundreds of green- and blue-eyed men, women and children strutting through multicultural Amsterdam like Dutch golliwogs, doling out *pepernoten* and sweets. And all along the route, you hear the zombified moan, the unifying wail of candy-mad urchins:

Peeeeeeeeeeeeeeeeeeeeeeeeeeeeeeeeeeeeeeeeeeeeeeeeeeeeeeeeeeeeeeeete!!!!!!!!!!

It's one big hallucinatory carnival, even without any chemical enhancement. God help the foreign tourists who stagger out of their coffee shops, stoned into space, only to find themselves confronted by a bewildering onslaught of marching music, hundreds of black cartoon characters doling out cookies and a bearded bloke on a horse who looks *vaguely* like Father Christmas. *Dude, I think we smoked too much!*

At the moment, though, the *Sint* is taking his place next to the mayor in front of the Maritime Museum, two tiny figures on the far side of the water, one in a red robe and a pointed hat, the other in a twinkling gold chain. Dozens of boats are amassed before them, bobbing up and down expectantly. All *Sinterklaas* would have to do is give the word, and he could bring the harbour to a halt with a kiddies' blockade.

In fact, he uses his address to praise the mayor, a Jewish Dutchman who has come under fire recently for not cracking down on extremism. Instead, he has adopted a more moderate approach, epitomised by his faintly desperate-sounding catch-phrase: 'I'm trying to keep the city together.' But at least the *Sint* is a fan. 'The mayor has been an example of how you can be there for all Amsterdammers and promote tolerance among them,' he declares over the loudspeaker, his voice ringing across the harbour. 'And I, in turn, will be there for all Amsterdam children!'

PART TWO:
BLACK AND BLUE

Having been among the first to circle the globe, the Dutch helped shape how we in the West view our place in the world. Consider this tale of two maps. In the middle of the Royal Palace in the heart of Amsterdam, the splendiferous Citizens' Hall depicts the Maid of Amsterdam as having the seventeenth-century cosmos at her feet, with the globe's hemispheres and the northern sky carved in marble on the floor and sculptures of Roman gods representing the planets around the perimeter.

However, if you travel to West Amsterdam, you'll find

another map set in an atmosphere that's a world apart from the picturesque city centre. A notorious open-air square, the Mercatorplein is located just south of Erasmus Park, a tribute to the Dutch prophet of tolerance. Although Mercator Square tends to be synonymous with urban strife in the national media, it was named in honour of the Flemish cartographer whose take on the world can still be found in classrooms today (and whose museum is located in Sint-Niklaas, Belgium). Mercator's innovation made it possible to display the globe on a flat piece of paper, the earth's curves conforming to straight lines of latitude and longitude. In doing so, though, the Mercator projection also distorted the size of Europe and North America. The red map splodged across Mercator Square shows the Netherlands and the rest of the Continent firmly at the centre of the world, with little Greenland almost as big as Africa. On the perimeter of the square, noble exotics carved in worn, twentieth-century concrete adorn modernist brick buildings, while the new citizens of Europe cross paths between the shops below: brown, black and white faces, alongside women in shawls and bearded men in skullcaps and robes.

Immediately after the Van Gogh murder, Mercator Square served as the starting point for what was undoubtedly the most extraordinary of the countless protests that took place around the country: a mosque-to-mosque bicycle rally. On the spur, or pedal, of the moment, an alliance of eighty Moroccan and Dutch demonstrators decided to *bicycle* from the Mercatorplein in the West to a park in East Amsterdam, stopping along the way to hand out orange buttons and posters bearing a kind of Just-Say-No-to-Extremism slogan – at *mosques*. 'The idea was to build a bridge between the West and the East,' says Ahmed Marcouch, one of the organisers. The itinerary included the controversial El-Tawheed Mosque. 'The official there was a little . . . *emotional* at first because he thought we were just targeting his mosque. But when we explained to him what we were doing, he accepted a poster and said, "We are also against extremism."'

I'm back in the Netherlands for *Sinterklaasfeest* and, while I'm here, I'm keen to see what Muslims think of the ongoing tensions. Ahmed has invited me to attend a community meeting of Dutch and Moroccans. A former police sergeant, he's the youth-and-safety coordinator at a community centre in the *Indische Buurt*, the 'Indonesian Quarter' close to where Van Gogh was murdered. Ahmed's also spokesman for the alliance of Moroccan mosques in the Netherlands; as such, he projects the moderate face of Islam. He wears a handsome grey suit, and his beard and moustache are shaved to the point of disappearance. Talking beforehand, he mentions how shocked he was to hear of the murder – 'In the Koran, it's not legal to kill anyone' – and outlines the experience of Moroccans in the Netherlands. Ahmed came here when he was nine years old, when his father and other guest workers took the risk of bringing their families to live among the godless Dutch. 'The problem is not fundamentalism. The problem in Europe – in Holland – is that Dutch people do not accept Islam at all as a religion in society,' he says, adding that there's a perception among some Muslims that 'Westerners will *never* accept you as a Muslim, no matter what you do. They will only accept you once you fall away from your religion.'

We drive over to a graffitied council estate in North Amsterdam and spend the rest of the evening in a room that has wires curling off the walls, a naked fluorescent tube drooping from the ceiling and a floor full of scabbed concrete that's been patched with tiles – or maybe it's the other way round. It's the scrag end of a building, the bit that no one could think of anything else to do with. Presumably the neighbourhood already had an illegal abattoir-cum-gangland torture chamber, so the locals said, 'What the hell? Let's turn this room into a community centre.'

Despite the grim ambience, roughly sixty people have turned out for the panel discussion, mostly middle-aged Moroccan men, but also a few youths and some white Hollanders making up the difference. The seven panellists include a policeman, a Dutch-Moroccan from the Mercatorplein, two imams plus a trainee in beards and anti-extremist buttons, a right-wing politico conforming to the skinhead stereotype (Aryan cheekbones, Mussolini pout and *Übermensch* muscles) and a caring-sharing white woman named Joke*. The moderator has such a fashion-defying haircut, I can't work out whether he's a Muslim or a Mennonite . . . then again, there aren't many Amish called Mohammed. Wonky hairstyle aside, he has mastered the art of talk-show presenting, weaving in and out of the audience, making big, circular, inclusive gestures and pausing every so often to check his notecards. Clearly, Mo watches a lot of daytime TV. He's a regular Mo-prah.

The event quickly turns into one long talking shop, though I do catch some interesting bits, thanks to Ahmed's on-the-spot translations.

One of the imams mentions that a Moroccan kid had told him it was good that Van Gogh had been killed. 'But I said to him, "What would you think if a Dutchman had killed one of your family because he was Muslim?" The boy was silent.'

---

* No joke – it's a common Dutch name.

The Dutch Aryan pipes up, telling the audience that he went to a mosque where an imam told him that all homosexuals should be killed.

'I don't believe him,' Ahmed mutters to me.

Neither does a Moroccan kid in the row behind us. He's got gelled hair and an American varsity-style leather jacket. 'You say that about imams, but why didn't we hear you speak out when Van Gogh said similar things against Muslims?'

This line is taken up by the councillor from the Mercatorplein district. 'Society operates on a double standard. When Van Gogh said offensive things, no one spoke out against him, but when a Muslim kid told national TV that he wished a right-wing politician would die of cancer, the government began an investigation.'

A granny in the audience throws in her two cents, clutching her handbag as she stands to speak (she's not taking *any* chances in this crowd). 'Living together starts by speaking the same language and celebrating the same festivals, such as *Sinterklaas*.'

After more than two hours of talking, we hear some final thoughts from Joke: 'The Netherlands is a country of conferences, and we need to have more conferences.'

More talking? She must be jok—

Keen to get some fresh air, I go outside to talk to Mustapha, the politician from the Mercatorplein, while he smokes and I sip some tea. It's my chance to put my pet theory to him: that Muslims in modern Europe are in a similar position to that of Catholics in England after the Reformation. Basically, they faced a choice between showing loyalty to the Crown or to a 'foreign' belief system led by the Pope. I suggest somewhat hesitantly that mainstream society might be much more accepting of Muslims if they actively demonstrated their loyalty by shopping extremists; not just turning a blind eye or ostracising them within their communities, but by actively reporting potential troublemakers to the authorities.

As it happens, he's glad to inform me, his district has just starting doing this, drafting a 'contract' between local mosques and the government. So far, though, only a Turkish and Pakistani mosque have signed up. The Moroccans are still mulling it over. 'And I can understand that, because the purpose of a mosque is prayer. People don't want to go to pray and feel they're being spied on.'

'I imagine that in some cases, it might involve reporting on a distant relative.'

He nods, somehow encouraged by my analogy. 'So if someone commits a crime in England now, no one cares whether they're Protestant or Catholic, do they?'

'Not really. But it took a long time to reach that point. Years of bloodshed.'

He stubs his cigarette on the ground and smiles. 'Hopefully we'll be able to avoid that.'

It's the Friday morning before 5 December, and schools throughout the Netherlands are gearing up for their visit from the *Sint* and his helpers. At one primary in south-east Amsterdam, though, *Sinterklaas* arrives solo. In the assembly hall, the black and Asian kids can barely contain themselves. They're wearing their handmade hats for the occasion – red mitres with crosses and puffy Pete numbers made of crêpe paper – and sitting cross-legged on the floor, buzzing and giggling with excitement.

Drafting in a couple of volunteers, the *Sint* lugs his burlap sacks onto the podium, flanked by two gigantic gift boxes.

'*Sinterklaas*, why have you come all alone?' a teacher with a microphone asks.

'I couldn't find my Petes.'

A gloved hand peeks out of one of the boxes.

The kids roar in unison: 'There he is!!!'

'Where?' The teacher and the *Sint* look in the wrong direction. '*There!!!!*'

As the *Sint* checks the first box, gloved fingers flutter above the other one. The children scream with delight, relishing the back-and-forth of the pantomime, until finally the boxes are removed and out pop – not two Black Petes, but *Red Pete and Blue Pete!*

For the kids, this chromatic anomaly doesn't make a blind bit of difference, so long as Pete delivers the sweet, sweet payola. But for teachers and parents at the Blauwe Lijn, Pete's complexion nearly split the school apart. The Blue Line was one of the first schools in the Netherlands to adopt an other-coloured Pete, way back in 1983, and it's one of barely half a dozen stalwarts that continue the alternative tradition. Despite its name, the Blue Line is quasi-officially classified as a *zwarte* – or black – school in the district known as Little Suriname, where more than sixty nationalities rub along together, trying to avoid friction. Barely 15 of the Blue Line's 200 pupils are white, and its roll-call has nearly halved over the past few decades, so the progressive primary has been forced to share its original campus – a disjointed U – with a Christian school owned by the state and another run by an evangelical group from Suriname. This juxtaposition makes *Sint* visits tricky. The Blue Line doesn't want its students to see the Black Petes frolicking across the way at the Christian school, and the black evangelicals don't want their children to see any Petes at all –

Black or Blue – not to mention the *Sint*. 'So we have to divide the two *Sints* and *Piets*,' says Kees van Veen, a former *Sint* who ushers *Sinterklaas* through the backdoor at the Blue Line.

A tech-friendly jack of all trades, Kees is also a veteran of the Battle of Black Pete. I met him just after the Van Gogh murder, when many white liberals from the Sixties were questioning their ideals. 'We have a very long history of tolerance in Holland, but it's based on trade,' he told me, explaining that the Netherlands was a commercial nexus between northern and southern Europe, as well as the Eastern and Western hemispheres. For the Dutch, tolerance of other cultures wasn't just a virtue, it was good business. 'We're not so tolerant as an ideal. It's all about making money.'

Back in the Eighties, Kees was one of the teachers who fought to change Pete after black parents complained to the school. 'At that time, there was a lot of idealism. When people came to you, you said, "Hmm, let's listen."' So he started to research Pete's roots, unearthing a songbook from his childhood that showed Pete with a chain on his ankle. As a boy, he remembered seeing Pete carry off another kid in his sack. 'When I was a child, you were afraid of *Zwarte Piet*,' he said. 'My father would call the *Sint* to report bad behaviour.' Since then, Pete had been rehabilitated, and his blackness attributed to chimney soot. 'But soot doesn't change your facial features.'

Kees found himself with a crisis of conscience. 'Once you know about the problem, what do you do?' The decision to turn Pete blue resulted in a 'big fight' that divided teachers and parents alike, regardless of their colour. 'It ended with neither side talking to each other for a year.' To this day, one of the veterans of the row keeps one fingernail painted black, in mourning for *Zwarte Piet*.

Last time we talked, he told me that many black parents didn't see anything wrong with Black Pete. 'If we were to ask parents now, I think we would have Black Petes again. I'm sure of it.'

'So what's stopping you?'

'We just don't talk about it.'

To their credit, though, the kids aren't afraid of asking *Sinterklaas* some awkward questions as he and Red and Blue Pete visit each classroom.

'Why don't you have any *Black* Petes?' asks an eight-year-old in braids.

A pause. 'Wellllll, we do . . .' The *Sint* hesitates.

Red Pete jumps in to save him. 'They're at *other* schools.'

Next question.

A boy raises his hand.

'Do you have a brother, the *Kerstman*, who lives at the North Pole?'

The *Sint* blanks him. 'No, I don't know that guy. Who's he?'

In another classroom, a black teacher with dreadlocks whoops with joy when the *Sint* arrives, throwing a hula hoop round her waist and encouraging the Petes to pretend they're going to drag her away. 'No, no,' she screams, 'I don't want to go to Spain!'

Outside the door, Kees frowns, telling me her play-acting is what used to happen in the bad old days of Black Pete. 'We don't do that any more. You can try to change the story, but it's hard because it's what they did in their youth.'

As we speak, I notice that some of the children have painted heretical images of Black Pete amid the decorations.

'I know – it's terrible isn't it?' he laughs. But he's stubborn to the end. 'I still think it was the right decision,' he says, watching Red and Blue Pete entertain the kids. 'It makes Pete even more of a clown. There's nothing to be angry or scared about.'

I wish I had that much conviction.

When Henk first suggested that I dress up like Black Pete, I have to admit I was tempted – for all the wrong, ornery, reasons. Of course, I could try to justify it by arguing that I wanted to explore the ethno-econo-psychological role of Black Pete in Dutch society. The truth is, I just wanted to wear the costume. I wanted to see what it was like to be Black Pete, purely out of instinctive, killed-cat curiosity – political correctness be damned. Over the past few weeks, though, I've begun to lose my nerve, particularly after witnessing the gobsmacked reaction of a Nigerian friend in London when I told her about the dark secret at the heart of a Dutch Christmas. What would my friends think? Then again, I had already been whipped by a boy Oil Wrestler in Turkey, felt up by a Sicilian coprophile and made an honorary Arse Blower in France. So it's unlikely that I could disgrace myself any further by playing the part of Black Pete in the Netherlands.

Even so, I'm a little on edge as I enter the wood-beamed pub that serves as the canteen, dispatch office and dressing room for *Sinterklaas Centrale*. It's 4 December, and today and tomorrow are its busiest days of the year, with all thirty teams of *Sints* and Piets doing the rounds of Amsterdam from ten a.m. to ten p.m. If my residual guilt weren't giving me grief, the scene at Sintcentral would be comical. Period gear hangs on racks at the back, guarded by a woman with a cigarette stuck to her lip, while the rest of the room is strewn with clerical robes, mitres and staffs, wigs and beards, burlap sacks and any number of doublets and breeches. At least a dozen male and female Petes are lounging around on their lunch break, carefully smoking and sipping coffee through straws, while a couple of others perfect their make-up in front of light-bulbed vanity tables on the sidelines. A posse of Petes is one thing, but there's also something here that no Dutch child should ever see: several *Sints* together, all in the same room, in varying degrees of dress and undress. One robed figure is completely bald, but with his big strap-on beard, it looks like his hair is upside down. Another has just a long, flowing white wig on his head: the very image of a geriatric rock god.

I seem to add to the comic effect, having wandered into the festive jollity with such a po-faced, stricken expression that somebody can't help but heckle me.

'Uh oh! It's the tax inspector!'

I search for sympathy from the nearest figure I can find: a tall, lean *Sint* in full bishop's uniform with white make-up smeared on his nose and cheekbones to make him look older. Surely he won't make fun of me. He assures me that Henk should be returning from his morning rounds shortly. 'But *I'm* the real *Sint*,' he confides smilingly. 'All these others are impostors.'

None too soon, Henk blusters in off the streets. He pauses in the doorway, a vision of Sint Nicolaas, before whipping off his fake hair and firing up a cigar. He grabs a newspaper from one of the tables and holds it up. 'Finally we made the front page!' he growls to anyone who will listen. 'It's just a shame about the picture.'

The photo on the front of *Algemeen Dagblad,* a major national newspaper, shows two Petes doing their rounds . . . with the *Sint* in an undignified pose, crouching to retrieve his hat from the ground.

'We don't want any more mistakes like this! It doesn't look professional!' Henk bellows, though many of his listeners scoff at how seriously he takes it all.

This probably isn't the best time to tell him about my misgivings, and anyway, they begin to disappear once he introduces me to his sidekick.

'This is my chief Pete,' he says, proudly clapping his hands on the shoulders of a young man who's wearing a plumed cap, gold loop earrings, a frilly cravat and a black, eighteenth-century-style coat in luxurious velvet with slash pockets and silver embroidery. The dandy's make-up accentuates his broad, chiselled nose and full, sculpted lips. Beneath his curly black wig, his own hair is dense with coils. I can't tell whether he's black or Moroccan. His name should be a clue, but even then I'm not sure. It's only when I ask him outright that Youssouf tells me he's the son of Moroccan immigrants. With time to kill before the afternoon shift, he takes off his coat and headgear to sit down and talk. A university student, twenty-one-year-old Youssouf has been a part-time Pete for the past four years, moving up the ranks to become Henk's righthand man. 'He thinks very highly of me,' he says coolly, lighting the first of many cigarettes. 'He always wants to have good Petes around him.'

When Henk goes into a rough neighbourhood, Youssouf turns into Bad-Ass Pete, scaring off any would-be Muslim attackers. 'I go in and tell them, "Fuck off!" and they say, "Oh, shit, he speaks Arabic!"'

However, in his frilly neckcloth – with painted lips that any woman would kill for – Youssouf doesn't look like much of a bruiser to me. In fact, in many ways, he's a model of East-meets-West integration for Europe, an Arabic-speaking Dutch

Moroccan who feels so at home in the Netherlands that he helps safeguard the country's most cherished tradition. Very few Moroccans manage to qualify for the elite high school he attended, let alone go to university, making him the kind of minority member who regularly receives admiring remarks from those in the majority: *If only all of them were like you . . .* It's meant to be a compliment, but it just underlines how different he is. 'Most of my friends are Dutch,' he says, in a neat reversal of the old bigot's defence: *Some of my best friends are black!* As for religion, Youssouf's parents are Muslims, but he's reluctant to associate himself with the faith of his fathers. 'I don't see fate as a way of living,' he says, exhaling smoke.

Yet Youssouf's eyes flare when I mention the calls for Moroccans to integrate more. 'They don't mean integrate, they mean assimilate one hundred per cent into Dutch culture,' he says. 'The Netherlands up until now has been very high-minded, but now it feels like people are saying, "You have to be like us, or you don't belong here."' In the current climate of suspicion and resentment, though, even he feels like more of an outsider. Maybe it's his imagination, for instance, but he's noticed that if he's sitting on a crowded tram, next to the only free seat, the other passengers are reluctant to take it; they would rather stand than sit next to a Moroccan. And he bristles as he talks about the double standards that apply to minorities: if an imam says something outrageous, there are calls for him to be punished, but if a Dutchman like Van Gogh does the same, the majority chalks it up to free speech. 'And if you say I'm a goatfucker, I'm not going to say, "I want to be your friend."'

Fair enough.

He cups his hands to light another cigarette, explaining that no matter where he goes, he's a foreigner – even when he visits

Morocco. 'Sometimes it stretches my legs so far, it's like standing between two cliffs that are moving apart, and I think I'm going to fall between the middle of them.' He forces a smile. 'If you thought too much about it, it would give you a headache.'

I ask whether he has any doubts about playing Black Pete.

'The fact is that Black Pete is black because he goes down the chimney,' he replies. Case closed. Then he pauses for another ruminative smoke. 'What I do find offensive is when you do it with brown make-up, because then it's not like going down the chimney. That is very offensive.'

It occurs to me that he may object to brown facepaint because it's the same colour as his own skin, but I'm in no position to judge. In any event, I'm feeling more at ease, given that there are at least two other people in the room who could claim first dibs on being offended. The other guy is actually black, and he's darkened his skin further, so that he looks for all the world like one of those grinning statues of 'exotic Negroes' that were all the rage in the boom years of European colonialism. The genuine Black Pete is making fun of a white Pete at the bar in dreadlocks: 'Hey, Rasta Pete!'

What I'm most concerned about now is my nose. I've had a cold for the past two weeks, and I don't know if I can get through the afternoon without having to sneeze or blow my nose, botching my blackface. I'd be the freakish equivalent of Rudolph the Red-Nosed Reindeer: JR the White-Nosed Black Pete.

With only half an hour to go, Youssouf sorts me out a sixteenth-century-style costume: a flat cap with a feather, a short red jacket with puffy sleeves, a pair of matching knee-length breeches and tights, and a crêpe-paper ruff, plus black gloves, and, of course, a curly black wig. I rush into the toilet to change, struggling to get to grips with the tights, as they get a grip on me, and take my place at one of the make-up tables. Youssouf hands me a plastic glove, a grubby sponge and a can of *schmink* that looks like shoe polish. The key to getting that perfect tar-baby complexion, he tells me, is to daub on the greasepaint rather than smear it. Unfortunately, though, I keep shmeering my *schmink*. A couple of girl Petes take pity on me, dampening the sponge in water to build up a glossy accretion of black all over my head. The Petes take their faux blackness incredibly seriously, daubing paint even on the backs of their necks and behind their ears, then using cotton swabs to finish off tricky bits such as eyelids, nostrils and the cartilage canyons of the ears. The final touch is a gash of red lipstick, applied as artfully as time allows. The goal is for children to think that Pete is actually black, as opposed to a white guy in make-up.

'If you miss a spot, just tell the kids it's a white freckle,' a burly Pete advises me.

Equally important is your hairpiece. My wig seems comfortable, but Youssouf swaps it for a bigger model. 'If your wig's too tight, you'll get a headache after an hour.'

Henk is raring to go, having donned his beard and mitre. He stops in the doorway again, this time to bid a farewell *Dag!* to his merry employees (as a rule, only one *Sint* can leave the building at a time so as not to traumatise passing children). We make our way out of the pub-cum-dressing room to our Sintmobile: a clapped-out box of a car known as an Opel Kadett – the equivalent of a Vauxhall Astra in the UK. We crowd into the plaid seats, Henk and Youssouf up front, me and another Pete in the back, with the *Sint*'s gold crosier wedged in between us, a literal cross-bar that runs the length of the interior. Henk's itinerary identifies Youssouf as his chauffeur, while the other Pete is in charge of the *Sint*'s book and spectacles, as well as the ever-present bag of *pepernoten*. Me, I'm Superfluous Pete, or maybe Notepad Pete, though that's gonna be a tough sell to the kiddies: *Gather round children, while I amuse you with my shorthand!*

I try to strike up a conversation with my fellow flunkey, apologising for my lack of Dutch, but apparently he's playing the role of Surly Pete today. He's supremely uninterested in talking, apart from covetous remarks about other cars and regularly checking his make-up. While I was talking to Youssouf back at Sintcentral, Henk had interrupted us to tell him that Surly Pete wasn't up to scratch; he wants him shifted to another team tomorrow. Maybe Surly senses he's been given the chop; if you ask me, he deserves it. All he does is swig energy drink, sneak *pepernoten* and smoke.

Before I know it, all three of them are smoking – a cigar for the *Sint*, ciggies for the Petes. I'm already struggling to keep my nose from running, without any added irritants to stimulate my hyper-twitchy nostrils. Of course I could ask them to stub out their smokes, and they probably would, though it wouldn't do much for transatlantic relations. Instead, I hold out in the hope that the decongestant I took this morning, combined with the smog in the car, will somehow clot up my nose. I cock my neck in anticipation and glance sideways out the window.

When I'm not fighting the urge to sneeze or scratch an itch, I'm grappling with an even baser psychological urge. 'You can do anything you want to, because you're behind a mask,' Youssouf had told me, explaining Pete's appeal. And I'm quickly learning that Pete manifests himself in different ways through different people. I'm aghast, for instance, to find that the first thing I want to do as Black Pete is make a rude gesture to someone on the street – something that would normally never cross my mind, even if I were in a foul mood – purely for the juvenile pleasure of seeing their shocked reaction: *Black Pete just gave me the finger!*

For Youssouf, possession by Pete turns him into the driver from hell, made worse by the fact that we've got only fifteen minutes between each visit, and we're not entirely sure where we're going. While he's bombing around the 'Old South' of Amsterdam, lurching over speed bumps, weaving in and out of bicycles and honking at lesser mortals, Henk is barking directions, telling him to get into the left lane, or turn right at that canal, or cross the street – no, not that one! – President Kennedylaan. They've both got their windows cracked to keep the windscreen from fogging up. Youssouf's feather is fluttering in the air, and Henk's head is a fountain of curly white tresses overflowing in the passenger seat. He's balancing his collapsible mitre on his knees and trying to read a bunch of photocopied streetmaps to find our first stop of the afternoon.

'We're not so lucky with the traffic,' he grumbles.

A girl on a bike starts to pull out, but Youssouf honks at her furiously. She laughs and glances at her companion. *Black Pete just cut me off!*

Despite our erratic driving, most of the other drivers – and especially their kids – smile, wave and occasionally ask for *pepernoten* (they're not gettin' any). One woman pulls up alongside and tells the *Sint* that his robe is caught in the door. Less helpfully, a wiseguy sees Henk fumbling with his photocopied maps and shouts, 'Hey, *Sinterklaas*! For your birthday, why don't you ask for a satnav system?'

Henk chooses to ignore him.

Our first destination is a middle-class block of flats in South Amsterdam, where two neighbouring families are hosting a *Sinterklaasfeest* for their kids. To my surprise, a passing Surinamese man spots us and waves excitedly: '*Sinterklaas*, one minute! Let me just get my kids and take a photo of them with you!'

'Sorry, we don't have time,' Youssouf says.

This *Sint*'s on the clock. The drill goes like this: as soon as our Kadett jerks to a halt, Surly Pete and I jump out (making sure to lock our doors) and ring the doorbell or knock. One of the parents then lets us in and hands us bags of presents to carry into the house – as if we've brought them fresh from Spain – as well as a list to slip into the *Sint*'s book. Surly Pete then scatters *pepernoten* before the *Sint*, who strides in with his big red book and golden staff, taking a seat in the fanciest chair available. Henk's get-up merits such exalted seating. Besides the scarlet cloak and mitre, he's wearing a clerical stole and a chunky jewelled cross over a white robe, with lavender gloves and a ruby ring on his right hand. When he sits, his legs are nothing but frilly lace from the knees down, with red leg warmers and slip-on shoes painted gold.

Number One Pete helps him put on his specs.

'Do you know what's in my book?' the *Sint* asks the children.

Given that it's actually a volume of the Catholic Encyclopaedia, I'm guessing a lengthy defence of papal infallibility. But also tucked inside is the list the parents gave us, with the kids' names and hobbies alongside jokes about their behaviour.

The smaller children take turns on the *Sint*'s lap, while teens-and-up stand before him for some gentle teasing. Occasionally it's the kind of adult banter that might be permissible for a

Catholic bishop but would get your average department-store Santa thrown out of his grotto and straight into court.

'Why do you need a double bed?' the *Sint* enquires of a gangly boy barely eighteen years old.

'Uh . . . so I can lie down more comfortably.'

The *Sint* lowers his head to glower at him over his spectacles. 'You're lying,' he grumbles with mock severity. '*Sinterklaas* was not born yesterday. Tell me – do you have some . . . *tricks* to get people into bed?'

The teen comes clean. 'That's also a reason, *Sinterklaas*.'

Sex talk with the *Sint*: now there's an erection-killer. The kid might as well torch the mattress now.

Sinterklaas lets him off after he sings one of the half-dozen *Sint* songs that loop through the air like a communal soundtrack at this time of year. After twenty minutes, the family sings us out – '*Dag, Sinterklaasje, dag, dag . . .*' – and we cram back into the car, crosier first, and start careening across town.

Surly Pete turns to me. 'Can you see any white on my neck? Because one of those little girls, she was *staring* at me.' His eyes widen worryingly as he takes another slug of energy drink.

Great. Now he's Paranoid Pete. *Dude, have some more sugar.*

Personally, I couldn't drink a thing. Besides my nose leaking and an itch spreading its tentacles across the side of my face, I'm carsick from Youssouf's driving. I try to talk to Henk. While he clutches the safety bar overhead to keep from being thrown through the window, he tells me that *Sinterklaas* bookings rebounded at the last moment to match last year's levels. 'I was very surprised. Despite the economic slump, people have decided that if they're going to cut spending, it will be on presents, not *Sinterklaas*.'

This seems logical enough: if Hollanders feel their culture is under fire, they're going to dig in over their Dutchness. Obviously, this is good for business, but Henk's work is also a personal mission. '*Sinterklaas* is one of the last few traditions to remain in Holland, so I am very keen that it continues.' After each visit, Henk makes a point of congratulating the family on supporting the *Sinterklaas* tradition. 'We must not let it die.'

I watch enviously as he removes his wig and beard and gives his head a two-handed, all-over scratch. *Oh, to be the Sint.* He does this several times throughout the afternoon. Without the fake face-hair, Henk could be a stereotypical bishop, his double chin testifying to a preference for feasting rather than fasting. Whenever we stop at a traffic light, though, he quickly turns into the *Sint*, snapping his headgear into place with all the nonchalance of a boy pretending his hand isn't caught in the cookie jar.

As the sky darkens, a fine drizzle begins to fall. 'Be careful not to get the rain on your face,' Youssouf advises me. I'm not sure how to do that without an umbrella, so I try to walk with my head down, Dejected Pete, taking my chances whenever I cross the street. Our housecalls cover the range of housing in Amsterdam, from utilitarian apartment buildings and suburban homes to a gabled townhouse with original features and a candlelit houseboat floating on a canal. All of the families are white and well-to-do − renting a *Sint* is still relatively rare in Holland − and all but a few of the children are blonde and adorable. They jump up and down when they see us and sing *Sinterklaas* songs on cue. One seven-year-old even plays a tune for Henk on her harp. 'She has so much faith in *Sinterklaas*,' her English father tells me. 'She kneels in front of the chimney every night asking him to come. But I doubt she'll believe in him much longer. She's like a . . . like a *spot* that's about to pop.'

Not an ideal metaphor – *come 'ere, you little pimple* – but I see what he means. Everywhere we go, Henk explains to the adults that Notepad Pete is writing a book on European traditions. Rather than send this Pete packing back to Spain – which, come to think of it, was the actual starting point for my journey – they respond with an openness and friendliness that's very much of the season and somehow very Dutch. With the combination of friends and families, fireplaces and candles, as well as seasonal food and drink, the homes exude a cosy glow, attaining that Dutch nirvana of warmth and well-being: *gezelligheid.* Every language has its untranslatable words – or concepts that native speakers like to think are unique – and *gezellig* is one of them. Insofar as I can understand it, it's a cosy togetherness that relies more on goodwill and genuine affection than the relative expense of the event or size of the presents. More often than not, the gifts are small items, sometimes no more than a chocolate letter representing the recipient's first name. Of course, the Dutch aren't known for being big spenders. What strikes me as very European, though, is the emphasis on cherishing what you have rather than always looking past the present to a golden future that may never come.

But there's not much time to soak up the atmosphere. We're running late. After a flying visit to a private party in a restaurant – where Henk refreshes himself with a Coke (and even a smile) – we dash away to our next destination. Trouble is, we're lost. To make matters worse, Henk has run out of cigars, making him increasingly irritable.

Youssouf's phone jingles to life: the ringtone is 'Conga' by

Miami Sound Machine. 'I know. We can't find the place,' he says abruptly. We swerve into a petrol station – a BP – and Black Pete jumps out to ask directions. Henk snaps on his wig and beard again and gets out to buy some cigars, leaving us two flunkeys in the car. Surly's smoking next to me, his eyelids low and red-rimmed.

'That is *so* stupid,' he scoffs.

I'm shocked. I'd given up hope that he could speak, let alone have opinions. I don't know what to say.

'He shouldn't go around without his beard and wig on, not even in the car. The most stupid thing is that he thinks if he's in the car no one can see him. We were stopped at some lights and there was a little girl looking at us from the car in front. People look in and see three Petes, of course they know he's supposed to be the *Sint*! And he's the *Sint* driving around in an *Opel*! This kind of thing should at least have tinted windows so nobody can see inside.'

He takes another long, peevish drag on his cigarette. 'I've gone to corporate *Sinterklaas* parties – now that's the real thing. This – this is just going to people's houses and making silly jokes. It's stupid.'

With typical Dutch forthrightness, Surly doesn't bother lowering his voice as Henk lowers himself into the car. Youssouf guns the engine and we're off.

'How's my make-up?' Surly asks me.

'Fine,' I say, sensing it's actually meant as a reciprocal question. 'How's mine?'

'It's all right. But you might want to keep your head down in your collar, so the kids can't see your neck.'

'Oh – okay.' *Jerk.*

'But your make-up is okay,' he offers after a moment's

silence. 'We're not meant to be Negroes. We're meant to look like we came down the chimney.'

As we roar through the leaf-strewn streets, rocketing over speed bumps and zooming around corners, it soon becomes apparent that we're as lost as ever.

'We just made a complete circle,' Surly mutters.

Don't I know it. My stomach's chasing its tail.

The *Sint*'s so frustrated he throws the book at us, or at least tosses it into the backseat, rummaging through the clutter to find his trusty photocopies.

Meanwhile, Youssouf starts accosting bemused pedestrians. 'Excuse me, do you know where such-and-such *straat* is?'

Several smirks and shrugs later – *if the* Sint *doesn't know, who does?* – we eventually find a kindly woman who goes out of her way to help. I opt to leave at the next stop, before I sneeze my face off.

Once we reach our destination, Henk announces to the roomful of adults and teenagers – a liberal Jewish family – that I'm interested in *Sinterklaas* and other traditions.

'How about *Suikerfeest*?' one of the men laughs, referring to the Muslim festival also celebrated this week. 'That's also a Dutch tradition!'

I say goodbye to Henk as he hustles off into the night (Youssouf is already gunning the Sintmobile's engine). Still in my Black Pete get-up, I hop into a cab.

'Where do you need to go?' the driver jokes. 'Madrid?'

His name happens to be Pieter, and he claims he knew Theo Van Gogh. 'He was a nice guy: exactly the same in person as he was in the media.'

I don't see how a Muslim- and Jew-baiter can be called 'nice' – if anything, I'd have hoped that Van Gogh's provocations were just an act – but the truth is, I'm only half listening. As I head back to Sintcentral, I picture Henk and his two Petes, one loyal, the other mutinous, bombing helter-skelter through the rain-slicked streets. Though it may not run on time, nothing will stop Henk's quixotic mission to perpetuate a 'fairy tale'. And in his own way, maybe Pete represents the face of things to come. Whether he's black, brown or blue, played by a white girl, a black man or a Moroccan immigrant, he and the *Sint* will adapt to their surroundings so that they survive, without causing too much offence. It's a long shot, but maybe – just maybe – that will be the Dutch solution to the problem. And it's people like Henk – and all the Washerwomen, Arse Blowers, Rooster Runners and Oil Wrestlers I've met – who will keep Europe's deep-rooted diversity alive . . . if only through sheer human cussedness.

Thanks

After nearly two decades in this line of work, you'd think I'd have gotten over it by now: the incapacitating fear that takes hold when I'm faced with asking strangers strange questions, knowing that I have absolutely no right to expect an answer. I've lost count of the times I've been tempted to hole up in my hotel room and draw the curtains, trying desperately to convince myself that *Actually, Spanish/Swiss/Italian TV isn't that bad*. What if the locals won't talk to me? What if they tell me to get lost?

For the most part, that hasn't been the case. Thanks to everyone in this book for taking the time to humour a tongue-tied foreigner who wandered around making awkward enquiries. Hopefully none of them will regret having helped me.

I also owe a debt of gratitude to the people behind the scenes who made all this possible in the first place: namely, the triumvirate of Lizzy Kremer, Mark Booth and Tim Andrews, as well as the countless folks at Random House who have supported this book and its predecessor, often anonymously. The ones I do know about are Rob Waddington, Ron Beard, Faye Brewster, Charlotte Bush, Susan Sandon, Ellie Clarke, Claire Round, Jonathan Sissons, Claire Lawler, Paul Herbert, Leslie Leigh, Katie Duce and Alex Kirby. Thanks to Adam McCauley for his racy artwork, as well as to Will Richards and Abby Hawkins for their virtuoso web designs skills.

Country by country, a hearty *Dank u* goes to Hans de Jongh

and Abigail Levene in the Netherlands for coffee, conversation and challenging me when I got it wrong, and to Priscilla van Leeuwen, Henk van der Kroon, Kees van Veen and Frits Booy (author of *Sint Nicolaas van A tot Z*) for their help on the story of *Sinterklaas*. *Merci beaucoup* to my brethren Arse Blowers in Nontron, particularly Michel Meyleu, Fabienne Lastere, Franck Angelliaume, Marc Battistel and Ramon Adam, as well as to Patricia and Philippe Emonet for their overwhelming hospitality in Martigny and to Veronique and Jonathan Lewis for tea and translation in London. In Greece, Jean Baker gave me the big-picture perspective on Kefaloniá, while Evangelia Fotiadi, Demetri Tashie and Dimitris Xygalatas provided insights into Greek Macedonia. Across the border, Aydemir Ay proved to be a superhuman guide to Edirne, and Suna (and Jill) Erdem and Firat Kayakiran went out of their way to help me in Istanbul. In Germany, *Weiberfastnacht* and *Karneval* wouldn't have been the same without Anja Kranz, Evi Zwiebler, Martin Sauerborn, Karl Schönball, Georg Fenninger, Max Benz and Dr Ulrich Ruh. Whether it was Goat Tossing, Baby Jumping or Rooster Running in Spain, I relied on the help and hospitality of Maribel and Paco Franganillo, Pedro and Angela Prieto, José María García, José Manuel Martínez García, Luis Miguel de Dios, Angel Manso, Leo Pérez García, Mónica Torres and Duncan Chard. Elsewhere in Iberia, Miguel Midraj gave me inside knowledge of the Portuguese, while Célia Azevedo spoiled me with more information about Amarante and the Phallus Festival than I could ever have hoped for.

I also want to thank all the family, friends and friends-of-friends whose support has ranged from the odd drink and meal to advice and accommodation, not to mention the discreet rearrangement of bookshop displays. First and foremost are my parents and Jeff and Julie Buck for their divine intercessions, as well as Tony Roddam (your blue plaque's in the post), Matthew and Nancy Galimi, Andrew Young, Charlie 'Bestseller' Connelly, Andy Hall at the Beeb, Jonathan Birt, Bob Mann, Dr D.R. 'Doc' Rowe, James Brooke, Bruce Hunter, Laura West, Kate Watkins, Sarah Bennett, the divine Ms Yoko Spungeon, Mike Butti, George and Binita McClintock, Adam and Stephanie Frankel, Recai Gunesdogdu, Michiko Fox for her Standards and the book club headed by Kerry Evans and Stephen Reid.

Finally, I would also like to thank Alin and my two little girls for their continued love and support.

Don't forget – if you'd like to find out more about these events, feel free to visit www.daeschner.com.

JR Daeschner
London